PRAISE FOR *THE NONES*

"Pastors and church leaders need to steward well our understanding and use of statistics, especially when it comes to understanding and explaining the rise of the nones. In this most helpful book, *The Nones*, Ryan P. Burge provides an aerial view of the American religious landscape as well as an amplified view of the rise of the nones—America's fastest-growing demographic. When you're finished reading this book, you will see the American religious landscape as it is—not as you think it is."
  —Ed Stetzer, executive director, Wheaton College Billy Graham Center

"A great temptation of this age is to label people, to turn individuals into categories that we can automatically dismiss or approve. The growing ranks of the diverse, religiously unaffiliated demographic are especially vulnerable to this reductionism. Against this trend, Ryan P. Burge deploys his expertise as a sociologist and his experience as a pastor to provide an invaluable, insightful, and detailed portrait of the nones. They turn out to be quite something and a reality that anyone involved in ministry or interested in society ought to understand. *The Nones* is an excellent guide."
  —David Gibson, director, Center on Religion and Culture, Fordham University

"Every time I talk to Ryan P. Burge, I learn something. He is one of the sharpest academics studying religion in the country. He brings both a sharp eye for data and a small-church pastor's insight into the changes affecting the American religious landscape. If you want to understand the rise of the nones—those who claim no religion—and how faith groups might respond, this is the book for you."
  —Bob Smietana, journalist, Religion News Service

"You can't minister to those you don't understand. *The Nones* will expand your knowledge of the rapidly growing 'religiously unaffiliated' population. Using straightforward analysis and rich graphics, Ryan P. Burge masterfully uncovers the origin, character, and future of this diverse but influential group. This analysis concludes with advice for addressing the spiritual needs of the 'nothing in particular' nones. *The Nones* belongs on every pastor's bookshelf."
  —Scott Thumma, professor and DMin director, Hartford Seminary; director, Hartford Institute for Religion Research

"A skill church leaders could develop, even if it spins the leader into some pain, is to listen to the disaffected, those who grew up in the church or near the church and who as young adults have walked on a different path. Anecdotes learned from listening then need to be enhanced and complicated with the kinds of data and interpretation that Ryan P. Burge sorts out in *The Nones*. Statistics and helpful graphs abound in this book and provide us with graphic displays of an unpleasant, complicated reality. Every section in this book brings me pain as a confessing Christian, but I want to know what is being experienced among those who find my faith inadequate or unhelpful. Be prepared to be distressed and disturbed, but take heart—the pain will lead you to what the gospel has the power to create anew."

—Scot McKnight, professor of New Testament,
Northern Baptist Theological Seminary

"With so much data coming at us, there is a need for reliable sources of data based upon rigorous, trustworthy research. To receive that data in a digestible and plausible form seems too much to ask, but Ryan P. Burge has done just that. From the '3 Bs' to the 'nothing in particulars,' *The Nones* is chock-full of nuggets for both the avid researcher and the responsible citizen."

—C. Jeff Woods, interim general secretary,
American Baptist Church, USA

"Clearly written with even clearer illustrations, *The Nones* by Ryan P. Burge explains who the nones are, why their numbers are growing, and what this means for the church. You need not be a 'numbers person' to read this book. You need only to care why the religious landscape has changed so much over the past forty years."

—Arthur E. Farnsley II, author of *Flea Market Jesus* and
The Bible in American Life; former executive officer,
Society for the Scientific Study of Religion

"For years pastors and Christian leaders have talked almost glibly about the *none*-ing of America. Finally, here's a book that can help them better understand both the rise and the diversity of spiritual nones. As a social scientist and a local church pastor, Ryan P. Burge is uniquely qualified to help pastors make sense of the huge shifting religious landscape of America. This book will become a recommended resource of the Send Institute as we help denominations and networks strategize starting new churches for the future."

—Daniel Yang, director, Send Institute,
Wheaton College Billy Graham Center

THE NONES

THE NONES

Where They Came From, Who They Are,
and Where They Are Going

Ryan P. Burge

FORTRESS PRESS
Minneapolis

To my wife,
whose support and care has been more than I deserve.
And to my two boys,
who give me more joy than I thought possible.

Contents

Preface

TWO FACTS WILL HELP PLACE THIS BOOK IN A PROPER CONTEXT. I have been pastoring American Baptist churches for the past fifteen years, and I also have a PhD in political science, having published fifteen articles in peer-reviewed academic journals. What that means is that I have constantly straddled the world of faith and academia. I realize that makes me pretty atypical. I'm no fun at dinner parties because I refuse to talk about my work—as a pastor or an academic—in a social setting. Way too many landmines. But it does make me pretty well suited to present data about American religion to pastors.

More specifically, I think it makes me an ideal voice to write about one of the most important shifts that has occurred over the last forty years in American religion—the rise of the religiously unaffiliated. As a pastor who is also an academic, I have firsthand knowledge of the power of statistics for people of faith. I have written dozens of pieces for *Christianity Today*, Religion News Service, and Barna Group that are all grounded in data and receive an overwhelmingly positive response from a variety of audiences.

Unfortunately, as powerful as statistics are, I can't tell you how many sermons I've heard, books I've read, and tweets I've seen in the past few years from well-meaning pastors that are just not statistically accurate. Pastors are supposed to be in the business of preaching the Truth (about not only Jesus Christ but also the social world), but a lot of them need to stay in their lane.

Let me be clear: I don't blame pastors for wanting to use statistics to try to make a point about how church membership is in decline and the religiously unaffiliated are becoming an increasingly important factor in American religion. Pastors want to leave their flock with one thing they can discuss when they sit down for lunch after church, and a good data point sticks in the brain in a way few other things do. People want to have unbiased facts explained in a way that they can understand. Pastors need to be steady sources of accurate information, but unfortunately, some of them aren't taking the time to fact-check everything that goes into the weekly sermon.

However, one of the most valuable things I learned in graduate school was how little I—and all of us—know about most of the world, which is why data in untrained hands can be a dangerous thing. Just as I wouldn't want one of my political science colleagues to try to explain the evolution of Trinitarian thought in Protestant Christianity, I don't want pastors to try to explain how Karl Marx thought about religion or expound on the implications of internet-based polling.

At the same time as I learned to be humble about what I don't know, I also learned to speak confidently in areas to which I have devoted years of study. Charting the course of American religion for the past five decades has been my life's work up to this point. Still, being a quantitative social scientist as well as a pastor often puts me in an awkward position. Sometimes I am asked to present my work to denominational leaders. Inevitably during the question-and-answer time, someone in the audience will bring up a particularly thorny topic and want me to weigh in on it. I almost always preface my response by asking, "Would you like me to answer that as a pastor or as a quantitative social scientist?"

In this book, I try to do both. I live in the data, creating charts and graphs almost every day. But in between recoding variables and specifying regression models, I carve out time to work on my sermon or visit one of my members in the hospital. My focus over the last few years has been twofold: publishing enough to earn tenure at my university and helping pastors and denominational leaders understand the world around them a bit better. My goal is to take all the education I have had in the social sciences to make the theory comprehensible and the data accessible. So pastors and committed lay leaders, consider this book a resource to get it right when talking about American religion—a little cheat sheet for your work.

Introduction

IT ALL STARTED WITH A TWEET.

A lot of social scientists I follow on social media were noting that the General Social Survey (GSS) had just released the raw data from the 2018 wave, and scholars were already cranking out quick analyses of some of the top-line changes in American political and religious life. For social scientists who study religion, the GSS is the most important survey instrument for analyzing changes in American society. It's the gold standard in measuring religious change in America. That's largely because the GSS has been asking the same religion questions in essentially the same way since its creation in 1972. If a researcher wants to know what share of Americans never attended church in the 1980s, the GSS is the place to go. As soon as I read the news, I immediately downloaded the cumulative data file and started doing some analysis.

My primary objective was simple. I wanted to know how the seven major religious traditions in the United States had shifted over the previous two years. I had already published several pieces about religious measurement, so I had all the code I needed stored on my hard drive. All I had to do was run it on the updated data file and visualize the results. But by the time I had gotten home from work, my two boys needed dinner and a bath. I could hardly contain myself, so I moved quickly. As soon as both of them had filled their bellies with peanut butter and jelly and were happily playing in a bubble bath, I bounded down the stairs to my office and ran the more than two hundred lines of computer code that would calculate the size of all seven religious traditions in every survey year of the GSS dating back to the early 1970s.

And I saw it immediately.

The percentage of religiously unaffiliated people had steadily risen since the early 1990s. Previously, the "nones" had zoomed past 10 percent of the population by 1996, crossed the 15 percent threshold just a decade later, and managed to reach 20 percent by 2014. That rise had not abated in 2018. It had finally happened: the nones were now the same size as both Roman Catholics and evangelical Protestants. That meant that the religiously unaffiliated were statistically the same size as the largest religious groups in the United States.

I had to let the world know, but I was on a time crunch. My boys were starting to get restless in the bathtub. So I quickly put together a graph, picked a premade color scheme, and added the names of each religious tradition to the visualization. I wrote up a quick caption, noted that there was "some big news" about the religiously unaffiliated, and hit the tweet button.

I went back upstairs to get my boys ready for bed, helped them get pajamas on, brushed their teeth, and read a quick bedtime story before lights-out. Then I looked down at my phone. The graph had already been retweeted nearly a hundred times. It was going viral.

What followed was one of the busiest periods of my life. Before this, I had spoken to two or three reporters in my entire academic career; now I was fielding two or three interview requests per day. That one simple graph took on a life of its own. It was picked up by most major media outlets in the United States, including the *New York Times* and the *Washington Post*, and it landed on the front page of CNN's website. Reporters from Europe were intrigued, and the story ended up in the *Times* and the *Daily Mail*. It made the front page of Reddit, receiving over thirty-six thousand upvotes and over two thousand comments. I appeared on C-SPAN on Easter Sunday. Journalists, podcasters, and pastors were all asking me the same questions: How did this happen? And what does this mean for the future of American religion? I didn't know it at the time, but my entire life had led me to this moment.

My career path has been a bit unusual. While I have been a quantitative social scientist for over a decade, I have also been in Christian ministry since just after my twentieth birthday. Wrestling with questions about the future of American religion is not just some cold and calculated academic exercise for me. It's something I experience every Sunday when I get behind the pulpit.

I grew up Southern Baptist. My mother was a Sunday school teacher, and my father drove the church bus. My grandmother was the church secretary, and my grandfather was an usher. We went to church every time the doors were open. I was the kid who was there every Sunday morning and Sunday night. When I entered junior high, the youth group of First Baptist Church of Salem, Illinois, became my home away from home. I went to as many church camps, youth rallies, spaghetti fundraisers, and lock-ins as I could. As I moved into high school, I began to lead Bible studies for the younger kids. I was all in.

During the spring of my sophomore year of college, I was confronted with a problem. I didn't have a summer job lined up. Through a series of seemingly random events, I became aware that a church just twenty miles from my hometown wanted a youth ministry intern for the summer. I applied, was interviewed, and accepted the job at the tender age of twenty. I had no idea what I was doing. That three-month internship turned into a three-year position that I left only after I decided I wanted to pursue a graduate degree in political science. In graduate school, I began pastoring a small church of about thirty retirees. A year later, I was called by First Baptist Church of Mt. Vernon, Illinois. Thirteen years later, I am still behind the pulpit. I constantly wonder how all this happened.

While at First Baptist, I finished a master's thesis, got married, bought a house, defended my dissertation, and had two children. And my church went from having about fifty people in the pews to just over twenty. What was happening in American religion was also happening right in front of me.

This book is an effort to understand and explain how the number of religiously unaffiliated went from no more than a rounding error to nearly a quarter of the US population. While others have tried to make these seismic changes about doctrine and dogma, that's not the approach I will be taking. Instead, I will use both the theory and methodological tools put forth by social science to explore what demographic, religious, and political factors have and are giving rise to the nones.

My work is unapologetically quantitative. That means you will find a lot of charts and graphs throughout these pages. Here's why I think that's essential: no one can accurately conceptualize what American religion looks like today, let alone what it looked like thirty years ago. We all live in our own social, cultural, and religious bubbles. The human mind often clings to anecdotes that represent the extreme cases, not the average ones. It's nearly impossible for any one individual to have a high-level view of American religion. While surveys are not foolproof (and we will discuss some of their flaws in just a few pages), they are one of the only ways to generate an objective assessment of people's beliefs and behavior over time.

If you are scared off by math, there's nothing to fear. I have taken great care to present simplified visualizations that are not based on complicated statistical models. More often than not, I am just doing simple arithmetic. A lot of social scientists seem to forget how much we can learn by simply counting things. However, if you are still struggling to understand a graph, the text will explain the visualization. I am going to point out findings you may have missed, and I will use the text to provide some additional information about the visualization.

The data for this work comes from a variety of sources that I have collected and organized over the course of my academic studies. Two primary surveys will appear frequently. The aforementioned GSS is an invaluable resource when looking at religious trends that stretch back for decades. However, the smaller sample size of the GSS can create problems related to statistical uncertainty. The Cooperative Congressional Election Study (CCES) is huge in comparison. While the 2016 wave of the GSS contained about three thousand respondents, the CCES conducted in the same year had a total sample size of sixty-four thousand. Despite its tremendous survey sample, however, the CCES suffers from one major problem: it was not created until 2006. Therefore, doing long-term trend analysis is not possible.

The structure of the book is as follows: the first chapter is a deep dive into the seven religious traditions that are identified by scholars of American religion. I describe each tradition in broad strokes and track the change in its size over the past four and a half decades. Explaining why the religiously unaffiliated have risen in the United States will be the aim of the second chapter. Topics of discussion here will include grand theories of social science, issues with survey methodology, and the rise of the internet. The remainder of the book will be focused on sketching the outlines of the three types of religious nones: atheists, agnostics, and those who identify as nothing in particular. Finally, the book will end with a discussion of the future of American religion. My aim here is to direct pastors and denominational leaders to think about ways to respond to the rise of the nones by understanding which factors can't be changed in American society and which ones can.

One of the lessons I try to impart to my students is that the role of a social scientist is not to describe the world as we wish it were, or hope it could be, but instead to describe it as it actually exists. That's my goal here. The data will be my guide, and providing simple and clear explanation will be my focus. I am reminded of the words of St. Paul when he wrote, "For now we see in a mirror, dimly" (1 Cor 13:12). It's my hope that after this book, the mirror will be slightly more illuminated.

CHAPTER 1

What Does the American Religious Landscape Look Like?

IT'S ALWAYS AMAZING TO ME HOW PEOPLE SPEND THOUSANDS OF hours and millions of dollars on just classifying things. For instance, in late 2018, scientists from more than sixty countries around the globe met in Versailles, France, faced with an unbelievably important problem: defining how much a kilogram weighed. The reference measure was literally a block of metal that was held under glass. The International Bureau of Weights and Measures chose that hunk of material to be a kilogram, a reference that is used untold millions of times a day around the globe. But they were facing a problem—the kilogram no longer weighed a kilogram. It was losing its mass very slowly over time. The reference was no longer accurate, and science had to make a change. They eventually adopted a resolution to move to a more precise and consistent measurement.[1]

In the United States, there's an entire industry that has cropped up called "tariff engineering." Those who engage in this practice try to convince the United States Court of International Trade that a raw material, a children's toy, or any other item imported into the country should be placed in a different classification in US tax code. For instance, several costume companies sued the federal government because some of the higher-end Santa Claus suits that they had imported were being taxed as "fancy dress" instead of a "festive costume," which resulted in their having to pay millions of dollars in additional taxes to the government. After a two-year legal process, the court ruled that the Santa Claus suits were, in fact, "fancy dress" and must be taxed at the higher rate.[2]

Being a researcher who studies American religion often feels like being a tariff engineer or a scientist trying to decide what a kilogram actually means—except in our case, the hunk of metal or expensive Santa costume actually has very strong opinions about its place in the world as well. It's like trying to define a bowl of gelatin after it has been mixed and as it sits in the refrigerator; by the time you have come to a consensus on a term for the bowl of neon-green soup, it's become something else entirely.

That's not to say that social science hasn't done its best to try to nail down a definition of religious affiliation, because it has. Beginning in the 1990s, a group of political scientists who were pioneering the study of American religion and politics began to articulate a classification scheme that became known as "the three Bs": religious behavior, religious belief, and religious belonging. (It bears noting that several of the authors of this typology were themselves evangelical Protestants and so had likely sat through hundreds of sermons that were structured around three central points that all began with the same letter of the alphabet.) Each of the Bs has its own set of theoretical and methodological strengths and weaknesses.

THE THREE *B*'S

Behavior

Religious behavior is tangible evidence of an individual's faith. For instance, it takes no leap in logic to assume that someone who attends church several times a week is likely more religious than an individual who attends only when she visits her grandmother every few years. However, church attendance is not the only dimension on which social scientists measure religious behavior. Things like how frequently an individual prays, how often or how much they donate to their church, or if they try to convert their friends and neighbors to their flavor of religion are all forms of religious behavior.

From a social science standpoint, using church attendance as a measure of religiosity makes sense. If someone says that they are Catholic but attend mass only once a year, they will be much less likely to be exposed to the theology and the religious culture of Catholicism than someone who is a faithful weekly attender. On the other hand, religious behavior, especially church attendance, is not without its deficiencies. For instance, many incredibly devout elderly people are physically unable to attend services, which means that they would score lower on a religiosity index. Another issue with using religious behavior to rate religious devotion is that some religions place a greater emphasis on attendance than others. For instance, evangelical and Mormon culture strongly encourage it, but it is not so important among Hindus or Buddhists. Also, religious behavior measures may undercount people who have moved to a new area and haven't found a church where they feel comfortable yet, or people who have young children whom they may not want to fight to keep quiet during a worship service.

Belief

Religious belief is what most people think about when they are asked to describe the goal of religion. I have heard many people state very forcefully that there is only one real reason to go to church and that is to strengthen one's relationship with the divine. This viewpoint presupposes a faith that is completely vertical in orientation—that faith is about an individual's relationship with God—and largely writes off the relationship one can have with other people in the congregation. From this perspective, the way an individual thinks is the most important dimension for social scientists to measure. The question most often used to measure religious belief relates to an individual's view of a holy text. For instance, the General Social Survey (GSS) asks respondents which of three statements comes closest to describing their thoughts about the Bible:

- The Bible is the actual word of God and is to be taken literally, word for word.
- The Bible is the inspired word of God but not everything in it should be taken literally word for word.
- The Bible is an ancient book of fables, legends, history, and moral precepts recorded by men.

Biblical literalism has become a proxy for a whole host of conservative religious beliefs. However, this measure is also incredibly problematic. The primary reason is that it is biased against people who don't practice Protestant Christianity. While there are many devout Catholics in the United States, the official position of the Catholic Church is not biblical literalism but instead that the Bible should be interpreted in light of the church's teachings on different theological issues. Therefore, many theologically conservative Catholics do not classify themselves as literalists and therefore are not counted as having high levels of religiosity, although they might be very religious by other measures. In addition, dozens of other faith groups—including Jews, Muslims, and those of Eastern faith traditions—have a difficult time answering a question about the Bible. While other questions have been used to measure an individual's religious belief—like asking about the existence of Satan, an afterlife, or evil in the world—many of them fall prey to the same issues that plague the question about biblical literalism: they are specific to one type of Christianity.

Belonging

The final *B* is that of religious belonging, which is the one that will be used as the unit of analysis in the remainder of this chapter. One of the primary problems that social science has to face is this: How do people know who they are and what they are about? That is, how do people orient themselves in social space? How do they define who may be friendly and who could potentially be hostile? One way people do this is by setting down markers, both visible and invisible, denoting what types of groups they want to affiliate with and what groups they see as undesirable. Think about someone who wears a camouflage shirt even when they are not going out to hunt. Or a man who wears a suit and tie to a wedding where others are wearing blue jeans. Some people proudly display their political affiliation on the bumper of their car, while others make it clear who they voted for by the content they share on their Facebook page. These are subtle ways for people to signal to others who they are and what type of people they would like to associate with.

A social scientist who uses religious belonging to sort people into categories does so based on the notion that religion is a decidedly social affair and that choosing a religious group is an intentional way of anchoring oneself in the social, religious, and political world in which they live. The preeminent political scientists Larry Bartels and Christopher Achen contend that people's driving principle as they move through life is, "What would people like me" do in a given situation?[3] That includes at the ballot box, in the pews, or on social media. If this is the proper way to understand the social world, then the primary question that social science has to answer is, How do individuals pick who are "like them"? I would argue that religion is an ideal way, an incredibly visible one, for citizens to orient themselves as part of the social world.

Consider this: there may be no more easily malleable demographic factor in American life than one's religious affiliation. For the vast majority of Americans, concepts like race and gender are incredibly concrete and fixed. For most, education is a pursuit that occurs only during a short period of their lives. And while one's income can drastically fall due to downsizing or recession, that usually is not followed by a drastic change in social or political behavior. Age is obviously a function of time. Other things like a change in marital status may happen once or twice, and people become parents just a handful of times.

Religion doesn't work like that. None of the demographic factors just mentioned can be changed as easily as religious affiliation. As an example, consider someone who took a survey a year ago and noted that they were Presbyterian, but when they were asked the same question about religion this week, they indicated that they had no religious affiliation. Did their actual religious behavior change dramatically between last year and now? More than likely, the answer is no. What is more plausible is that they were rarely attending services before but still clung to that religious identity. But for reasons that can never be completely understood, they made the conscious choice to say in the most recent survey that they have no current religious affiliation. It required not a conversation with their pastor or a public pronouncement to their friends and family but instead just a subtle shift in their mind: from seeing themselves as a Protestant Christian to someone who has no attachment to any religious group. That one simple shift can be indicative of a tremendous amount of change in the way that person thinks about their place in the world.

So how do social scientists sort the menagerie of religious affiliations into categories that are not so broad that they lose all conceptual clarity or so large that they would be impossible to easily remember? The most widely adopted system in use today is called RELTRAD. It was developed by a team of social scientists nearly two decades ago as a way to sort individuals in the GSS into different religious classifications. It's fair to say that no one, including the creators of RELTRAD, loves the classification scheme. However, its usage has become pervasive in American social science, with dozens of peer-reviewed books and articles using the typology every year. It's the best that we have.

Here's how it works. It takes a series of questions about religious affiliation in the GSS and places each specific religious tradition in one of seven categories: evangelical Protestant, mainline Protestant, Black Protestant, Catholic, Jewish, observant of other faith traditions, and nonaffiliated. Those seven categories are what I will discuss in some detail in the remainder of this chapter. But first, I wanted to provide a broad sense of what American religion has looked like over the past forty-six years.

In broad terms, the graph in figure 1.1 shows two dominant religious traditions: evangelical Protestants and Catholics. Three traditions are smaller: Black Protestants, observants of other faith groups, and Jews. And finally, there are two traditions that have had a great deal of volatility over the past four and a half decades: mainline Protestants and those without

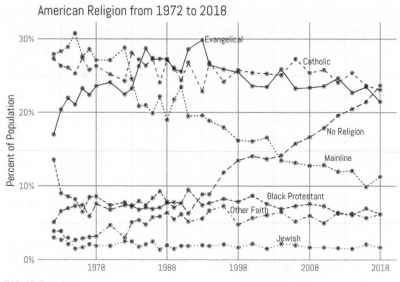

FIGURE 1.1

Data from the General Social Survey, a project of the independent research organization NORC at the University of Chicago, with principal funding from the National Science Foundation, https://gss.norc.org/Get-The-Data.

a religious affiliation—the nones, as I call them. While this book is focused on those who claim that they have no connection to a faith tradition, it's important to understand what options are available to people who desire to join a religious community—before they check the "none of the above" box. Some may be selecting the "no religion" box because they feel as if they have no better options on the survey. It's crucial to understand what those other options are. To that end, what follows is a brief discussion of some of the major features of these seven groups as well as an explication of how their share of the American population has shifted over the past forty-six years. This is by no means an exhaustive description of these groups, but I hope it will serve as an entrée into picturing American religion through a wide lens.

THE SEVEN RELIGIOUS TRADITIONS
IN THE UNITED STATES

Evangelical Protestants

It's fair to say that when the average American thinks about Protestant Christianity, they likely conjure up images of evangelicals. However, the term *evangelical* itself is hotly debated by scholars and laypeople alike. In just the past few years, there has been fierce discussion among historians, social scientists, and theologians about what it actually means.[4] The RELTRAD scheme classifies several denominational groups as evangelical. The largest is the Southern Baptist Convention, which is also the largest Protestant denomination in the United States, with nearly fifteen million members in 2019.[5] Other traditions classified as evangelical include the Assemblies of God (as well as other Pentecostal traditions), the Free Methodist Church, and the Lutheran Church—Missouri Synod. In addition, most people who say that they attend a nondenominational church are also placed in the evangelical category. The race of churchgoers is taken into account as well. For instance, Black Southern Baptists are classified as Protestants, not evangelicals. That means that this tradition is overwhelmingly, but not exclusively, white.

Speaking theologically, evangelicals hold to a conservative view of the Bible. In the past decade, the share of evangelicals who believe that the Bible is the literal word of God has hovered between 55 and 65 percent. These churches almost uniformly do not allow women to become pastors. Instead, they practice what has been called "complementarianism," an interpretation of the Bible that indicates the genders are not equal but instead complement each other through their use of different skill sets. Additionally, a hallmark of evangelical theology is its emphasis on a born-again experience. This is described as a dramatic, often emotional moment when an individual gives themselves over to the call of God and the Holy Spirit enters their heart. The result of this event is expected to be a transformation in belief and behavior.

It's impossible to talk about evangelicals without a discussion of their politics. For example, the fact that 81 percent of white evangelicals voted for Donald Trump in 2016 has been widely reported by those in the media.[6] However, what many reports miss is that four in five white evangelicals also voted for the Republican candidates for president in both 2008 and 2012. The close kinship between evangelicals and the GOP dates back to the formation of the religious right by a small group of influential evangelical pastors in the late 1970s. Many of them began to espouse a message of free markets, low taxes, and social

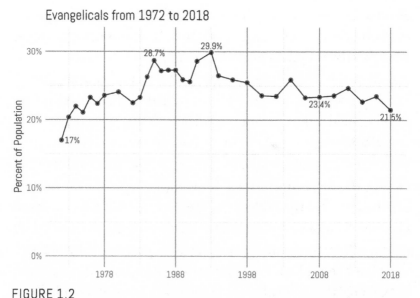

FIGURE 1.2

Data from the General Social Survey, a project of the independent research organization NORC at the University of Chicago, with principal funding from the National Science Foundation, https://gss.norc.org/Get-The-Data.

conservatism. Abortion and gay marriage have persisted as the key issues for many evangelicals, with two in three evangelicals opposing abortion and same-sex marriage in 2016.

As can be seen in figure 1.2, the trend line for evangelicals over the past forty-six years serves as an interesting litmus test for those who try to interpret the data. One set of responses is typically along the lines of "Look how far evangelicals have fallen in the last twenty-five years." This perspective is rooted in comparing the high-water mark for evangelicals in 1993, 29.9 percent, to their current share of the population, 21.5 percent. That's an eight-percentage-point decline in two and a half decades. But there's another way to look at this data: that the period from 1983 to 2000 was somewhat of an outlier. If those years are eliminated, then evangelicals have basically held the same share of the population for the entire forty-six years. However, it's also accurate to say that evangelicals have seen an erosion in their share of the population since the beginning of the millennium. Their share has declined by about two percentage points in twenty years—a small amount, but one that may be worrisome for evangelicals.

Mainline Protestants

While evangelicals are the conservative form of American Christianity, mainline Protestants are perceived as the more moderate flavor. Their name comes from the fact that many of these churches were built on the Main Streets of towns and cities across the country. The largest denominations are often called the "Seven Sisters": the United Methodists, the Evangelical Lutheran Church in America, the Presbyterian Church (USA), the Episcopal Church, the American Baptist Church, the Disciples of Christ, and the United Church of Christ. While many of these church denominations are relatively new, they often trace their history back hundreds of years. For instance, the modern Episcopal Church finds its roots in North America in the early 1600s, when the Church of England was the official church of the Virginia colony.[7] Mainline Protestants are also largely white and are rapidly aging; the average mainline Protestant was nearly sixty years old in 2018.

As previously hinted at, mainline Protestants occupy the middle ground in matters of theology. They aren't as liberal as Unitarians, for instance, but their view of the Bible is not as strict as that of their evangelical brethren. While nearly two in three evangelicals are biblical literalists, just one in three mainline Protestants believes that the Bible should be read literally. Mainline denominations are also open to having women in the pulpit. In fact, that may be the touchstone of mainline Protestantism—a belief in "egalitarianism," which contends that women and men were created equally and therefore should have the same opportunities in ministry. Several of these denominations also support same-sex marriage. For instance, the United Church of Christ allowed couples of the same sex to wed as early as 2005.[8]

People often assume that because mainline Protestants are more religiously liberal, they should also side with the Democrats at the ballot box. However, the reality is often more complicated than that. Some of these traditions do lean to the left. For instance, nearly six in ten members of the Disciples of Christ identify with the Democrats, along with simple majorities in the Episcopal Church, the American Baptist Church, and the United Church of Christ. However, 53.7 percent of the largest mainline denomination in the United States, the United Methodist Church, are Republicans; just 35.1 percent are Democrats.[9] Often this partisan affiliation has more to do with economic issues than social topics, however. Mainline Protestants are typically white-collar workers who enjoy higher incomes and therefore want to see lower tax rates and less government bureaucracy.

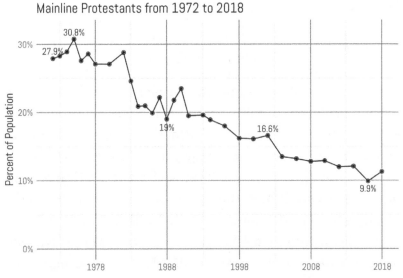

FIGURE 1.3

Data from the General Social Survey, a project of the independent research organization NORC at the University of Chicago, with principal funding from the National Science Foundation, https://gss.norc.org/Get-The-Data.

While evangelicals have had a roller-coaster pattern of growth and decline, the mainline trajectory has almost entirely been downward, as can be seen in figure 1.3. A statistic that always stands out to me is that from 1972 until 1983, the largest religious tradition in the United States was mainline Protestant Christianity. In fact, none of the other seven religious traditions in the past forty-six years has broken 30 percent of the population—except for mainline Protestants, who made up 30.8 percent of Americans in 1976. However, in a span of just twelve years, mainline Protestants lost a third of their members, dropping to just 19 percent in 1988. Since then, the decline has slowed somewhat. By 2004, they were below 15 percent and then in 2016 fell into the single digits—9.9 percent of the population. They have seen a small rebound in 2018; however, that may be just an aberration in the data.

Black Protestants

The final type of Protestant to consider is those who attend historically Black churches in the United States. The fact that an entirely different category is needed just because of the color of a worshiper's skin makes many people bristle at first blush. However, there are solid historical, social, and political reasons to separate Black Protestants. Many of those are rooted in the history of slavery and Jim Crow, as well as the racial discrimination that still persists in America today. Even after the Civil War, freed Black Americans were not afforded the same rights and access to social organizations as their white neighbors. Because of that isolation, the Black church evolved into an entirely different type of institution from white Protestantism.

If white Christians wanted to join a social club, they could simply become members of the Lions or the Rotary or the American Legion. They would be embraced with open arms, and these clubs provided a network of connections to people in the local community who could help in times of trouble. This was not the case with Black people, as these clubs resisted integration for decades. Instead, Black people would use the church not just as a center for spiritual growth and practice but as a place to socialize and share a meal. In much the same way, Blacks were shut out of the political party process. If a Black person wanted to run for office, the parties often would not allow them to speak at the functions they held. As a way to circumvent that, the Black churches allowed these politicians to use the church's pulpit as a way to drum up support for their campaign. The thought of a politician using the Sunday service as a means to politic seems completely inappropriate for most white Christians, but for the Black church, this was the only option that they had.

To further complicate matters, Black Protestants are theologically conservatives, sharing many of the same positions as their evangelical neighbors. Black Protestants are just as likely to believe that the Bible is literally true as evangelicals, and there is no difference in the two groups' views on same-sex marriage. Yet their politics are completely at odds. While vast swaths of evangelicals vote for Republicans, typically nine in ten Black Protestants vote for the Democratic candidate for president. The reasons for that are obviously complex, but much of the divergence can be found in the history of oppression that Black people have experienced in the United States. While evangelicals are often wary of the size and scope of the government, Black Protestants believe that the government has been one of the few institutions that has in any way supported their voting rights and access to education.

Demographically, Black Protestants have seen a slow downward drift over the past three decades, which is displayed in figure 1.4. In the mid-1980s, almost one in ten Americans was affiliated with a Black Protestant tradition. That share has declined in the past twenty years. Now approximately 6 percent of Americans are Black Protestants. Why the decline? A big part of it is that while just 5 percent of Black people said that they were religiously unaffiliated in 1980, that number has quadrupled in 2018 to 20.8 percent of the Black population—which, coincidentally, is almost the same trajectory as the rise of the nones in the entire American population. Coupled with the fact that the share of Americans who identify as African American has stayed stagnant over the past three decades, this will lead to an inevitable decline. In chapter 3, I will discuss how several demographics, including race, impact the rate of disaffiliation.

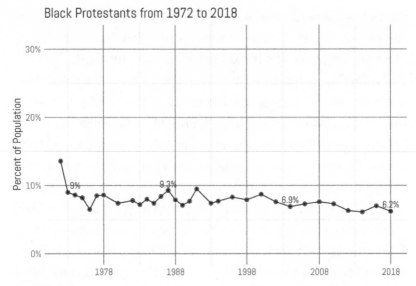

FIGURE 1.4

Data from the General Social Survey, a project of the independent research organization NORC at the University of Chicago, with principal funding from the National Science Foundation, https://gss.norc.org/Get-The-Data.

Catholics

The Catholic Church has always played a tremendous role in the religious landscape of the United States. Many eighteenth- and nineteenth-century immigrants came to this country from countries where the Catholic Church was the only choice for people seeking out a faith tradition. Many of the Irish fleeing from the potato famine landed in America wanting to build a new life but also retain the teachings and trappings of the Catholic Church. This was true for immigrants from the rest of Europe as well. Many of the largest cities in New England are overwhelmingly Catholic as a result of this great migration that occurred during the eighteenth and nineteenth centuries.

More recent immigrants to the United States have come from Central and South America, countries where the Catholic Church has been especially strong. However, this group of immigrants is more racially diverse. While the American Catholic Church had been overwhelmingly white for centuries, that is changing rapidly. In 2018, a quarter of all US Catholics were not white, and that share could grow exponentially in the coming decades as white birth rates slow compared to nonwhite Americans.

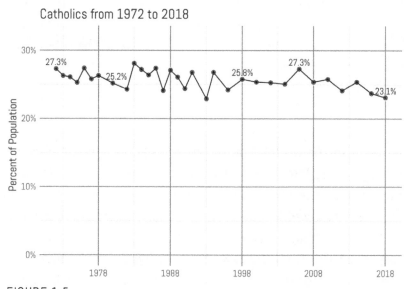

FIGURE 1.5

Data from the General Social Survey, a project of the independent research organization NORC at the University of Chicago, with principal funding from the National Science Foundation, https://gss.norc.org/Get-The-Data.

The Catholic Church is still one of the dominant religious institutions in the United States, but it seems to be in decline, especially in the past decade, which is apparent in figure 1.5. The Catholic share of the population was surprisingly stable from 1972 until the mid-2000s, when their portion of the population hovered between 25 and 27 percent. However, that number declined to 23.1 percent in 2018. While it would be unwise to pin this on any one cause, it's impossible to ignore the recent scandal involving cases of sexual abuse by priests. Many of these allegations began to receive media attention when the *Boston Globe* launched an investigation into them in the early 2000s. It's noteworthy that the share of Catholics who say they never attend church services has risen from 7 percent in 1973 to 14.3 percent in 2016. So it would appear that the number of nonpracticing Catholics is growing, though the number of people who identify as Catholic has declined only slightly. American Catholics were statistically the same size as evangelicals and the religiously unaffiliated in 2018.

Jews

Judaism in the United States has had a long and complicated history. Many Jews arrived from Europe during great waves of migration in the 1800s. While Jewish synagogues can be found all over the United States, they are typically concentrated in the Northeast, as many settlers put down roots in New England and the Rust Belt. American Jews have always been a numerically small portion of the population but have had an outsized role in American society and politics. Jewish Americans serve as an interesting puzzle for political scientists because they possess many of the traits that should lead to a Republican affiliation, such as earning solid family incomes and being almost completely Caucasian, but despite this, they are a strong Democratic voting bloc. The reasons for this are not entirely straightforward; however, one theory is that Jewish people see themselves as outsiders in their society and think the Democratic party has consistently tried to cater itself to marginalized population groups.[10]

It's crucial to remember just how small the Jewish population is in the United States, which is clear from figure 1.6. According to the GSS, they made up 3 percent of Americans in 1972,

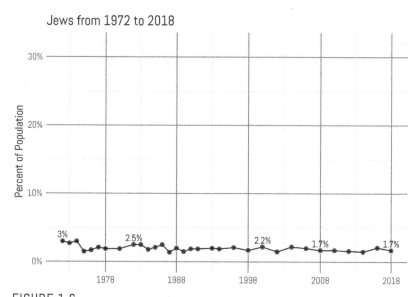

FIGURE 1.6

Data from the General Social Survey, a project of the independent research organization NORC at the University of Chicago, with principal funding from the National Science Foundation, https://gss.norc.org/Get-The-Data.

and that number declined to 1.7 percent in 2018. To put that in perspective, that's about the same percentage as Buddhists and Hindus combined or about the same as Latter-day Saints. Because the decline has been so slight (just 1.3 percent over forty-six years), the size of the Jewish population was not statistically different in 2018 compared to 1972. However, Judaism is not just a religious affiliation but also a cultural identity, so many Jews who are not religiously active may still check the box for Jewish on surveys because of their ethnic ties to Judaism.

Observants of Other Faith Traditions

One of the primary difficulties in classifying religion in the United States is that once one moves away from the largest religious groups (mainly Protestants and Catholics), lots of small religious denominations must be classified. RELTRAD uses "other faith tradition" as a catchall for a variety of religious groups that are not large enough to justify their own category. Those who fall into this group come from a menagerie of backgrounds, including Muslims, Mormons, Buddhists, Hindus, pagans, and people who indicate that their religious affiliation is "other" on the GSS. Consequently, it's not possible to speak in broad terms about the contours of this politically, racially, and religiously diverse category.

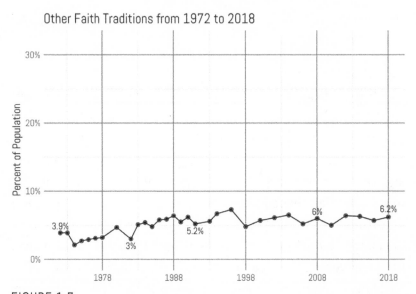

Other Faith Traditions from 1972 to 2018

FIGURE 1.7

Data from the General Social Survey, a project of the independent research organization NORC at the University of Chicago, with principal funding from the National Science Foundation, https://gss.norc.org/Get-The-Data.

What is notable, though, is that this group is consistently growing in size, which is visualized in figure 1.7. In the mid-1980s, just 3 percent of Americans were of another faith tradition, which was essentially the same size as the Jewish population.

That share has risen slowly and steadily over the past several decades—reaching a peak of 6.2 percent in the latest wave of the GSS. There are several reasons for this increase. For instance, the Mormon church has grown about 1.5 percent per year in recent years.[11] But what is also fueling this increase is immigration to the United States. While a great many in the past came from regions of the world where Christianity was the dominant force, many recent arrivals to the United States have been from Asia. With them they bring a Buddhist, Hindu, or Muslim affiliation, which is also boosting these numbers. Additionally, more and more Americans are rejecting traditional labels like Protestant, Catholic, or Christian and are instead saying that they are merely spiritual, a choice that puts them in the "other faith tradition" category.

The Nones

Having surveyed the rest of the American religious landscape, we now turn to the subject of the inquiry—those who say that they have no religious affiliation. Consider this: of the six religious traditions that were detailed in this chapter, five are smaller today than they were in 1972. Just one—other faith traditions—is larger, and the increase there is just 2 percentage points. Between 2016 and 2018, those without religious ties rose 1.5 percentage points. The growth has not always been so exponential. For instance, from 1972 to 1990, the rate of increase was a total of 2 percentage points. However, something changed from 1991 to 1996, when the share of the nones jumped from 6.3 percent to 11.9 percent. To put it bluntly, 5 percent of the population disaffiliated in a five-year period. From that point forward, the nones have enjoyed what venture capitalists have called "hockey stick" growth, which is visualized in figure 1.8. With very few exceptions, the nones have grown consistently year over year since the mid-1990s, and it would appear that there is no end in sight.

FIGURE 1.8

Data from the General Social Survey, a project of the independent research organization NORC at the University of Chicago, with principal funding from the National Science Foundation, https://gss.norc.org/Get-The-Data.

Religious demography is a zero-sum game. If one religious tradition gets larger, then others have to get smaller. We can't add any water to this bathtub; we can only swirl it around. So where have the nones come from? The easy answer is mainline Protestant Christianity. As previously noted, mainline Protestants have declined from 30 percent of the population to just 10 percent in about four decades. It would be convenient to claim that this explains the entirety of the rise of the nones, but that would be too simplistic. Consider the fact that evangelicals were 29.9 percent of America in 1993 but are now 21.5 percent. That eight-percentage-point drop has to affect another part of the bathtub as well. Couple this with the fact that Black Protestants, Catholics, and Jews have seen small declines as well, and we begin to see that the religiously unaffiliated have come from a variety of sources—not just moderate Protestants. This phenomenon will be explored in greater depth later on.

HOW MANY NONES ARE THERE REALLY?

All these results from the GSS need to be understood in the context of the way other surveys ask about religious affiliation. The GSS's approach is to ask respondents, "What is your religious preference? Is it Protestant, Catholic, Jewish, some other religion, or no religion?" Most of those response options lead to follow-up questions about specific religious affiliation. For instance, if someone says that they are Protestant, then they are asked to specify their broad denominational family (Baptist, Methodist, etc.), then are asked an additional question that tries to identify their specific tradition (e.g., United Methodist or Free Methodist). However, if someone chooses the "no religion" option, then that portion of the survey ends, and they move on to a different topic. Note that the GSS does not ask if someone classifies themselves as an atheist or agnostic.

The approach the Pew Research Center takes is entirely different. Instead of offering just five options up front like the GSS does, it has twelve different choices, ranging from the typical options of Protestant and Catholic to smaller groups like Mormons, Buddhists, and Muslims. In addition, the Pew approach offers a total of three options for people to select if they are religiously unaffiliated—atheist, agnostic, or a category simply titled "nothing in particular." So instead of just stating that an individual has "no religion," as in the GSS, the Pew approach delineates different types of religious "nones."

This approach has been adopted by the Cooperative Congressional Election Study (CCES), which is based at Harvard University and has been done at least biannually since 2006. The CCES is a wonderful resource for studying religion for three reasons. First, it is publicly available to anyone who wants to download the data and do some analysis. Second, it asks about religion in the same way the Pew Research Center does, which counts the aforementioned three types of religiously unaffiliated people. But most importantly, it has a huge sample size. While each wave of the GSS is around 2,500 people, the 2016 sample of the CCES was 64,600. That means that even a population that makes up about 5 percent of all Americans (like atheists) still gives us a larger sample size than the entirety of the GSS sample. That allows a researcher to look at atheists by gender or race or any number of variables and still have a sample size with good statistical power.

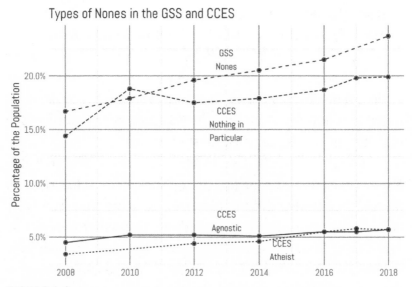

FIGURE 1.9

Data from Stephen Ansolabehere, Brian F. Schaffner, and Sam Luks, Cooperative Congressional Election Study, Cambridge, MA: Harvard University, http://cces.gov.harvard.edu.

However, this difference in methodology leaves researchers with a significant statistical discrepancy, which is clear from figure 1.9. If one collapses the three categories of the religiously unaffiliated in the CCES (atheist, agnostic, nothing in particular) into one group and compares that to the overall estimate of "no religion" from the GSS, the CCES estimate is much larger. The CCES indicates that a total of 31.3 percent of Americans have no religious affiliation. Of that, 5.7 percent are atheists, 5.7 percent are agnostics, and another 19.9 percent are "nothing in particular." The divergence between the estimates of the unaffiliated from the GSS and the CCES was 7.6 percent in 2018, which is up from a 5.6 percent difference in 2008. To translate that to actual numbers—the CCES indicates that twenty million more Americans are religiously unaffiliated than the GSS.

So what's going on here? How can we explain this discrepancy? It's impossible to know exactly which estimate is correct. A good portion of survey research is trying to get inside the mind of the person who is participating in the research. One possible reason for the divergence is that the addition of the "nothing in particular" category seems to be giving permission to people who are very marginally attached to religion to go ahead and select that option. Maybe it appears to be less judgmental than the "no religion" option in the GSS. To explore that possibility, I checked the number of Protestants and Catholics who say they never attend church in the GSS and the CCES. The data shows twice as many never-attending Protestants in the GSS as in the CCES and slightly more never-attending Catholics. To me, this provides support for the theory that the CCES makes it easier for people to indicate their honest assessment of their religion—they are unaffiliated.

Therefore, moving forward, I will typically be using the classification scheme put forth by Pew to describe the religiously unaffiliated as three distinct groups—atheists, agnostics, and those who believe in nothing in particular. Because the GSS only gives one overarching category—those of no religion—it's impossible to make distinctions among the different types of "nones." One of the primary goals of this work is to illustrate, in some detail, that nones are not created equal. Lumping atheists together with those who say that they are "nothing in particular" is both theoretically and practically inappropriate, as the two groups think, act, and vote in completely different ways.

To summarize, American religion is both incredibly volatile in some segments and also highly consistent in others. While most traditions have seen small shifts in size over the past four decades, two groups have changed rapidly—mainline Protestants and the religiously unaffiliated. On average it seems that many people who would have identified as mainline thirty years ago now say they have no religious connection. In essence, moderate Protestants are going extinct, while conservative Christianity is holding the line. In 2018, the GSS indicated that the "nones" were now the same size statistically as Roman Catholics and evangelical Protestants, with simple projections suggesting that the nones will likely be the largest religious group in America inside a decade. Despite the fact that at least a quarter of all adults are religiously unaffiliated, scholarship on this growing religious segment has lagged far behind work that tries to explain the social and political worlds of other religious groups, like evangelicals and Catholics.

I've spent quite a bit of time explaining what has happened to American religion over the past four decades. However, I have not yet tried to answer an even more difficult question: Why is it happening? More specifically, Why are the nones on a path to being the largest religious group in America in the next decade? As is often the case in the social science world, the answer is "It's complicated." It's crucial to remind ourselves that nearly 20 percent of Americans didn't decide to move away from religion at the same time or for the same reason. Everyone who became a none got there by their own path. While I can try to illuminate some of the broadest and most well-trod avenues for this shift, it's impossible to understand all the side roads and back alleys that some people have taken as they've moved away from religion. However, a more robust view of the cultural, political, and demographic changes in the United States over the past four decades can hopefully shed some light on this area.

CHAPTER 2

A Social Scientist Tries to Explain Religious Disaffiliation

"SO WHY IS ALL THIS HAPPENING?"

It's a question that haunts my dreams, to be honest. In every interview I do about American religion, eventually it will all come back to that question. A lot of the time, I'm scheduled for an eight-minute radio spot and know that to answer that query with any measure of scientific precision, I would need at least an hour. So I give the kind of very abbreviated and overly reductive answer that I'm sure makes a lot of my academic colleagues cringe, leaving out a lot of the nuance that exists in the social world and completely ignoring well-established work by many of my friends. I feel terrible about doing that, but that's the nature of talking to the media.

The truth is, I can't point to one single causal mechanism for the nones' astronomically growing numbers, and no other academic can either. The problem with social science is that it's the study of people. People are emotional, unpredictable, and completely unintelligible most of the time. When I teach a course in American voting behavior, I impress upon my students that tens of thousands of pages are written every year trying to understand what goes through a person's mind when they cast a ballot on election day. They might be reflecting on months of thorough research and careful consideration of the future of

American monetary policy. Or it could be that they didn't like one candidate's haircut.

The same challenges arise when studying American religion. One individual can leave a church after years of spiritual soul-searching because they have a sophisticated theological disagreement with the pastor about transubstantiation. Others leave because the congregation moved the Sunday service half an hour. Broad strokes are the name of the game for all social scientists. Those of us who study American religion are not in the business of understanding why a specific individual left or changed religious affiliation; instead, we are trying to understand, at a broad level, what factors lead most people to leave church behind. Some of you will surely read the following pages and think, "I didn't leave church for *any* of those reasons." And you're right. Each individual who walks away from religion has their own reasons and their own spiritual journey. Social science can't get too hung up on explaining the outliers; rather, we have to strive to understand what happened to the average person. It's just the nature of the discipline. However, I would caution you to think carefully about some of the larger unseen forces in American society that may make the decision to change religious affiliation easier or more difficult. Those invisible factors can be cultural, political, theological, or just the spirit of the times. And as a pastor, I never want to discount the work of the Holy Spirit in people's lives, which can push them in a variety of spiritual directions. With all those caveats laid out, let's turn to some of the major theories that explain the rise of the nones.

SECULARIZATION

One of the oldest theories in the sociology of religion is called secularization. This theory contends that as a society gains higher levels of educational achievement and economic prosperity, the result will be a gradual move away from religion. This theory was written about extensively by some of the most influential and foundational social scientists, including Max Weber, Émile Durkheim, and Karl Marx. The overarching implication of secularization theory is that eventually, all countries on Earth will reach a point where religion is either largely marginalized or completely nonexistent.

To give some historical context for this view of modern society, it's crucial to understand how some anthropologists think about the role religion played in ancient societies. For almost the entirety of recorded human history, civilizations have been formed around and endured because of their ability to feed their citizens. Feeding oneself used to require living a nomadic lifestyle, following livestock around as they grazed the countryside. At some point (which is fiercely debated among academics), human beings began to grow crops in an organized fashion, giving way to an agrarian society.[1] The ability of individuals to reap a bountiful harvest was an essential component of the growth and advancement of human civilization.

If the survival of an entire species is predicated on their ability to raise enough crops, it's no surprise that humans became obsessed with the weather. Too much rain, a prolonged drought, inadequate sunshine, or an insect infestation could lead to not just a disastrous harvest but also a large percentage of your town nearly starving to death until the next growing season. In an attempt to stave off such a calamity, civilizations began to look for explanations for droughts, pestilence, and other natural disasters. Naturally, many of those explanations related to the divine. If the rain came at the proper time, that was God rewarding good behavior, but if some disaster befell the community, that must be evidence of wrongdoing in their midst.[2]

German sociologist Max Weber argued that as rationality and scientific discovery began to explode after the Enlightenment, human beings began to see the error of their ways and came to understand rain as the outcome of scientific processes, not the result of divine intervention. The German word Weber used to describe this shift in understanding, *Entzauberung*, is often translated "disenchantment" in English, but the literal translation seems much more fitting: "de-magic-ation." Thus Weber argues that civilizations used to understand their world through superstition but now have the tools of science and rationality to guide their activities.[3]

The founder of communist theory, Karl Marx, believed that religion was an artificial structure created by those in power as a means to keep the underclass subservient to the whims of the bourgeoisie. Marx famously wrote, "[Religion] is the opium of the people."[4] For Marx, religion was a tool of oppression used by those with power and a way for people with less power to psychologically cope with the poor treatment they were receiving as they worked in factories full time. Thus the goal for Marx was to get people to realize that they were being subjected to violence by the rich and well-connected elites. Marx believed it was his duty to help promote class consciousness—to make the working class aware of how they were being exploited by the ruling class. The famous last words of *The Communist Manifesto* make this plain: "Workers of all countries, unite!" For Marx, class consciousness was elusive but inevitable, and when it was achieved, religion would lose its utility and recede from society.

The primary evidence that supports secularization is seen in Europe and is visualized in figure 2.1. In many countries on the European continent where dozens of religious wars have been fought over the past several hundred years, very few people actually attend church with any regularity. I calculated

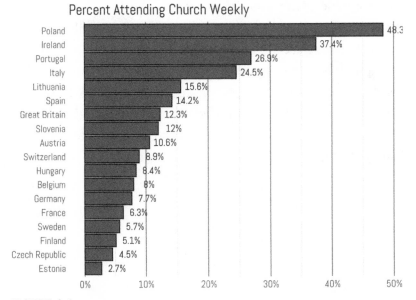

Percent Attending Church Weekly

Country	Percent
Poland	48.3
Ireland	37.4%
Portugal	26.9%
Italy	24.5%
Lithuania	15.6%
Spain	14.2%
Great Britain	12.3%
Slovenia	12%
Austria	10.6%
Switzerland	8.9%
Hungary	8.4%
Belgium	8%
Germany	7.7%
France	6.3%
Sweden	5.7%
Finland	5.1%
Czech Republic	4.5%
Estonia	2.7%

FIGURE 2.1

Data from the European Social Survey, https://www.europeansocialsurvey
.org/.

the share of people in several European countries who attend
church once a week or more. Notice that Poland and Ireland have
high levels of religious attendance—and that those are clearly
outliers. In Italy, the center of Catholicism, religious adherence
matches that of the United States, with just one in four attending
services once a week. Other populous European countries like
Spain and Great Britain have attendance rates in the low teens,
while in Germany and France, fewer than one in ten of their
citizens attend church once a week or more. While there are no
reliable measures of European religiosity before the 1970s, the
hundreds of vacant churches that exist across the continent bear
witness to the reality that Europe has become an overwhelmingly
secular continent since World War II.[5]

Yet despite all the evidence that developed democracies have
cast off religion as they have gained higher levels of educational

and economic advancement, one case is clearly an outlier from this trend—the United States. To visualize that, I grabbed some World Bank data related to the gross domestic product (GDP) per capita from eighteen countries, as well as data from the Pew Research Center about the percentage of people in each country who said religion was very important. I then created a scatter-plot of the relationship between those two variables, which is displayed in figure 2.2.

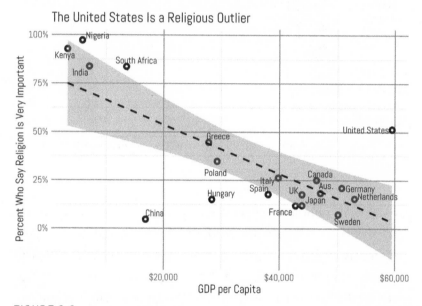

FIGURE 2.2

Data from World Bank, "GDP per Capita (Current US$)," accessed August 19, 2020, https://tinyurl.com/y967okgt; and Pew Research Center, "The Global Religious Landscape," December 18, 2012, https://tinyurl.com/y6gqdfl4.

Notice that the trend line is high on the left side of the graph and low on the right side, which indicates a clear negative relationship between GDP and the importance of religion. Said another way, as a country becomes more economically prosper-ous, it is less religious. This confirms the theories laid out by

Weber and Marx. However, there are two major outliers on the graph. In the bottom left, we see China, which according to the linear model should be much more religious than it is currently, based on its economic output. We can easily chalk that up to the communist government that went out of its way to discourage religious belief in the past seventy-five years.[6] However, the other outlier is on the right side of the graph—the United States. According to this simple model, the share of American citizens in the United States who should rate religion as very important is less than 5 percent based on the country's economic prosperity.

There are several explanations for why secularization theory doesn't work in the case of the United States. One argues that the United States is an exceptional country, so the social science theories about religion and economic advancement just don't apply. Some have argued that American society is a decidedly individualistic one where authority is distrusted, and the low-church ethos of many Protestant churches appeals to the antiestablishment predispositions of many Americans.[7] Another explanation comes from the French social scientist Alexis de Tocqueville, who visited the United States just a few years after its founding and was surprised by the strong separation of church and state. As de Tocqueville put it, "Religion cannot share the material might of those who govern without incurring some of the hatred they inspire."[8] In essence, American religion dodged a bullet by not being sponsored by the state. Finally, some social scientists credit the religious pluralism of the United States as the cause of American exceptionalism. The fact that no one tradition encompasses more than 30 percent of the American population might insulate religion from a national backlash against all expressions of faith.[9]

Another way to think about the issue is that the United States is experiencing secularization but that it is several decades delayed in comparison to countries in Europe. The evidence that was laid out in the prior chapter related to the astronomical rise in the religiously unaffiliated does provide tacit evidence that the United States is seeing a wave of delayed secularization and that the United States will likely look more and more like Europe as time passes.

SOCIAL DESIRABILITY BIAS

One of the great things about academia is that we create fancy terms for things that are very simple. "Social desirability bias" is a nice way of saying that people lie. More specifically, it refers to the well-documented phenomenon that people don't tell the truth when asked survey questions because they want to look good in the eyes of the person conducting the survey. When I describe this concept to people, often a few chuckles erupt around the room—an understandable reaction. However, for social scientists, this is an especially pernicious problem that weakens our ability to be certain about the results we collect when we put a survey into the field.

What do people lie about on surveys? Controversial areas of American social life are the usual suspects. For instance, if you were asked by a female survey administrator whether women are less qualified than men to become president of the United States, would you answer yes if that was your honest answer? Or if a Black person asked if you think Black people are lazier than white people and you did hold that belief, would you say what you really think? Of course, lots of people are going to mask their true feelings while being questioned by a survey collector. But racism and sexism are not the only areas in which people consistently misreport their true feelings. Social scientists who study things like sexual behavior struggle to get a true measurement of how much pornography people watch, how frequently they masturbate, or whether they have ever had an affair. Those who study drug use also know that most people underreport their actual behavior. We know that many people will not admit that they have smoked marijuana, and it's very likely that they will significantly downplay how much alcohol they consume as well.

However, ground zero for social desirability bias may be religious activity. Despite the fact that more and more Americans are indicating that they are religiously unaffiliated, US culture still holds to a sense of a civil religion—the assumption that Americans should believe in God and attend church.[10] For instance, Pew has published survey research indicating that the majority of Americans believe religion does more good than harm, strengthens society, and brings people together.[11] This sense that being involved in church is a positive social behavior provides clear evidence that any survey that asks religious questions is going to be shot through with social desirability bias.

One of my favorite examples of this problem is the case of Ashtabula County in northeastern Ohio. A team of researchers conducted a telephone poll of adults in the county to ask a series of questions about respondents' religious activity, including church attendance. Overall, 35.8 percent of Protestants said that they attended church weekly. After the survey had been administered, the research team created a database of every Protestant church in the county using telephone books, property records, and newspaper advertisements. Having organized this list, the researchers then sent a letter to each church asking them to report their average attendance over the past year. If churches didn't respond, surveyors counted cars in the parking lots and used both collection methods to generate an estimate of overall attendance. The researchers concluded that the average percentage of Protestants who attended church in Ashtabula County was just 19.6. In essence, half of the people who said they attend church once a week lied about it.[12]

The effect of social desirability bias on the ability of researchers to obtain a full and accurate count of the religiously unaffiliated cannot be overstated. The clearest implication is that lots of people are actually not religious at all, but they are afraid to say as much to a survey researcher. In effect, there are many more nones than surveys indicate. But trying to pinpoint the pervasiveness of social desirability bias is nearly impossible. To illustrate just how difficult it is to isolate, I calculated two things: the share of Americans who say that they have no religious affiliation as well as the percentage of Protestants and Catholics who say they never attend religious services. The results are displayed in figure 2.3.

Part of being a social scientist is trying to make educated guesses about how respondents will reveal their preferences in a survey without explicitly asking them for their real opinions. In this case, it seems possible people would be more likely to admit that they are a "never-attending" Protestant or Catholic than to just say the truth: they have no religious affiliation. What the data should indicate, then, is that the share of Christians who say that they never attend church has declined as the percentage of the religiously unaffiliated has risen. However, that's not what the data indicates. In fact, somewhat surprisingly, the share of the religiously unaffiliated has skyrocketed (as previously described), but at the same time, the percentage of people who say they are Christians but also say they never attend services is also up (from about 10 percent in 1993 to just over 15 percent in 2018).

Social desirability bias could still be having an effect here but possibly in a more subtle way. Consider this explanation

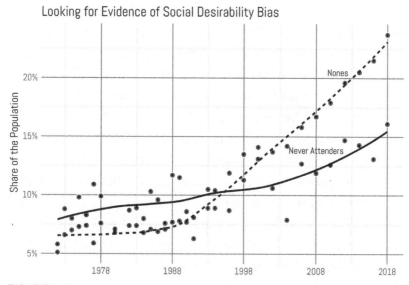

FIGURE 2.3

Data from the General Social Survey, a project of the independent research organization NORC at the University of Chicago, with principal funding from the National Science Foundation, https://gss.norc.org/Get-The-Data.

of religious affiliation. In reality, there is a continuum from affiliation to disaffiliation. On one end are people who report both a religious affiliation and some level of church attendance. On the other end are those who say that they are not attached to religion, nor do they attend church. In the middle are those who are affiliated or indicate religious attendance. It's possible that the erosion of social desirability bias has led some people who were never-attending affiliates to disaffiliate but has also led to some marginally attached Christians (like those who say they attend once a year) to now say that they never attend religious services. In effect, the erosion of social desirability bias pushes large portions of the population to report their actual religious affiliation and behavior. A logical prediction is that as social desirability bias becomes less noticeable, then even more of the never-attending affiliates will become nones.

From a social science standpoint, this is unquestionably a good thing. If social desirability bias is actually waning—and the evidence seems to indicate that it is—academics are increasingly able to accurately identify the religiously unaffiliated in their survey samples. That leads to a more accurate portrait of American social life. But what does this mean for those who do the hard work of preparing to preach and lead worship every Sunday? How should pastors feel about the fact that nearly a quarter of Americans are unaffiliated and an increasing number of Catholics and Protestants say they never attend services? It's easy to look at those skyward-pointing trend lines and get discouraged, but it's possible, and probably even likely, that many millions of people were just not being honest with the survey administrators decades ago. Now we are seeing an accurate picture of American religion. Not to be overly cliché, but the first step in recovery is recognizing you have a problem. Maybe an individual who is willing to be honest about where they stand in matters of spirituality is more open to reconsidering their future than someone who is not being honest with themselves.

THE INTERNET

Social desirability bias is important because social science needs to find a way to explain why it has become more socially acceptable in recent years for people to be religiously unaffiliated or to report their actual level of church attendance to a survey administrator. Obviously, it's not a good idea to ask people taking a survey, "So why did you lie on previous surveys, and are you lying now?" Yet there are always forces in society that make telling the truth a little bit easier or more difficult. One primary development may explain a great deal of this shift toward more honesty in American society surrounding religion: the internet.

Imagine if someone was born in 1960 in rural Mississippi, a place that is overwhelmingly politically conservative and also nearly unanimously Christian. If that individual, for whatever reason, began to doubt the existence of God and eventually viewed themselves as an atheist, would they want to make that belief known to their friends and family? It's highly likely that this individual would go their entire life never meeting a fellow Mississippian who shared the same beliefs about God. The academic community has a term for this experience: *the spiral of silence.*

The German political scientist Elisabeth Noelle-Neumann described the spiral of silence in the late 1970s. Noelle-Neumann believed that every individual has an inherent desire to blend into a group and to avoid social isolation at all costs. Therefore, people are attuned to what opinions are being espoused with confidence in the public square. If an individual's view of the world is in line with the one they hear being discussed, they will join in boldly. However, if one perceives that their opinion is not held in high regard by their community, then they will become willfully silent. People naturally assume that silence is agreement, and therefore, the people who hold the majority opinion will become louder and more forceful, while those who initially stayed silent will have even less incentive to voice their disagreement as time passes.[13]

There is some scientific evidence to support a belief that the spiral of silence theory may not function the same way on the internet. In fact, some studies have shown that minority opinion holders are even more apt to speak up in an anonymous online environment.[14] However, on social media, where users are more often identified by their real names and share photos and other personal information, the spiral of silence still persists, just as it does in the face-to-face.[15] But the internet does seem like an ideal space for someone who is struggling with religious belief to find a community that will either help them work through their doubts or give them permission to walk away from their faith entirely. For instance, Reddit, an anonymous social media platform, has a number of forums that could reinforce users' belief systems. Parts of the site entitled "Debate a Christian" or "Debate an Atheist" have tens of thousands of subscribers, and a subreddit entitled "Atheism" has 2.5 million members. In comparison, the "Christianity" subreddit has just 215,000 subscribers. Clearly, if the aforementioned hypothetical Mississippi atheist was born in 1990 instead of 1960, they would be much more likely to find compatriots in the digital realm.

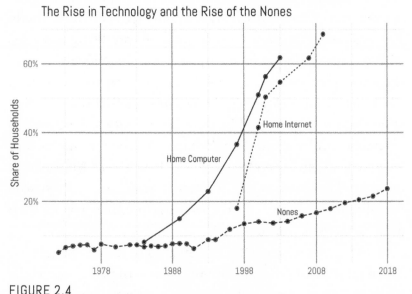

FIGURE 2.4

Data from the United States Census Bureau, "Computer and Internet Use in the United States: 1984 to 2009," February 2010, https://tinyurl.com/yyv54yv7.

But does the rise in the share of internet users directly translate to the explosive growth of the nones? The data just doesn't tell a clear story. I visualized the share of Americans who owned a personal computer as well as those who had internet at home and then compared that to the rise of the religiously unaffiliated for figure 2.4. First, it's important to note just how quickly home internet became common in the United States. While just 18 percent had a connection in 1997, that share jumped to 41.5 percent in just three years; the total number of households who had internet access in their homes tripled in just six years. Yet the religiously unaffiliated rose from 7 percent to 13 percent from 1990 to 1998, when just small shares of Americans had access to that technology.

It is likely that many millions of Americans now declare they are religiously unaffiliated because of things that they have seen or read on the internet. It's very possible that without its widespread adoption, the trend line for the nones would be much flatter. However, the problem for social science is that as the internet changed, so did a lot of other parts of American society. It would be irresponsible not to mention that the internet has likely also had a polarizing impact on other parts of American life as well, especially politics. It's possible that this polarization has galvanized Americans, so many people feel they have to pick sides—Republicans versus Democrats, believing in something versus having no religious affiliation.

POLITICS

Maybe I am slightly biased because I am a trained political scientist, but I have always felt that the best and clearest explanation for the rapid rate of religious disaffiliation can be traced back to the recent political history of the United States. In recent years, everyone who studies religion and politics has been constantly confronted with the same statistic: 81 percent of white evangelicals voted for Donald Trump in the 2016 presidential election.[16]

While many political observers were quick to note that the GOP and white evangelicals have consistently had a strong relationship, many pundits viewed the 81 percent figure as some sort of statistical aberration when in reality it was just business as usual. In fact, in 2008, 79.1 percent of white evangelicals voted for John McCain for president, and 77.4 percent of them cast a ballot for Mitt Romney in 2012.[17] Outside of Black Protestants, there is no more politically homogeneous religious group than white evangelical Protestants.

It's important to understand that the connection between the devoutly religious and the Republican Party hasn't always been this strong. In fact, in 1978, half of all white weekly churchgoers identified as Democrats, while today, just one quarter do.[18] This shift to the right side of the political spectrum among the devoutly religious may have ignited a backlash whereby political moderates and liberals fled church in droves when their political beliefs were challenged.

So how did this happen? How did white Christianity (especially white evangelicalism) become synonymous with conservative politics? The answer is one that is hotly debated among religious historians. Perhaps the most widely cited theory is that a group of conservative evangelical pastors who had gained a great deal of notoriety by becoming televangelists began to use their media platform to speak of the ills of American society. Discussion centered around issues like homosexuality, pornography, and abortion. Using these issues as flashpoints, they organized what became known as the religious right, which sparked widespread protests against the Equal Rights Amendment, homosexuality, and abortion.[19]

However, other scholars have questioned whether these culture war issues were really the impetus for such a potent political movement. Dartmouth professor Randall Balmer has detailed a counternarrative about the religious right that focuses not on morality but instead on racism. More specifically, Balmer argues that the most important Supreme Court case for the religious right was not *Roe v. Wade* in 1973 but one that was decided two years earlier: *Green v. Connally*. It concerned Holmes County, Mississippi, which had chartered three private Christian schools in the wake of public-school desegregation. As a result, not a single white student attended a public school in Holmes County by the mid-1960s. The IRS denied the three schools a tax-exempt status, and the schools sued, losing at the Supreme Court. Following this, Bob Jones University, a fundamentalist school that did not admit Black students, also had its tax-exempt status revoked. Many in the religious right found this to be an encroachment on religious freedom, using it as a rallying cry to whip up more support for their cause of racial segregation.[20]

One final explanation comes from the Princeton historian Kevin Kruse, who believes that the true genesis of the movement lies in not morality or racism but instead economics. Kruse contends that a group of wealthy, well-connected businessmen were growing tired of the high levels of taxation and regulation imposed upon them by Roosevelt's New Deal programs. If they tried to fight these regulations directly, they would look self-interested and greedy. Instead, they began to encourage and mobilize pastors all over the country to decry the evils of social-ism and extol the virtues of free-market capitalism. It was this movement that led to the addition of "under God" to the Pledge of Allegiance and the printing of "In God We Trust" on our cur-rency. In essence, these were efforts to inoculate the American public against the encroachment of atheistic communism.[21]

It's possible that all three of these—morality, racism, and economics—have played a role in the fusion that exists between white American religion and political conservatism in the twenty-first century, but no matter the cause, the melding of these two groups is almost complete. For instance, in 2018, 93 percent of all white Protestants attended a church in which Donald Trump's approval rating was above the national average of 40 percent. Additionally, sixteen of the twenty largest Protestant denominations moved toward the right end of the political spectrum between 2008 and 2018.[22] In essence, devout Protestant Christians are Republicans, with very few exceptions.

The belief that politics was having an unmistakable impact on the American religious landscape emerged in scholarly literature as early as 2002, when Michael Hout and Claude Fischer published a paper titled "Why More Americans Have No Religious Preference: Politics and Generations," in which they began to explicate, using statistical data, the fact that disaffiliation was occurring almost entirely among people who placed themselves on the left side of the political spectrum. To illustrate that, they broke the General Social Survey (GSS) up into five different ideological groups—liberals, those who lean liberal, moderates, those who lean conservative, and conservatives—and then calculated the share of each group that reported that they had no religious affiliation for each year in the GSS.[23] Their data ends in 2002, but I have replicated and extended their analysis in figure 2.5.

What can be observed is clear and unmistakable—disaffiliation is directly related to political ideology. In fact, there's no deviation in the pattern as one moves from the left side of the ideological spectrum to the right: the rate of disaffiliation drops significantly. To put some numbers from 2018 on it, the unaffiliated included 43.6 percent of liberals, 30.5 percent of those who lean liberal, 21.7 percent of moderates, 13 percent of those who lean conservative, and just 9.8 percent of those who identified as conservative. A liberal is twice as likely as a moderate and four times more likely than a political conservative to

Political Explanations for Religious Disaffiliation

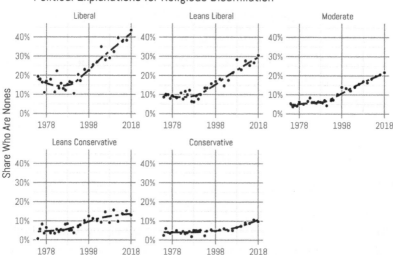

FIGURE 2.5

Data from the General Social Survey, a project of the independent research organization NORC at the University of Chicago, with principal funding from the National Science Foundation, https://gss.norc.org/Get-The-Data.

be unaffiliated. It's crucial to consider that it's not always been like that this. For instance, in 1988, 15.2 percent of liberals were unaffiliated, but for the remaining four categories, the range was between 5.1 and 8.5 percent, and the differences weren't statistically significant. It's fair to say that liberals have always been more likely to be unaffiliated, but the disparity has never been so large.

There is a strong counterargument to be made on this point, though. One of the most difficult problems that researchers face in studying religion and politics is endogeneity—the idea that we can never be sure which way the causal arrow goes. To put it more simply, we cannot answer this question: Do our politics impact our religious affiliation, or does our religiosity have an impact on what political party we identify with? Recent scholarship seems to be pointing more and more to an understanding of politics as the first cause and religious affiliation lying downstream of that. Instead of deciding who they will cast a ballot for based on their religious tradition, most Americans pick a church that lines up with their view of the political world.[24]

SOCIALIZATION

While political differences may be a leading cause of religious disaffiliation, another more basic concern is also worth discussion: social isolation. Easily one of the most important books written in social science in the past fifty years is by the Harvard political scientist Robert Putnam. In his 2000 book *Bowling Alone: The Collapse and Revival of American Community*, Putnam lays out in painful detail a stunning shift in American society: people are retreating from an active social life. Using mountains of meticulously collected data on membership in organizations like the Lions Club and the Elks Lodge, he shows that America is becoming more socially fragmented. Putnam calculates the share of Americans who bowled in bowling leagues dating all the way back to 1900. He finds that in the 1960s, nearly 8 percent of all adult males bowled in a league, but by the early 1990s, that rate had collapsed to just about 3 percent. The book paints a portrait of increasingly isolated Americans who live on islands far from the rest of society.

The main concern for Putnam is what he describes as "social capital," the invisible bonds that hold a community together. Social capital makes people care about the local school district even when they don't have school-aged children. It's the reason people volunteer to pick up trash on the highway or set up a fundraiser to buy new playground equipment at the city park.

Social capital is what gives people a sense of place, purpose, and belonging. With the reported decline in social activities, Putnam worried that the ties that bind people together would begin to fray, and communities would suffer as a result.

Seen through the lens of *Bowling Alone*, the decline in church affiliation and attendance is not unique to just the religious arena but part of a decrease in social activity in all areas of American life. In essence, people stopped joining groups, and church was just caught up in the wave of the desocialization of America. Interestingly, according to Putnam, the main culprit of this social retraction is the introduction of technology, specifically cable television. The book was written in 2000; therefore he was unable to include the full impact of the internet in his

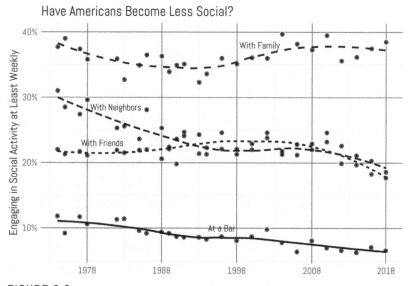

FIGURE 2.6

Data from the General Social Survey, a project of the independent research organization NORC at the University of Chicago, with principal funding from the National Science Foundation, https://gss.norc.org/Get-The-Data.

work, yet he hinted at the individualizing impact it would have on people's leisure time.[25]

Does the data from the GSS bear out Putnam's conclusions? The GSS asked several questions about social behavior, including how often people socialize with their friends, family, and neighbors along with a question about how frequently they go to a bar or tavern. I calculated the share of Americans who said that they engaged in each activity at least once a week for figure 2.6. The results are somewhat mixed. It's clear that Americans spend just as much time with their families today as they did forty years ago. However, there has been a significant decline in how often Americans socialize with their neighbors, down from 30 percent to 20 percent over four decades. There has also been a noticeable decline in socializing with friends in the last decade as well. Finally, patronizing bars has dropped almost in half since 1972. So yes, it does seem like Americans are less social now than they were in the 1970s, but they are still very committed to spending time with their families and almost as likely to spend time with their friends.

The issue that arises with the bowling-alone hypothesis is that it may not have a direct impact on all types of religiosity. As described in chapter 1, social scientists think of religion in terms of behavior, belief, and belonging. If people are more reluctant to engage in social activity, that would likely lead to a decline in religious behavior, specifically church attendance. However, it may not necessarily lead to a drop in religious affiliation, because the internet has made it easier to watch church services or religious programming in the comfort (and isolation) of one's home. Thus if Putnam's assertion is true, then the data should indicate a steep drop in religious attendance, which could potentially be followed by a rise in religious disaffiliation. The problem with using a theory of social isolation to explain why people leave religion is that the data just doesn't support it.

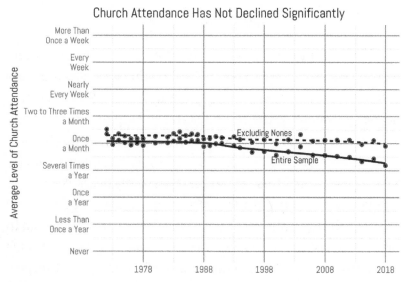

FIGURE 2.7

Data from the General Social Survey, a project of the independent research organization NORC at the University of Chicago, with principal funding from the National Science Foundation, https://gss.norc.org/Get-The-Data.

I calculated the average level of church attendance for two groups in the GSS—the entire sample and a subsample of people who say that they are affiliated with a religious tradition in figure 2.7. While the rise in those with no religious belonging clearly appears in the data, the decline in religious behavior is largely imperceptible. If all respondents are included, the average drop in church attendance over the past forty-six years is 14 percent. Just for reference, the nones have risen eighteen percentage points in that same time period. If I exclude those who claim that they have no religious affiliation, then the drop is just 7.8 percent. That means that every six years in America, church attendance has dropped a single percentage point. Recall that many of Putnam's measures dropped much more rapidly. In short, this theory of social isolation seems persuasive, but in reality, the data doesn't tell such a convincing story.

LOSS OF TRUST

Another force may explain Putnam's data about social isolation: people have lost trust in most societal institutions, including the American government. When Franklin Delano Roosevelt was elected president of the United States during one of the worst economic crises to face the country in its history, he was harboring a secret—he could not walk. Roosevelt had been struck by polio as a child and was rarely able to walk any distance without significant help. This fact was rarely reported by the press, and very few photographs of FDR in a wheelchair were published in national newspapers.[26] Other presidents have engaged in rampant philandering in the White House while the press turned a blind eye. Warren Harding paid secret child support payments to a number of women he had had relationships with. John F. Kennedy had numerous affairs, as did his successor, Lyndon Johnson. None of this ever made the national news.[27] It makes sense that the American public had a great deal of trust in the government for most of the nineteenth century. However, all that changed with Richard Nixon's Watergate scandal. It laid bare for many Americans that the government was being run not by statesmen of noble character and sound decision-making but by morally dubious, self-interested politicians.[28]

Fast forward just a few years, and twenty-four-hour cable news begins in earnest right around the same time that Bill Clinton's affair with Monica Lewinsky becomes national news. No longer would the press turn a blind eye to indiscretion, instead describing the details of leaders' encounters in often lurid detail. The press took on a more investigative role, with many media outlets establishing teams whose role it was to poke and prod every corner of American life. It comes as no surprise that while that 77 percent of Americans trusted government to do the right thing at least most of the time in 1964, that share has dropped to

17 percent in 2018.[29] Other scandals soon began to tumble out. As previously noted, in the early 2000s, the *Boston Globe*, along with other newspapers, began to print a series of painstakingly reported stories about how the Catholic Church had systematically been covering up numerous incidences of priests sexually assaulting minors in parishes across the country.[30] Americans were left with a terrifying question: Whom can we trust?

It only makes sense that many people who read the news of the Catholic Church scandal would not only stop attending church entirely but also renounce any religious affiliation so as not to be associated with such activities. Such events are often cited when one reads social media chatter written by people who say that they have no religious affiliation. The data does bear this out, to a point. Not many surveys ask about the Catholic Church's sex abuse scandal specifically, but I found one that was conducted by ABC News in 2002.

The survey asked respondents if they approved or disapproved of the way the church was handling the scandal. A huge majority (nearly 80 percent) disapproved of the way that the Catholic Church was dealing with the problem, which can be seen in figure 2.8. However, the differences by religious tradition are telling. The most support for the church's response unsurprisingly came from Catholics: 27.8 percent approved. However, just one in five Protestants and just one in ten of the nones approved. The religiously unaffiliated had the strongest level of opposition to the Catholic Church's response. But does this evidence provide support for the theory that the rise of the nones is a direct result of the loss of trust that Americans have in institutions?

The *Boston Globe* ran its first story about the scandal in 2002, so it would seem likely that if this were the driving factor leading many Catholics to become religiously unaffiliated, then they would have done so soon after the stories began being reported in the United States. The GSS asks respondents about the religion

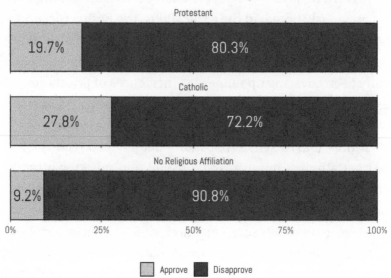

How Do You Feel about the Way the Catholic Church Is Handling the Sexual Abuse Scandal?

FIGURE 2.8

Data from ABC News / *Washington Post*, "Catholic Church in Crisis Poll," ICPSR, last modified June 27, 2002, https://tinyurl.com/y5tcg9y8.

they were raised in, as well as the tradition that they affiliate with as an adult. We would expect to see those taking the surveys in the 2000s to be more likely to defect than in the decades prior; however, that's not what the data indicates. In fact, Catholics taking the survey in the 2000s were just 1 percent less likely to be Catholic as adults than Catholics taking those same surveys before the church was embroiled in the scandal. There was a significant rise in defection between 2010 and 2018. However, this does not support the narrative that the primary driver of disaffiliation was a loss of trust in the Catholic Church, because both mainline and evangelical Protestant defection jumped significantly during this period as well, which is clear from figure 2.9.

I think it's fair to say that the lack of trust that people have in institutions may be a piece of the puzzle, but the evidence does not point to it being the main culprit. It seems plausible that many people have walked away from a religious affiliation since 2000 for a variety of incredibly personal or totally trivial reasons that they may not want (or be able) to describe to survey administrators or their friends and family. Mentioning the Catholic Church scandal may have become an easy way to shut down discussion regarding reasons for leaving religion. I don't want to minimize those who have been affected by sexual abuse in the Catholic or Protestant churches; their stories need to be told, and reforms need to be taken seriously by all religious organizations across the country. But it seems quite a statistical stretch to say that tens of millions of Americans were so affected by the scandal that they left not just the Catholic Church but other faith groups as well.

In What Religious Tradition Did People Raised Catholic End Up?

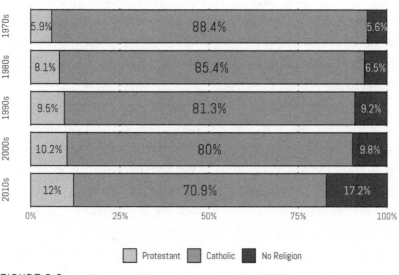

FIGURE 2.9

Data from the General Social Survey, a project of the independent research organization NORC at the University of Chicago, with principal funding from the National Science Foundation, https://gss.norc.org/Get-The-Data.

CHANGES IN FAMILY STRUCTURE

One other possibility seems worth discussion, and that is the fact that the American family does not look the same in 2018 as it did in the mid-1970s. A raft of social science research concludes that being part of a religious community is more likely when someone comes from a stable household environment. This may be because of a perceived hostility in churches toward single mothers or divorcées.[31] It could be that people see religion as a luxury for people who have a weekly routine, something that falls out of the reach of many Americans.[32] As just one example of that, I calculated the share of Americans who said they were married in the GSS dating back to its first iteration in 1972. Figure 2.10 tells a potent story. In the 1970s, nearly three-quarters of all adults in the United States were married. That dropped below half in the late 1990s and has continued a downward trajectory. In 2018, just 42.5 percent of all Americans said they were married. Put another way, if you selected ten random adults in 1972, seven of them would have been married. A random sample of ten adults in 2018 would only contain four married individuals.

While marital status is an important part of the religious affiliation puzzle, it is not the only family-related variable that can drive disaffiliation. One of the most well-cited theories in the sociology of religion is called the "life-cycle effect," which is the understanding that religious attendance waxes and wanes over a person's lifetime.[33] Specifically, children are often very religious, with many growing up in youth groups and attending church camps and other religious events. However, when they graduate from high school, they move into a more adventurous stage and try to find their own identity. Often, this leads to less-frequent church attendance. However, this disaffiliation is short-lived as many begin to settle

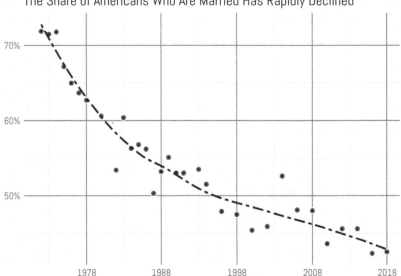

The Share of Americans Who Are Married Has Rapidly Declined

FIGURE 2.10

Data from the General Social Survey, a project of the independent research organization NORC at the University of Chicago, with principal funding from the National Science Foundation, https://gss.norc.org/Get-The-Data.

down in their late twenties or early thirties, a life stage often characterized by marriage and child-rearing. Many want their children to grow up with a moral foundation like they did, so they regain a religious affiliation. If the life-cycle effect applies, the societal institutions of marriage and family should draw people back into the pews.

In fact, that is exactly what the data from the GSS shows in figure 2.11: it's clear that the group of people who are most likely to be religiously unaffiliated are people who are not married and do not have children. In fact, 35 percent of that group said they had no religious affiliation in 2018, which is twelve percentage points higher than the rate of the general public. Being married but not having children does make people slightly more likely to be religiously affiliated, with just under 30 percent of this group saying that they were unattached to religion in 2018. However, a larger impact can be seen on the right side of the graph, which looks at only people who have children. For those people who have children but are not married, just over 20 percent are unaffiliated, compared to 16 percent of Americans who are married with children. It's worthwhile to note that someone who is neither married nor a parent is twice as likely to be unaffiliated as someone who is both.

It's necessary to point out that while the rate of marriage has dropped substantially in the past forty years, the share of Americans who say they have no children has stayed remarkably stable. The data indicates that the rate of childless adults was approximately 24 percent in the early 1970s but rose to 28 percent by 1990 and has stayed at that level for the past

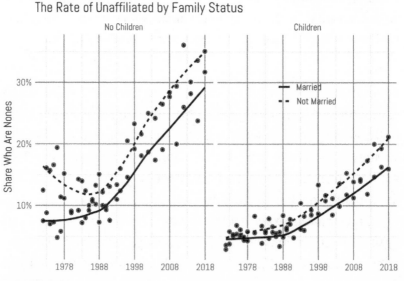

FIGURE 2.11

Data from the General Social Survey, a project of the independent research organization NORC at the University of Chicago, with principal funding from the National Science Foundation, https://gss.norc.org/Get-The-Data.

thirty years. The issue is not necessarily fertility; it's family structure. Americans are having as many children as they did three decades ago, but a much smaller share of those children are being raised in two-parent households. Note above that the difference in affiliation rates between the married and the unmarried was about five percentage points in 2018. However, recall that the unmarried are now making up a larger share of the population. If the share of Americans who were unmarried in 1972 were the same as it was in 2018, the disaffiliation rate in 1972 would have been just over 20 percent. Recall that the actual share of the American population with no affiliation in 2018 was approximately 23 percent, which means we can assume that about 3 percent of Americans are religiously disaffiliated because of the increase in unmarried adults.

CONCLUSION

To return to the central question of the chapter, Why are the religiously unaffiliated now 23 percent of the population? As with all things in life, it's complicated. I have detailed half a dozen of the most popular explanations, but as I have described, many of them seem to be only partially satisfactory. The problem is that the causal arrows hardly ever flow in one direction. Consider just two of these explanations for the rise in the nones: changes in politics and family structure. While it's clear that political liberals are more likely to be religiously unaffiliated, that is also true for people who aren't married and have no children. However, the data from 2018 indicates that Democrats are 10 percent less likely to be married than Republicans. So does one's marital status impact one's politics, or vice versa? The other question that emerges then is how much of the rise in disaffiliation is due to the decline in people being married and how much is related to partisanship? No matter how good a statistical model may be, it can't untangle these difficult causal problems.

If I were to have to point to a few factors, I think that secularization, politics, and the internet are the major causal factors that have given rise to the nones. It seems foolhardy to believe that Europe, a continent that is very similar to the United States in terms of educational attainment and economic growth, could see a massive decline in religious affiliation and that somehow the United States would avoid that same fate, at least to some degree. I do believe that America is a stubbornly religious country in ways that Europeans cannot adequately understand and social science can't completely explain. What that means is that I don't believe we will ever see a time where huge majorities of Americans are unchurched. However, to try to pinpoint where the march of the nones will end is a fool's errand.

While secularization might have put the pieces in place for America's disaffiliation, I think what accelerated the shift were changes in politics, fueled in no small part by the introduction of the internet. In every graph that looks at American religion, something unmistakable happens in the early 1990s. While the nones were slowly trending upward to this point, their rise accelerated dramatically around 1995. The biggest religious trend occurring at that moment was the rise of evangelicalism and the religious right. Recall that evangelicals hit their high-water mark in 1993, when they were 29.9 percent of the population. It doesn't take a huge causal leap to believe that as the loudest and most numerous voices in Protestant Christianity became more theologically and politically conservative, that drove off a lot of moderates. To make matters worse, evangelicals have continued to drift to the right side of American politics since the 1990s. The GSS always asks people to place themselves on a seven-point scale of partisanship that ranges from "strong

Democrat" to "strong Republican," with "Independent" as the middle option. In 1990, 42.6 percent of evangelicals identified as Democrats; today, just 29 percent do. As evangelicals have become more linked to one political party, that has naturally led to the alienation of a lot of people who think differently about politics.

I don't think any amount of rhetoric from social scientists or theologians will convince tens of millions of evangelicals to veer back to the theological and political center in the coming decades. Websites that derive millions of clicks per month focus on making the other side of the religious or political debate look silly. Human beings want to have their beliefs about the world confirmed. In many ways, the damage has already been done—the wave of the nones will continue to grow in size. However, what I think is unquestionably valuable is for both people of faith and those who claim no religious affiliation to understand the contours of this ever-growing bloc of American society. While each of the nones arrived at the same place through their own journey, it's helpful to understand what they hold in common—socially, politically, and demographically. What follows is a deep statistical dive into the world of the religiously unaffiliated.

CHAPTER 3

The Demographics of Disaffiliation

THE PRIOR TWO CHAPTERS HAVE BEEN FOCUSED ON HOW THE nones have grown so large and some possible explanations for their growth, but another question looms—Who are the nones? We all generate stereotypes in our heads when we think of groups of people; it's just how our minds work. It's easy to create a caricature of what an atheist or agnostic looks like: A young white male who spends a lot of time on internet forums calling Christians "sheep." Or a philosophy professor at a liberal arts college who wears a tweed jacket with elbow patches and tries to convince undergraduates that Nietzsche really was right—God is dead. However, you'll find that both of those mental images are fairly inaccurate once you look at the data.

Here's a reality that most people don't fully appreciate about the religiously unaffiliated. In 1972, just one in twenty Americans said that they had no religion. When a group is that small, it can be fairly homogeneous. The way that most groups grow (religious or not) is through personal connections, not because of grand, macrolevel shifts in philosophical or political sensibilities. To declare that you were a none in 1972 was to align your identity with a group that was very much the minority in American society. It took a tremendous amount of conviction to make such a declaration. For most people, publicly declaring a shift in religious affiliation just wasn't worth the social cost.

In 2018, nearly one in four Americans said that they didn't affiliate with a religious tradition. That means that about fifty million people in the United States would choose the "no religion" option if they took the General Social Survey (GSS). There is no way a group can grow that large without becoming much more diverse. That's why it's nearly impossible to give a simple description of who the nones are: they exist in large numbers in age, income, and educational spectrums. They now reflect the racial diversity of Americans as a whole and are more gender diverse than ever before. And while many people assume that the religiously unaffiliated are far-left political liberals who favor the Democratic party, that's become less and less true every election cycle.

In short, the nones look like the United States because they make up such a large part of this country. However, what that also means is that any strategy of evangelizing the religiously unaffiliated cannot be one-size-fits-all. In fact, my hope is that a lot of pastors and denominational leaders will come away from this chapter with the realization that they had no idea what the nones really look like. The data indicates that they come from all walks of life and represent what could accurately be described as the largest mission field in the United States today.

AGE-PERIOD-COHORT ANALYSIS

It's tempting to say that the growth of the religiously unaffiliated is a product of youth. That is, every succession generation has a larger share who are unaffiliated than the last, and this provides a straightforward justification for the steady increase of the nones. This explanation has the benefit of being somewhat true, but it is also incredibly oversimplified. The problem with age is this: it's an incredibly difficult theoretical concept to wrap your mind around. In fact, because of its complexity, social science has generated an entire methodological approach to this problem called age-period-cohort analysis. It's best to explain it by way of an example.

Everyone who lives to a full life expectancy will pass through all the typical age milestones. For instance, all Americans will become adults at eighteen, be able to gamble and buy alcohol at twenty-one, and be eligible to run for president at thirty-five. In this simple example, we are discussing just the biological concept of aging. People age and their hair begins to gray, they become more susceptible to disease, and their interests and hobbies begin to shift. I would venture to guess that when someone thinks of aging, this is what comes to mind.

However, that a person turns thirty-five may not have the same psychological and social impact in 2018 as it did in the past. Consider a thirty-year-old woman who was born in 1930 versus a one born in 1980. According to the US Census Bureau, that hypothetical woman born in 1930 celebrated her thirtieth birthday and her tenth wedding anniversary around the same time. For the woman who entered the world in 1980, there's a good chance she was still unmarried at age thirty, or if she had tied the knot, they would still be in the honeymoon phase.[1] Couple that with the fact that the average age of first-time moms has jumped nearly four years since the 1970s and it becomes clear that turning thirty today means something entirely different from what it did just a few decades ago.

To take this into account, social science has coalesced around the concept of a birth cohort, which usually means placing people who were born in a five-year time frame into a group that can be analyzed over their entire lives. By creating these birth cohorts, social science can to some extent control for the fact that people move through the life course at different rates today compared to the way they did in the past. Obviously, there are going to be outliers. Even today, some people get married straight out of high school, while others never decide to head down the aisle. But cohorts help social scientists generate coherent pictures about how the process of moving through life impacts different generations in different ways.

However, what throws a wrench into this whole tactic is what have been called "period effects." We know that not all years are created equal. Most go by without any sort of national or international event that will register on our psychological and sociological world. However, some time periods change the way that we think about the world in dramatic ways.

My grandmother Emma was born in 1912. She was seventeen years old when the stock market crashed, and she transitioned into adulthood when the United States was going through the worst economic depression seen in a century. It deeply affected the way that she saw the world. She never put more than an inch of water in the tub for bathing, and anything more than a five-second look in the refrigerator without grabbing something drew a harsh scolding for wasting electricity. She lived frugally because it had been necessary for her to survive. However, someone born just fifteen years later or earlier would have not been molded by economic struggle in the same ways.

Period effects account for the idea that there are specific moments in American history that can have a measurable effect on sociological behavior. Events like the Civil War, Pearl Harbor, the conflict in Vietnam, Watergate, and the September 11 attacks all changed the way that Americans think about themselves, their existence, and America's place in the world. Despite the fact that these events occurred when the members of a single birth cohort were roughly the same age, they each may have been shaped by these events in completely different ways. For example, those who were drafted in Vietnam and those who weren't may have vastly different outlooks on war and peace.[2]

The problem of understanding how the natural aging process and the reverberations of national or international events influence people sociologically is especially hard to disentangle when trying to understand American religion. As previously discussed, being an atheist in a deeply religious part of the country in 1980 was an entirely different reality from being in that same situation in 2019. The advent of the internet and social networks has had differential impacts on people's views on faith, religion, and spirituality. A Catholic who was raising young children in the church when the sex abuse scandal became national news likely had a different reaction from one who had no children or was far removed from the concerns of parenthood. September 11, 2001, drove a lot of people to return to church, but its long-term effect on religious behavior is statistically negligible. Seismic events like these can create outliers in the data concerning religious behavior and affiliation.

With that as context, I visualized the distribution of age in the seven religious traditions that were described in detail in chapter 1 as well as the distribution for the entire sample. Figure 3.1 represents data from 1972 through 1980 as a beeswarm plot. Where the plot gets wider, that represents a larger number of respondents bunched up around that age group. In addition, I included the average age for each faith tradition at the top of its plot. Note how that fatter part of the distribution for the entire sample is fairly wide at the bottom, which is reflective of the fact that 36.2 percent of adults were under the age of thirty-five in the 1970s. Many other traditions mirror this distribution. For instance, 34.8 percent of evangelicals and 39.3 percent of Catholics were in this age group as well. That is a strong indicator of the growth potential for these traditions, as these adherents are in peak fertility. But the numbers for the nones are clearly an outlier. Nearly six in ten of the religiously unaffiliated were under the age of thirty-five in 1972–80. No other faith tradition had above 45 percent of its adherents in that cohort.

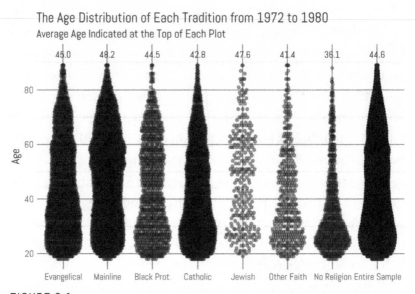

The Age Distribution of Each Tradition from 1972 to 1980
Average Age Indicated at the Top of Each Plot

FIGURE 3.1

Data from the General Social Survey, a project of the independent research organization NORC at the University of Chicago, with principal funding from the National Science Foundation, https://gss.norc.org/Get-The-Data.

However, things shift when the sample is restricted to just 2008 through 2018. Most notably, every tradition has gotten older because Americans have gotten much older in the past four decades. That's largely a function of fertility rates undergoing a slow and predictable decline. It's unlikely that we will see another baby boom in the near future. As a result, the distribution of age looks much different today. For instance, the largest bulge for evangelicals used to be under the age of forty, but no more. Now the wide part of the distribution is between the ages of forty and fifty. The shift for mainline Protestants is even more dramatic. Now the average mainline Protestant is 57.4 years old—an increase of 9.2 years, easily the biggest shift of any group. However, the nones have gotten older as well. The average religiously unaffiliated American is now six years older today than they were in the 1970s, which is larger than the median increase in age for all Americans. Said another way, America is getting older, but the nones are getting older more rapidly.

While 59.2 percent of nones were under the age of thirty-five in the first graph, that has dropped to 40.2 percent in the past decade, which is visualized in figure 3.2. At the same time, the share of the unaffiliated who are at least sixty years old has jumped from 10 percent in the 1970s to 17 percent since 2008. However, it would still be statistically inaccurate to say that the prototypical none is now starting to sprout a few gray hairs. The modal age for a none in the 1970s (meaning the age that shows up the most in the distribution) was twenty-three years old. In the 2008 to 2018 shift, the modal is still just age thirty—which just so happens to be the modal age of the average American. That's a small shift when compared to evangelicals. The modal age of an evangelical in the 1970s was twenty-four years old. Today, the age that appears the most among evangelicals is fifty-eight. For mainline Protestants the modal age is now sixty-seven years of age. So it's fair to say that the nones have gotten older, but that was inevitable given the trends going on in American society. The larger concern for Christians is that their median age is climbing quickly, and with fewer young people to pack the pews with children, that could lead to a membership cliff in the coming decades.

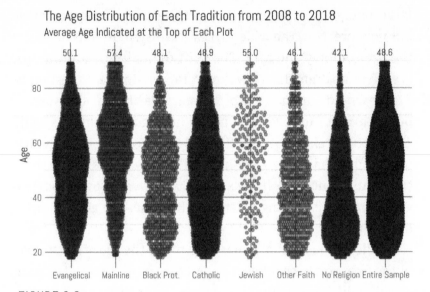

The Age Distribution of Each Tradition from 2008 to 2018
Average Age Indicated at the Top of Each Plot

FIGURE 3.2

Data from the General Social Survey, a project of the independent research organization NORC at the University of Chicago, with principal funding from the National Science Foundation, https://gss.norc.org/Get-The-Data.

However, there are other ways to look at the relationship between age and religious affiliation. As a way to get closer to the issue of birth cohorts, I grouped the sample into five generations: the Greatest Generation (1901–24), the Silent Generation (1925–44), baby boomers (1946–64), Generation X (1965–76), and millennials (1977–95). I then calculated the share of each generation that described itself as unaffiliated in each wave of the GSS, dating back to 1972 for figure 3.3. Because of how age interacts with these generational categories, the Greatest Generation has disappeared from the analysis because most of them have died, while millennials don't appear until the late 1990s, when the oldest of them moved into adulthood.

The trends for the Greatest Generation and the Silent Generation are similar but not identical. Note that the Silent Generation was always slightly more likely to be unaffiliated in the 1970s

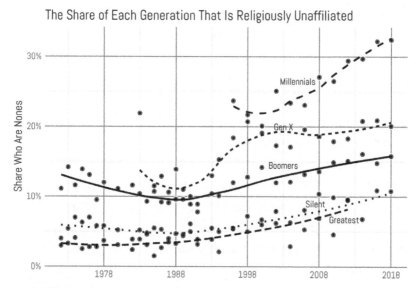

The Share of Each Generation That Is Religiously Unaffiliated

FIGURE 3.3

Data from the General Social Survey, a project of the independent research organization NORC at the University of Chicago, with principal funding from the National Science Foundation, https://gss.norc.org/Get-The-Data.

and 1980s; however, that gap narrowed in the 1990s. But it's also worth pointing out that for both it and the Greatest Generation, religiosity was not solidified at any age. As those from the Greatest Generation and the Silent Generation aged, they also became more likely to say that they were religiously unaffiliated. This may give some tacit support to the belief the social desirability bias (discussed at length in chapter 2) was masking people's true feelings on religion. As it became more socially acceptable to be a none, it looks like even people from these generations were more apt to state their true religious attachments.

The baby boomers show a progression that is completely unique to their generation. When the GSS began in 1972, the oldest baby boomers were just finishing high school, so the first portion of their trend line depicts the turbulence of youth. Note that about 13 percent of them said that they were unaffiliated in the early 1970s, but that figure actually dropped below 10 percent in the late 1980s, when many of them were getting married and starting families. However, from that point, the trend line rebounds and shows a steady upward trajectory. According to the most recent data, just over 16 percent of boomers are now unaffiliated.

That same trough is also apparent for Generation X but can be statistically deceiving. In the late 1980s, just a small fraction of Generation X had moved into adulthood, so the sample size included just the leading edge of Gen X. When all of them move into their twenties or early thirties, a clear upward trend is present. The share of Generation X who were unaffiliated nearly doubled from 1998 to 2003. However, from that point forward, the line has almost flattened out. The overall impression from the data is that about one in five members of this generation is unaffiliated, which is still below the average for the entire sample.

The same little trough that appeared around 1988 for Generation X appears about fifteen years later for millennials, when the oldest millennials were entering adulthood. But as more of them moved into their twenties, the line begins an unmistakable climb upward. It's notable how clear the data points are for the past decade, generating an incredibly consistent trend line. From 2013 to 2018, the share of millennials who were unaffiliated jumps 2.5 percentage points. Projecting these trends into the future is risky business, but with a trend that is so consistent, it seems safe to say that we have not seen a plateauing of the millennial nones. Just to put some clear numbers on this, in 2018, 10.8 percent of the Silent Generation were unaffiliated compared to 15.8 percent of baby boomers, 20.1 percent of Generation X, and 32.4 percent of millennials. The jump from Generation X to millennials is staggering in size.

One more essential piece of the puzzle is found by looking at generations that span fifteen to twenty years instead of sorting people into five-year birth cohorts. This helps zero in on period effects because while the oldest millennials were twenty-four when the Twin Towers fell, the youngest were just six years old. After dividing the GSS into twenty birth cohorts, the sample was clustered into six age ranges. The purpose of this is to understand if being someone who was thirty years old in 1980 has the same impact on religious affiliation as being thirty years old in 2000.

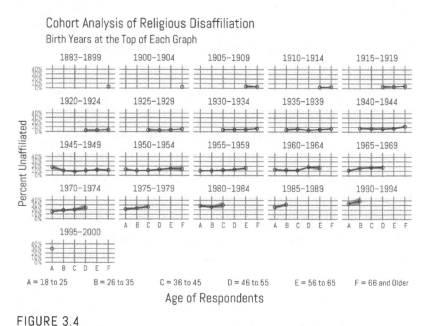

FIGURE 3.4

Data from the General Social Survey, a project of the independent research organization NORC at the University of Chicago, with principal funding from the National Science Foundation, https://gss.norc.org/Get-The-Data.

While the first row of figure 3.4 doesn't afford us the ability to see how individuals in those birth cohorts moved across the entire age range, the second row begins to reveal some interesting patterns as people aged. For those born between 1925 and 1944, the lines are essentially flat across the life course—meaning age had no impact on their rates of disaffiliation. But that begins to change for those born in the late 1940s. Many in this birth cohort seemed to drift away from religion in their early teens and midtwenties but then came back in large numbers and stayed there as they moved into middle age and retirement.

Then a new pattern begins to emerge in the third row of birth cohorts. The lines show an unmistakable trend—they move upward as these birth cohorts age. In essence, what this analysis reveals is that the older these people got, the more likely they were to walk away from religious affiliation. This wasn't a matter of being raised in a household without religion and never picking up a faith tradition along the way. These are individuals who identified as religiously affiliated but then begin to cast that aside as they age. But what amplifies this issue is that the y-intercept keeps going up. In other words, more people are entering adulthood without a religious affiliation, and they become more likely to stay a none as they age. To put a fine point on this, nearly a third of people who were born between 1990 and 1994 had no religious affiliation between the ages of eight and thirty-five. That's the highest share of any birth cohort at any age in the survey—and it jumps to nearly 40 percent as they moved into their late twenties.

As can probably be ascertained, age and time are difficult concepts to try to untangle methodologically. However, there seem to be a few clear messages that emerge. One is that the patterns that emerged from generations like the baby boomers and the silent generation are not that instructive when trying to understand religion among today's young people. Dozens of books on church growth have tried to glean insights from the way the baby boomers drifted in and out of a religious community, but the reality is that this was a unique moment in American history, and strategies for evangelizing millennials shouldn't be based on the findings derived from prior generations.

The other clear outcome is that no singular seismic event nudged Americans back toward a religious affiliation or toward becoming a none. Instead, the shift toward disaffiliation was gradual and unrelenting. It's clear that every successive generation starts out less religious than the one prior, but that's only a part of the puzzle. As these young people become more outspoken about their move away from religious affiliation, that gave permission to older people who had been sliding toward disaffiliation to finally declare their true religious attachments. If this is truly the case, then many more nominal Christians are going to check the "no religion" box going forward, and that's not necessarily true just among the youngest Americans.

EDUCATION

Recall that the preeminent sociologist Max Weber believed that education was antithetical to religion. Most well-educated European countries have been described as post-Christian because very few of their citizens see religion as an important part of their daily lives. As such, we would expect to see a similar pattern in the United States: more educated Americans disaffiliating from religion in larger numbers than those who had lower levels of educational attainment. Fortunately for social science, that's an easy theory to test given that the GSS also asks every respondent about their level of educational attainment.

I broke the sample into five educational groups, ranging from those who never finished high school to those who took graduate-level course work, and then calculated the share of each group who said that they had no religious affiliation between 1972 and 2018.

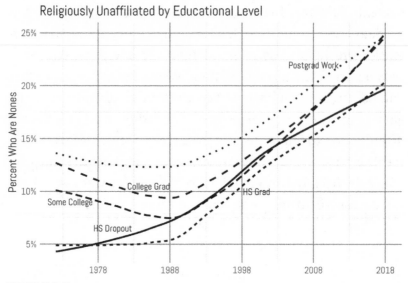

Religiously Unaffiliated by Educational Level

FIGURE 3.5

Data from the General Social Survey, a project of the independent research organization NORC at the University of Chicago, with principal funding from the National Science Foundation, https://gss.norc.org/Get-The-Data.

Figure 3.5 is fascinating because it really could be divided into two parts, before 1990 and after 1990. Before 1990, there's not a lot of movement to report and there's a near perfect relationship between education and religiously disaffiliation—the higher level of degree obtained, the more likely a respondent was to choose no religion. The gap between those who dropped out of high school and those who did graduate-level work is just about six percentage points.

But something happened after 1990, and all the lines begin to shoot up as the exponential rise of the nones emerges among all levels of education. However, the upward slope of the five lines is remarkably similar. Eventually, right around 2008, another interesting pattern begins to develop. Essentially two clear groups begin to form—those with a high school diploma or less and those who have attended at least some college courses or more. The difference in disaffiliation rates for the two groups stands at just about five percentage points, with about one in four of the high education group being religiously unaffiliated compared to one in five of those in the lower education group.

That seismic change in the early 1990s is also something worth dwelling on. While it's nearly impossible to put a finger on exactly why the nones were relatively stable until this point but then rose meteorically, there is a data point that seems relevant to this discussion. Recall from chapter 1 that evangelicals had seen a steady rise from the 1970s through the early 1980s, moving from 17 percent in 1972 to 22 percent by 1984. However, by 1984, evangelicals had hit 28.7 percent and then rose even higher to 29.9 percent of the population in 1993. This is also the period in which the religious right claimed their largest electoral victories. In the 1994 midterm elections, Republicans won fifty-four seats back in the House as well as eight Senate seats largely by campaigning on social values, many of which were included in the Contract with America.[3] It seems possible that this dramatic increase in disaffiliation is due, at least in part, to a backlash against conservative evangelical politics.

However, there may be something happening that is more subtle and impossible to detect in the prior analysis: that the impact of education has varied based on birth cohort. Consider the fact that just 4.6 percent of adults twenty-five and older had a bachelor's degree in 1940, but today that share has increased to 33.4 percent of adults. That indicates that earning a bachelor's degree may mean something entirely different today from what it did four decades ago and that rates of religious disaffiliation may depend more on birth cohort. To test that, I broke the sample into five-year birth cohorts and calculated the share of each educational level who had no religious affiliation.

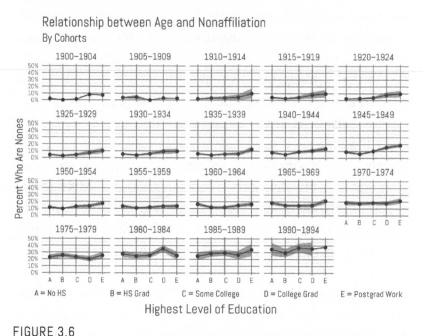

FIGURE 3.6

Data from the General Social Survey, a project of the independent research organization NORC at the University of Chicago, with principal funding from the National Science Foundation, https://gss.norc.org/Get-The-Data.

As can be quickly inferred from glancing at the line graphs in figure 3.6, there's not a clear and unmistakable relationship between education and being religiously unaffiliated. Said another way, this analysis does not provide clear support for Weber's secularization theory. However, it does find some support in a few of the birth cohorts. For instance, there is a pronounced upward trend line for those born in the latter half of the 1940s, so in this cohort, it is true that education did lead to secularization. This is also somewhat evident for those born between 1940 and 1944 but in a more muted way.

However, younger Americans (meaning those born in 1955 or later) seem to have a much flatter trend line, meaning that the relationship between higher levels of education and religious disaffiliation is nonexistent or very small. For instance, there's not a single birth cohort after 1970 in which those who have done some graduate work are statistically more likely to be unaffiliated than those who dropped out of high school.

Thus it's fair to say that if one meets a fortysomething with a master's degree, they are no more likely to be a religious none than someone they graduated high school with who didn't decide to pursue further education. These results provide only very minimal support for the idea that education and religious affiliation are negatively related. While that may have been somewhat true for generations that were born before 1950, the mass disaffiliation that appears in the data for those with college degrees largely abated in the last few decades.

Let me offer a possible explanation for the shift. As previously noted, the share of Americans who have earned a college degree has grown astronomically over time, which means that the type of people who went to college fifty years ago are likely much different from those who are attending classes today. A university education used to be reserved for those who came from upper-middle-class backgrounds, who may have been more inclined to shift away from religion anyway. Now people from all walks of life are earning bachelor's degrees. So while it still may be true that some people are lured away from religion after taking a few college philosophy courses, that's the exception, not the rule.

GENDER

What is, so far, an unexplored component of the rise of the nones is gender. Obviously, many of the demographic variables that have been discussed in this chapter are deeply impacted by gender disparities. While nearly 60 percent of all college graduates were women in 2016,[4] they are still making 85–90 cents for every dollar that a man makes in the workplace.[5] Additionally, while 86 percent of single-parent households were headed by a woman in 1960, that had only declined to 76 percent in 2011.[6] It's clear that women's financial and time constraints look much different from those of their male counterparts regardless of income, education, or parental status. But do women who are often struggling to make ends meet and raise children sacrifice religious commitment?

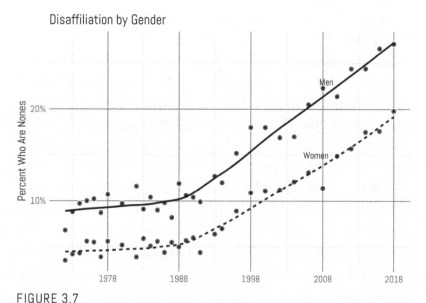

FIGURE 3.7

Data from the General Social Survey, a project of the independent research organization NORC at the University of Chicago, with principal funding from the National Science Foundation, https://gss.norc.org/Get-The-Data.

The data visualized in figure 3.7 clearly indicates that they do not. That characteristic "hockey stick" style of growth of the nones that appeared in my prior analysis is replicated here. Things were relatively flat until about 1990, when the rates of disaffiliation jumped for both men and women. And what is startling is how consistent the gap is between the two groups throughout the 1970s and 1980s: it's consistently roughly five percentage points during this time period. But as time passes, both groups disaffiliate more frequently, and the rate of disaffiliation for men begins to outstrip that of women. Since 2012, the gap has stood somewhere between seven and ten percentage points. Thus both genders are walking away from organized religion, but men are doing so at even higher rates. In 2018, 27.1 percent of men were nones compared to 19.8 percent of women.

One potential explanation for the religious disaffiliation gap between genders may be related to child-rearing. As previously mentioned, women are three times more likely to be in single-parent households today than men, which means that many more of them are faced with the question of whether they should make religion a part of their children's lives. As mentioned in chapter 1, having children can be a factor that helps limit the rate of religious disaffiliation, but what role does this play in keeping women in religious traditions? To test that, I broke the sample down by gender as well as by whether the respondents had children. Additionally, I limited the analysis to people under the age of fifty to concentrate only on those who would be wrestling with these issues related to child-rearing and religion.

Figure 3.8 is a fascinating look at the interplay between gender and parental status. It comes as no surprise that people without children are much more likely to have no religious affiliation than those who have children. In fact, nearly four in ten men who had no children in 2018 were a religious none, compared

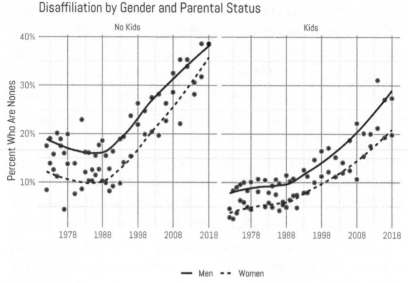

Disaffiliation by Gender and Parental Status

FIGURE 3.8

Data from the General Social Survey, a project of the independent research organization NORC at the University of Chicago, with principal funding from the National Science Foundation, https://gss.norc.org/Get-The-Data.

to just 28 percent of men with children. The gap for women was even larger—35 percent for childless women versus 20 percent for women with children. However, something peculiar has happened in recent years among the childless—the gender gap has closed. More specifically, the difference in religious disaffiliation rates for men and women without children has shrunk to zero in 2018 (although the trend lines haven't caught up yet). For those with children, the gap is much larger—nearly 9 percent. But comparing the two groups of women reveals a staggering fact—while 19.8 percent of women with kids were a none in 2018, the rate of disaffiliation among women without kids is 38.5 percent. In essence, a childless woman is twice as likely to be a none. For men, the gap is significant as well (eleven percentage points), but smaller than women.

This is worth some consideration. As noted previously, marriage and children are key touchstones that typically bring people back into religious communities. Marriage as an institution has declined significantly as part of a typical life course for younger Americans. However, the data indicates that while fewer people are getting married every year, the share of Americans who do not have children has stayed remarkably stable. That means that the vast majority of individuals who choose to be childless are making a conscious decision to pursue a lifestyle that stands in opposition to the dominant culture. It takes no huge theoretical leap to assume that this decision is much more difficult for a woman to make than a man. Consider the fact that until 2008, a majority of women said that they preferred staying home and taking care of their family, and just 56 percent of women in 2019 preferred a job outside the home.[7] A willfully childless woman has to fight against a great variety of societal pressures, many of which emerge from traditional religious beliefs about gender roles. Thus these women may feel even greater relief when walking away from religion, as they are no longer subject to messages that try to undermine their lifestyle choices.

RACE

As is the case with gender and religion, there is also a significant social component to race and religion as well. For most of the history of the United States, white Christianity was the dominant religious tradition. However, that has slowly begun to change as factors related to immigration and secularization have significantly altered American society.[8] For many racial groups, there is a strong cultural connection to a religious tradition. For instance, despite the fact that many Latinx have been in the United States for generations, they often still have a strong familial connection to a religious tradition.[9] Likewise, Black American culture has always placed a great deal of emphasis on Protestant Christianity.[10] However, those who trace their ancestry back to the Eastern religions of Asia have a different cultural sensibility from those with other racial backgrounds.[11] Because of these differences, the level of cultural acceptance of religious disaffiliation varies widely.

While the GSS only offers three racial options (white, Black, and other), the larger Cooperative Congressional Election Survey provides many more, including white, Black, Hispanic, Asian, and several other options. It also allows respondents to specify whether they are an atheist, agnostic, or "nothing in particular," as was previously mentioned in chapter 1. This affords us tremendous insight into not just the rate of religious disaffiliation by racial group but also what label people choose when they leave organized religion.

It's clear from figure 3.9 that Asians are an outlier compared to the other racial groups. In 2008, they were 10 percentage points more likely to be religiously unaffiliated than any other racial group. That upward trend has continued, and now four in ten Asians have no religious affiliation. The other racial groups (white, Black, Hispanic, and others) land much lower than the Asian sample. For instance, 20.8 percent of whites were nones in 2008; that has jumped to 33.4 percent by 2018, slightly higher than the overall average of 31.3 percent. Hispanic disaffiliation is more modest. In 2008, just 18.6 percent were nones; now the share is 29.7 percent. What might be the most surprising racial group is Black Americans, however. In 2008, they were the least likely to be religiously unaffiliated (17.7 percent). In just a ten-year time period, the rate of disaffiliation has jumped a staggering 14.4 percentage points to 32.1 percent. It seems possible that the share of Black people who are nones might double in less than fifteen years.

Disaffiliation by Race

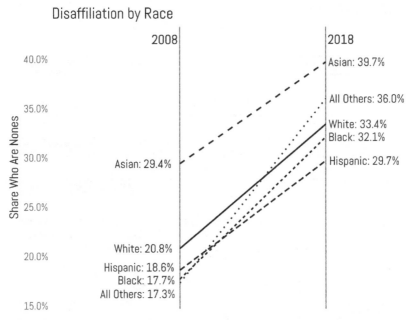

FIGURE 3.9

Data from Stephen Ansolabehere, Brian F. Schaffner, and Sam Luks, Cooperative Congressional Election Study, Cambridge, MA: Harvard University, http://cces.gov.harvard.edu.

While looking at nones as a general category provides a good starting point, digging into which label they choose can provide a window into how culture impacts religious disaffiliation. The three options of atheist, agnostic, and nothing in particular provide respondents the freedom to indicate whether they have truly walked away from religion to become an atheist or agnostic or just don't feel strongly about religion and fall into the nothing-in-particular category. As you can see in figure 3.10, this distinction does make a difference for some racial groups.

A significant number of white nones are comfortable with claiming an affiliation that is far from theism. In fact, over four in ten white nones are atheists or agnostics—the highest share of any racial group. On the other end of the spectrum are

Types of Nones by Race

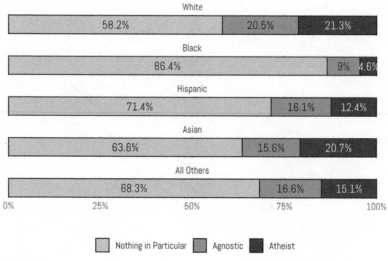

FIGURE 3.10
Data from Stephen Ansolabehere, Brian F. Schaffner, and Sam Luks, Cooperative Congressional Election Study, Cambridge, MA: Harvard University, http://cces.gov.harvard.edu.

Hispanics and Black people. Hispanics are ten percentage points less likely to say that they are an atheist or agnostic compared to white Americans. However, Black Americans are even more reluctant to totally reject religion, with 9 percent of Black respondents identifying as agnostic and just 4.6 percent claiming to be atheists. Consider this: a white none is three times more likely to be an atheist or agnostic compared with a Black person. The cultural forces that shape religious choice in minority communities look much different from those among white Americans.

CONCLUSION

Taken together, the data paints a chilling picture. There is no segment of American society that has been immune to the rise of religious disaffiliation. While it would be easy to say that this is largely driven by young people moving away from a religious faith, there's also some evidence that older Americans are moving away from faith communities as they enter their twilight years. While churches used to rely on many of their young people moving back toward a religious tradition when they hit their thirties and forties, that seems to be less and less likely with each successive generation.

The data indicates that less-educated Americans are only slightly less likely to move away from religion than those who have at least some college education, but as more and more Americans pursue course work at the collegiate level, the likelihood of disaffiliation does increase. At the same time, many of the societal factors that used to keep women in church have begun to fade. In 2018, a woman without children is just as likely to be a none as a childless man. That portends a bleak future for religion, as more Americans are choosing to be child-free. Some of the cultural influences that surround religion among racial groups have diminished as well. The rise in disaffiliation among Black Americans is alarmingly rapid, and now there is no racial group that is not at least 30 percent religiously disaffiliated.

I think comparing American churches to a foam cup of water is an appropriate analogy. Churches have always had pinholes punched in the sides of their cups. They would lose water through the deaths of their older members, but the water kept being replenished by young families bringing their children or by members converting people from the community. For many, the water being poured in vastly exceed the amount that was lost through the pinhole-sized leaks. Now those small drips have become gaping holes, and the water is leaving rapidly. Those holes represent a rapidly aging core demographic that is dying off, but those punctures also include those who grew up in the church but then left, never to return. At the same time, the flow of water that used to refill the cup has slowed to a trickle as churches continue to struggle to bring in new members.

If the flow of water into the cup slows down even more or the holes expand in diameter, the cup is going to run empty at some point in the near future. But all is not lost. The next chapter will focus on the three types of nones—atheists, agnostics, and nothing in particulars. If the church wants to increase the flow into its cup, there are potentially large reservoirs in the American population, some of which seem fairly easy to tap. Other data may also point toward ways to reduce the size of the holes that have formed in their cups. If less water flows out the bottom and more pours in from the top, churches can maintain their congregations far into the future.

CHAPTER 4

Nones Are Not All Created Equal

ONE OF THE MOST MEMORABLE TRIPS OF MY COLLEGE EXPERIENCE was a long weekend in Chicago as part of the required curriculum at Greenville College. The goal of the trip was simple: expose college freshmen to a broader range of religious expression than they likely experienced growing up. I can honestly say that it changed my life. The first stop was at an Episcopal church. As someone who had grown up Southern Baptist, I had no experience with the mainline tradition. Things only became more awkward when I realized that the priest who was going to conduct the service and serve Communion was a lesbian. As she gave me a sip of real wine (the first alcohol to touch my lips), I knew that I could never tell my very evangelical grandmother about my experiences in Chicago.

The experience only became more disorienting from there. We attended a Catholic mass at a large cathedral, and we sat in a synagogue and heard a rabbi read the Torah in Hebrew on Friday night. We wrested with the similarities between Christianity and Islam while visiting a mosque. I will never forget the sense of awe, wonder, and silence that pervaded the Bahá'í House of Worship as I stared up over one hundred and thirty feet to the top of their temple on the North Shore of Chicago. Before we boarded the buses to return to downstate Illinois, we also worshiped at St. Benedict the African Catholic Church, which features a truly unique combination of Catholic liturgy and Pentecostal song and dance.

I still wrestle with some of the things I saw, heard, and felt while on that three-day trip. But one thought that struck me immediately as we drove back home through the cornfields was that religion is so incredibly diverse that I will never truly be able to understand it all.

The same may be even more true for the various ways one can be religiously unaffiliated. Up to this point, I have largely treated all the nones as a single social group. Obviously, that's a total oversimplification. In fact, lumping all of them together is just as inaccurate as trying to analyze all Christians as a single group. My trip to Chicago made that painfully clear to me.

In some ways, the religiously unaffiliated are the most difficult groups to characterize in American society. At least Christians can agree that the Bible is a sacred text and that a worship service should contain some songs, Scripture reading, and prayer. The religiously unaffiliated are not a cohesive group in the same way. The reality is that the only thing that truly binds them together is the fact that they might all check the same box on the survey form.

What makes matters even more difficult is that the General Social Survey (GSS), which I have been using extensively in the last few chapters, affords only that one box for the nones: "no religion." That places someone who actively tries to convert people away from religion in the same category as someone who just doesn't think about matters of faith that much at all.

However, I have another data source that does allow for a deep dive into the different types of religiously unaffiliated Americans. The Cooperative Congressional Election Study (CCES), which surveyed over sixty thousand people in 2018, indicates that 35 percent of Americans are Protestants, while 31.3 percent are religiously unaffiliated. The Protestant group is further divided into seventy denominations. The religiously unaffiliated are broken down into three categories: atheists, agnostics, and nothing in particular. Clearly, those three options for identifying as a none are still unduly reductive, but they can provide more nuance than the one category that exists in the GSS.

Despite the fact that all the nones are lumped into just three groups, a great deal of insight can be extracted from these three categories. After analyzing these three groups for the past few years, I have developed a clearer picture of the nones. Obviously, an atheist has an entirely different outlook on religion, politics, and their place in the world from someone who merely selects the "nothing in particular" option. These choices have huge ramifications for denominational leaders and potential evangelists who wonder what type of people would be receptive to an invitation to attend a church service or openly talk about matters of faith.

What follows is a brief description of each of the three none groups, followed by some basic demographics to provide some broad details about the differences between atheists, agnostics, and nothing in particulars. Finally, I will discuss the religious characteristics of each group. The data tells a clear and unmistakable story: nones are not all created equal.

ATHEISTS

It's fair to say that when someone talks about the "nones," their minds likely jump to atheists. Often in discussions, I hear pastors and other religious leaders use the term *atheists* as a catchall for people who are not attached to a religious tradition. In many ways, atheists are an atypical, slightly extreme version of nones. As was discussed in chapter 1, atheists make up about 6 percent of the adult population of the United States—just one in five of all the nones. So while they are obviously vocal on internet forums, they don't speak for the majority of the nones.

The data indicates that there's a great deal of antiatheist sentiment among the American public, so to choose the term *atheist* on a survey means to accept all the baggage that comes with that term. The 2012 American National Election Study asked respondents to rate their attitudes toward twenty-two groups on a scale ranging from 0 (meaning very cool) to 100 (meaning very warm). The average score for each group is visualized on a single line in figure 4.1.

Working-class people do very well, scoring 83.1 on a scale from 0 to 100. Just behind them is the military at 80.5. Christians as a whole score 72.6, while Catholics come in about ten points lower at 61.1. Atheists are at the very bottom of the graph. The mean score for this group is 38.4, which is four points lower than the United States Congress. The religious group that is the closest in score to atheists are religious fundamentalists, and they are more than ten points higher at 49.1. Clearly, there's a great deal of antiatheist bias in the United States, so to voluntarily take on that moniker is to invite possible ridicule and ostracism. As such, atheists tend to be the most militant in their belief system.

AGNOSTICS

The term *agnostic* dates back to 1869, when Thomas Henry Huxley, the right-hand man to Charles Darwin, used it in a speech to describe his view of the supernatural. It comes from the Greek term *gnosis*, which means "to know" and, when combined with the prefix *a-*, indicates an uncertain view of the supernatural. Huxley stated, "It simply means that a man shall not say he

Thermometer Score of Various Groups

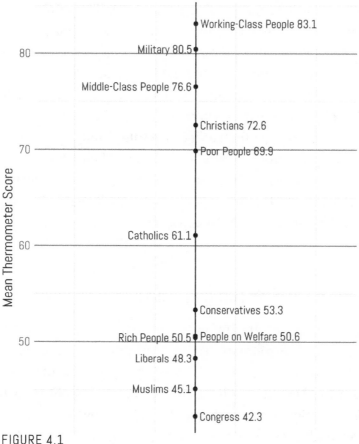

FIGURE 4.1

Data from the American National Election Study, "2012 Time Series Study," https://tinyurl.com/y2rncj8l.

knows or believes that which he has no scientific grounds for professing to know or believe."[1]

As such, agnostics are a step removed from the certainty that is espoused by atheists, who clearly believe that there is no Higher Power in the world. Often agnostics will use the language and construction of reason or scientific inquiry to indicate that because there can be no irrefutable evidence for God's existence, it would be improper for anyone with this worldview to say that God does or does not exist. Instead, agnostics are open to the possibility that either conclusion may be proven empirically true.

Agnostics, as will be described in the remainder of this chapter, are a hard group to understand from a data perspective. Just like atheists, they make up about 6 percent of the adult population. They also sometimes behave in ways that make them seem even more extreme than atheists, while through other lenses, they are much more moderate in belief and behavior. While few surveys ask specifically about people's opinions of agnostics, it does seem likely that they avoid some of the negative sentiment that is linked to the atheist label.

NOTHING IN PARTICULAR

The group that is often forgotten when talking about the nones doesn't have a sophisticated-sounding name like *atheist* or *agnostic*. In fact, this group is unified by a rejection of all labels. When the Pew Research Center asks people about their religious tradition, it gives them twelve options, beginning with the larger traditions like Protestant and Catholic. But after listing both atheist and agnostic, there's one more category: "nothing in particular." This group might be the most consequential religious group in the United States, and no one is talking about them the way they talk about atheists or agnostics.

What is a "nothing in particular"? My conception of this group is that when they are asked the survey question about religious affiliation, instead of feeling strongly one way or the other about being attached to a theistic religion—like Baptists, Mormons, or Muslims—or about having no religious inclinations, like atheists and agnostics, they just shrug their shoulders and check the "nothing in particular" box. Note that this is not the same as saying that they are a member of a religious group that is not listed on the survey, because the very last option after "nothing in particular" is "something else," which allows people to type their affiliation in a text box. So we know that these individuals are not Wiccans or Jedis. Instead, these are people that just don't feel strongly about religion one way or the other.

Nothing in particulars happen to be part of one of the largest religious groups in the United States. If all the nones were represented by just five people, one of them would be an atheist, another one would be agnostic, and three of them would be nothing in particulars. That clearly doesn't fit the image most people have of what the nones look like. In the general American population, one in five Americans is a nothing in particular.

While its size alone makes the nothing-in-particular group one to watch, another fact demands that people pay attention to them: they are the fastest-growing religious group in the United States. I visualized the three largest Christian groups: white evangelicals, white Catholics, and mainline Protestants in figure 4.2. Only white evangelicals have seen any growth in the past decade, and their increase has been very slight—just over 1 percentage point. At the same time, the nothing in particular group has grown 5.6 percentage points. Here's a staggering statistic: one in twenty Americans has become a nothing in particular over the past decade. That increase in their ranks alone is nearly the same size as the total share of atheists or agnostics in 2018.

However, while it is not easy to conceptualize what atheists and agnostics have in common, it's essentially impossible to find any true commonalities among the nothing in particulars. At least atheists and agnostics have a worldview they agree on; the same is not true for nothing in particulars. While the other two types of nones are often antagonistic toward religious beliefs and behavior, the same intensity is not present among nothing

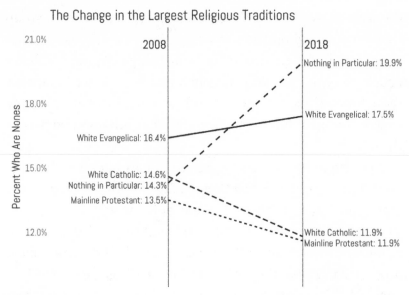

The Change in the Largest Religious Traditions

FIGURE 4.2

Data from Stephen Ansolabehere, Brian F. Schaffner, and Sam Luks, Cooperative Congressional Election Study, Cambridge, MA: Harvard University, http://cces.gov.harvard.edu.

in particulars. As the following analysis will illustrate, these are often the most distant, isolated, and checked-out members of society.

AGE

As previously described in chapter 3, age has a tremendous impact on the likelihood that individuals will disaffiliate from a religious tradition or change their overall church attendance. At the same time, it does not seem to affect the likelihood of their becoming a nothing in particular versus an atheist or agnostic. The average American in 2018 was 47.7 years old. In comparison, the nones are about six years younger on average. But the differences in the average age between the three kinds of nones are within the margin of error. For nothing in particulars, it's 41.8; for agnostics, it's 42.0; and for atheists, it's 42.1. Looked at merely through the prism of average age, it would be easy to think that the three types of nones are similar, but when the sample is divided up into age ranges, clear differences emerge, as is clear in figure 4.3.

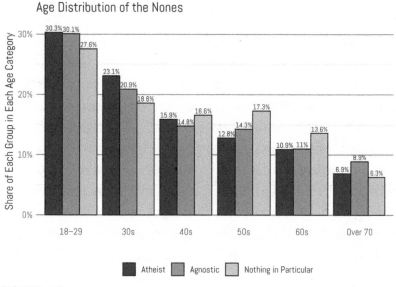

Age Distribution of the Nones

FIGURE 4.3

Data from Stephen Ansolabehere, Brian F. Schaffner, and Sam Luks, Cooperative Congressional Election Study, Cambridge, MA: Harvard University, http://cces.gov.harvard.edu.

For instance, the youngest adults in the United States, those under the age of thirty, are slightly more likely to be atheists or agnostics than they are to identify as nothing in particulars. Three in ten of all atheists and agnostics fall into this youngest age group. The same general pattern is evident for people in their thirties. Atheists make up the largest part of nones, followed by agnostics, and then nothing in particulars. However, things begin to shift when we look at people in their forties.

Those between forty and forty-nine years of age are more likely to be nothing in particulars than they are to identify as atheists or agnostics, but the overall differences are relatively small. For those in their fifties and sixties, there's a clear aversion to the atheist and agnostic labels. Both age groups are much more likely to identify as nothing in particular. Inexplicably, those over the age of seventy prefer the agnostic label to atheist or nothing in particular.

Looked at broadly, half of all atheists and agnostics and more than 45 percent of nothing in particulars have not seen their fortieth birthday. Fewer than one in five atheists or agnostics is over the age of sixty. Clearly, older Americans are less apt to be nones, but if they do disaffiliate from religion, the choice seems to be the "nothing in particular" category. Recall the previous data indicating a great deal of cool feelings expressed toward atheism. It's fair to assume that this may be particularly felt among older Americans, thus turning them away from adopting the atheist or agnostic label. The same coolness is not felt by younger people. It's possible that the erosion of social desirability bias may lead younger people to express their true position: they are atheists or agnostics.

GENDER

Here's a quick thought experiment: picture an atheist or agnostic in your mind. What gender are they? I'm going to guess that most people conjure up an image of a man. That does make sense. If you ask people who are interested in atheism to name authors who have had the most profound impact on their religious worldview, many of them will list Sam Harris, Christopher

Hitchens, and Richard Dawkins. In February 2020, I went on Amazon and looked at the top-selling books about atheism. Of the top thirty best sellers, just two were written by women. It seems that atheism is largely a male-dominated enterprise—and the data backs that up.

Gender Breakdown of the Nones

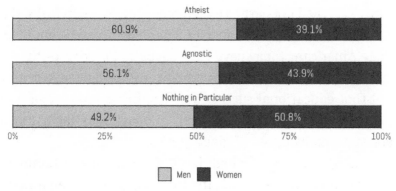

FIGURE 4.4

Data from Stephen Ansolabehere, Brian F. Schaffner, and Sam Luks, Cooperative Congressional Election Study, Cambridge, MA: Harvard University, http://cces.gov.harvard.edu.

A simple gender breakdown in figure 4.4 provides a clear and unmistakable picture—atheists are much more likely to be male. In fact, just two out of five atheists in 2018 were women. Agnostics have a slightly more equitable gender distribution, with 43.9 percent of this group identifying as female. However, the only group that represents any kind of gender parity is nothing in particulars, who are evenly split between the genders and thus mirror the general public. One has to wonder if atheism will have a hard time growing in the future because most women who convert to that label will have to be persuaded by male authors.

EDUCATION

Essential to understanding the differences in the types of religious nones is noting just how much they differ in overall level of education. One of the biggest shifts in American life that has gone relatively unnoticed because of how gradually it has occurred is the massive increase in educational attainment by the general population. For instance, in 1972, nearly four in ten Americans had not earned a high school diploma; by 2018, that number had declined to just 12.9 percent. In addition, many more Americans today have gained a bachelor's degree than in years past. Now one in three Americans has a college degree. But that educational success (and the increased income that typically comes with higher levels of education) has not been enjoyed equally by all religious groups.

Atheists have a very high level of educational attainment, as is apparent in figure 4.5. In 2018, nearly half of all atheists had earned a bachelor's degree (44.2 percent). In fact, there is no major Christian group in the United States that can say that they have higher levels of education than atheists. Agnostics follow closely behind atheists, with four in ten having completed a bachelor's program, which is the same level of education usually attained by mainline Protestants. But to find the last type of nones, the nothing in particulars, you have to move all the way to the bottom of the graph. Just one in five members of this group completed a bachelor's degree, which is thirteen points lower than the general population. Both agnostics and atheists are twice as likely to have met this academic threshold as nothing in particulars. It's obvious from this angle that nothing in particulars are not demographically similar to atheists or agnostics.

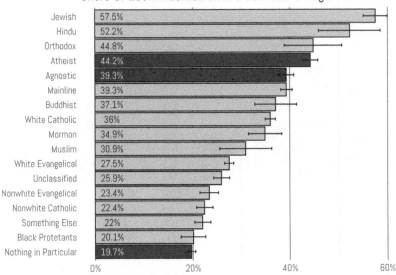

Share of Each Tradition with a Bachelor's Degree or More

FIGURE 4.5

Data from Stephen Ansolabehere, Brian F. Schaffner, and Sam Luks, Cooperative Congressional Election Study, Cambridge, MA: Harvard University, http://cces.gov.harvard.edu.

INCOME

The impact of this educational attainment on the income of the different religiously unaffiliated groups is profound. For instance, while half of the overall population of the United States earns less than $50,000 per year in household income, nearly 60 percent of the nothing in particulars earn less. That's much higher than the percentage of atheists or agnostics in that bracket. Consider this: a nothing in particular is 50 percent more likely to land in the lowest income category than an agnostic.

Those differences also appear at the top of the income spectrum in figure 4.6. One-quarter of all atheists have an annual household income of at least $100,000, while one in five agnostics does. Nothing in particulars lag far behind, with just 12.7 percent

Income Distribution among the Nones

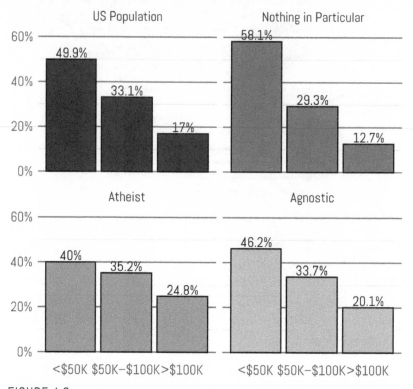

FIGURE 4.6

Data from Stephen Ansolabehere, Brian F. Schaffner, and Sam Luks, Cooperative Congressional Election Study, Cambridge, MA: Harvard University, http://cces.gov.harvard.edu.

making six figures per year. That is also nearly five percentage points behind the national average. From both an educational and income angle, the data tells an unmistakable story: while atheists, agnostics, and nothing in particulars are all classified as "nones," that term glosses over vast differences in the lifestyles, occupations, and political worldviews of these three groups. If anything, this finding underscores the fact that the nothing in particulars are one of the most educationally and economically disadvantaged groups in the United States today, while atheists and agnostics enjoy much higher levels of economic success. But does that play a role in their political behaviors and opinions?

POLITICAL PARTISANSHIP AND IDEOLOGY

Two concepts in political science—ideology and partisanship—help orient groups across the political landscape. Ideology is typically measured on a five-point scale that ranges from very liberal to very conservative, with the midpoint being labeled moderate. Partisanship spans seven points, with strong Democrat on the left side, strong Republican on the right side, and Independent in the middle. While it is true that these two measures are often correlated, many Americans consider themselves conservative Democrats, and there are even a few liberal Republicans in the mix as well. To get a sense of where the three types of nones fall on both dimensions, I generated a scatterplot of eleven different religious groups with partisanship on the horizontal axis and ideology on the vertical axis. The bottom left corner of figure 4.7 would indicate a very liberal strong Democrat, while the top right would be where a very conservative strong Republican would find themselves.

To orient ourselves in political space, I also calculated the mean partisanship and ideology for the entire sample. The average American finds themselves almost smack in the middle of both continuums; however, on partisanship, they are ever so slightly to the left of center. The top right of the graph is filled with the expected groups—white evangelicals and Mormons, but there is quite a bit of clustering around the middle of the graph. A linear relationship can be detected as well. The more a group identifies with the Republican party, the more likely that they are to describe themselves as conservative. There are a few outliers on this trend line though. For instance, Black Protestants are

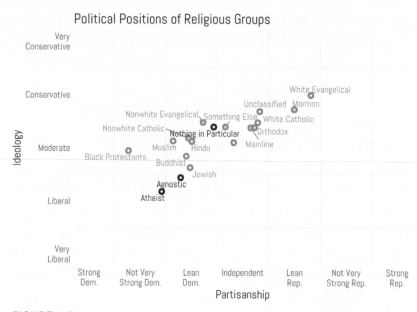

Political Positions of Religious Groups

FIGURE 4.7

Data from Stephen Ansolabehere, Brian F. Schaffner, and Sam Luks, Cooperative Congressional Election Study, Cambridge, MA: Harvard University, http://cces.gov.harvard.edu.

the farthest group to the left on the partisanship scale, but they describe themselves as moderates in terms of ideology.

Where do the nones fit into this mix? The nothing in particular group is right in the middle of the graph, not too far from the average for the entire sample. However, nothing in particulars are just to the left of the mean on partisanship but are also slightly more likely to identify as conservative than the average American. Atheists and agnostics are clearly outliers when it comes to religious groups. Atheists are easily the most liberal political group, with agnostics not far behind. However, on the partisanship continuum, it's fair to say that they not as solidly Democrat as would be expected. Black Protestants are quite a bit to the left of atheists and agnostics when it comes to identifying as strong Democrats. This analysis makes clear that while religious demographers lump the nothing in particulars, atheists, and agnostics into a single category, there are vast differences in their political viewpoints.

POLITICAL ACTIVITY

Another dimension to politics merits some discussion when it comes to the nones. While the prior graph indicates that the atheists and agnostics are fairly liberal and lean toward the Democratic party and the nothing in particulars fall somewhere in the middle on both dimensions, that matters little unless those groups are consistently engaged in political activity. Recall that the nothing in particulars had the lowest level of education of any religious group in 2018, with less than a quarter obtaining a four-year college degree. On the other hand, atheists and agnostics were some of the most educated people in the United States. How does that translate to the real world of politics? Do atheists and agnostics engage in political activity at a higher rate than the nothing in particulars?

A battery of questions in the 2018 Cooperative Congressional Election Study (CCES) listed six political activities and asked respondents if they had engaged in that activity in the prior twelve months. I calculated the share of atheists, agnostics, and nothing in particulars who said they did participate in those political activities, as well as visualized the percentage of the general public who participated in those six ways. This illustrates nicely the gulfs that exist among the nones.

First, note in figure 4.8 that atheists are clearly the most politically active none group. A quarter of them attended a protest or march, 40 percent had contacted a public official, and a quarter had displayed a political sign. All those rates are dramatically higher than the general population. Agnostics do not fall

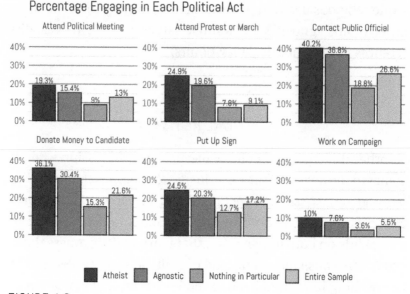

Percentage Engaging in Each Political Act

FIGURE 4.8

Data from Stephen Ansolabehere, Brian F. Schaffner, and Sam Luks, Cooperative Congressional Election Study, Cambridge, MA: Harvard University, http://cces.gov.harvard.edu.

far behind their atheist counterparts. Many engage in political activities at a much higher rate than the general public (often just a few percentage points lower than atheists).

Nothing in particulars are an entirely different story. For all six political activities, not only do they engage at lower rates than atheists or agnostics; they also are much less likely to participate than the general public. For instance, just 9 percent of nothing in particulars have attended a political meeting, compared to 13 percent of the general population and 19 percent of atheists. Atheists are three times more likely to attend a protest and nearly twice as likely to work on a political campaign.

Obviously, some of this difference can be attributed to the fact that nothing in particulars have much lower levels of education and income, as previously mentioned, but having a lower socioeconomic status does not preclude people from engaging in political behaviors, such as putting up a lawn sign or contacting a public official. On every measure of political participation, they fall far behind. But in addition to political activities, the survey also asked if the respondent had given blood in the last year. While 15 percent of atheists and agnostics said yes, just one in ten nothing in particulars said they did. While this group makes up nearly one in five Americans, they are largely politically forgotten because they do not engage in meaningful ways in the electoral process or society in general. While the nothing in particulars are obviously nones, they need to be understood as their own distinct group, with much different demographics and behavior from atheists and agnostics.

RELIGIOUS ATTENDANCE

While the data is clear that the nothing in particular group is much less likely to engage in social activities, such as attending college or giving blood, and political actions like putting up a political sign, does that mean that this group is also more hesitant to darken a church door for Sunday service? Here, the narrative changes somewhat. Looking through the lens of religion brings the picture into focus, revealing that the nothing in particulars as a group seem to be less averse to religious belief and religious activities than either atheists or agnostics. That's clearly true when it comes to how often they attend church, shown in figure 4.9.

It seems logical that atheists would be the least likely to attend services. Prior data indicates that atheists face some negative feelings in the general public, and to take on the label "atheist" means that it is embraced only by those who feel very far away from any type of organized religion. The data corroborates that position. In fact, 96.6 percent of atheists indicate that they "seldom" or

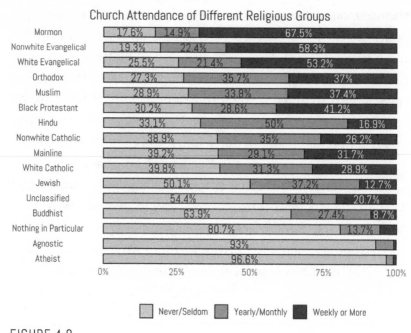

Church Attendance of Different Religious Groups

FIGURE 4.9

Data from Stephen Ansolabehere, Brian F. Schaffner, and Sam Luks, Cooperative Congressional Election Study, Cambridge, MA: Harvard University, http://cces.gov.harvard.edu.

"never" attend church. Agnostics are somewhat more apt to go to church but not by much. While nearly 90 percent of atheists report never attending, just seven in ten agnostics do. However, when the "never" and "seldom" responses are collapsed together, 93 percent of agnostics fall into these two categories. Nothing in particulars are more likely to participate in religious services at least sometimes. In fact, one in ten of this group attends yearly, and another 10 percent attend monthly or more. However, still half of nothing in particulars never come to church, and another quarter describe their attendance as "seldom." The data seems to indicate what an outside observer would guess: atheists are the furthest away from a faith tradition, while agnostics are somewhat closer, with nothing in particulars having a somewhat higher frequency of church attendance.

RELIGIOUS IMPORTANCE

Church attendance is just one aspect of religiosity, as was discussed in chapter 1. Another dimension is religious belief, and while the Cooperative Congressional Election Survey did not ask about specific religious doctrines, it did ask, "How important is religion in your life?" In figure 4.10, the same general pattern related to religious behavior seems to be replicated, with some small variations.

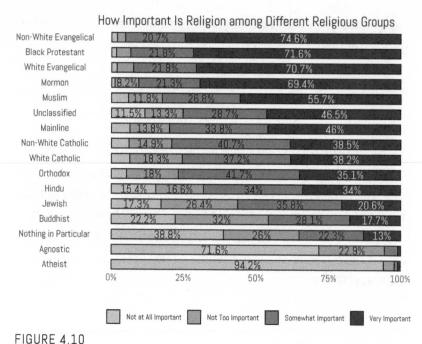

How Important Is Religion among Different Religious Groups

FIGURE 4.10

Data from Stephen Ansolabehere, Brian F. Schaffner, and Sam Luks, Cooperative Congressional Election Study, Cambridge, MA: Harvard University, http://cces.gov.harvard.edu.

For instance, nearly 95 percent of all atheists say that religion is "not at all important" in their lives. That largely tracks what appeared in the prior graph related to church attendance. However, that same sentiment is shared by just 71.6 percent of agnostics, but another 22.9 percent of them say that religion is "not too important." In essence, the difference between these two groups is just a few percentage points. However, we see that nothing in particulars seem to place more importance on religion. For instance, 35 percent of nothing in particulars say that religion is "somewhat" or "very" important in their lives, while at the same time, only 38.8 percent believe that religion is "not at all important."

From the standpoint of those who are interested in perhaps trying to convert a religious none into a Christian tradition, the data indicates that the group of people who are the most closed off to the possibility of religion are atheists, followed closely by agnostics. Consider the fact the 95 percent of atheists say that religion is "not at all important" and 90 percent of them never attend church: this group is not ambivalent about religion; they actively resist it. Nothing in particulars, on the other hand, seem to be at least somewhat open to the possibility of becoming part of a faith community. One in five of them attends church at least once a year, and a third of them say that religion is at least "somewhat important." But does that data mean that conversion is possible?

CONVERSION RATES

The vast majority of surveys in social science are longitudinal. What that means is that the survey administrators randomly poll a group of people every two years. Every wave of the survey represents an entirely new set of randomly selected individuals. This type of survey helps us understand how the size and composition of religious groups have shifted over time, but it does not tell us why those shifts occur. For instance, the GSS indicates that 23.1 percent of Americans are nones today, but it cannot tell us where they came from. Panel data helps pull back the curtain on those questions. Instead of asking a different set of people a series of questions every two years, a panel survey asks the same questions to the same people more than once over time. While panel surveys are not perfect, they are well suited not only for tracking the shifts in the sizes of religious groups but also for telling us how those shifts occurred.

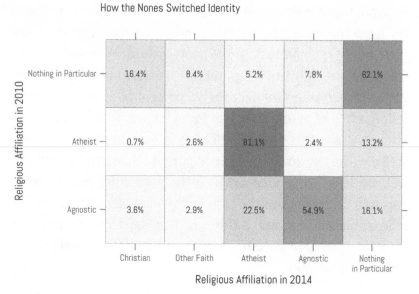

How the Nones Switched Identity

FIGURE 4.11

Data from Stephen Ansolabehere, Brian F. Schaffner, and Sam Luks, Coop-erative Congressional Election Study, Cambridge, MA: Harvard University, http://cces.gov.harvard.edu.

The CCES team did a panel survey that began in 2010 and was followed up in 2012 and 2014. That means that researchers can track how people moved across the religious landscape, jumping from being Catholics or Protestants to nothing in particulars or agnostics to atheists over a four-year period. It provides us an unprecedented look at how the none groups work and how individuals move in and out of these categories as time passes.

To get a sense of how the three types of nones shift their affili-ation, I looked at where people who had identified as agnostic, atheist, or nothing in particular in 2010 ended up when they took the final survey in the fall of 2014. The results (visualized in figure 4.11) tell a fascinating story of what American religion really looks like.

For people who were agnostics in 2010, just over half of them were still agnostics in 2014 (54.9 percent). However, if an agnostic shifted their classification, the group that they were most likely to defect to was atheists, which occurred among a quarter of agnostics. In contrast, just 16.1 percent of agnostics became nothing in particulars, while 3 percent converted to a non-Christian faith group and 3.6 percent identified as Christians in 2014. For atheists, the retention rate was much higher. In fact, four out of five people who identified as an atheist in 2010 were still an atheist in 2014. If an atheist did change their affiliation, they most likely moved to nothing in particular, which happened for 13.2 percent of atheists, while another 2.4 percent became agnostic. However, just 2.6 percent joined another faith tradition, and less than one in one hundred became a Christian (0.7 percent). Stories of atheists having a dramatic born-again experience seem to be common in evangelical circles but appear in this data to be very rare events.

Nothing in particulars seem to represent something different compared with the other two none groups. Their retention rate is fairly high, with 62.1 percent still identifying as nothing in particular in 2014, which was somewhat lower than atheists' and just slightly higher than agnostics'. However, where did the nearly four in ten who changed their affiliation over time go? The data says that about 13 percent of them became atheists or agnostics. However, over a quarter of them moved toward a religious tradition. Nearly 9 percent joined a non-Christian faith group, but 16.4 percent identified as Christians at the end of this four-year period of time.

If a Christian is trying to be strategic about reaching out to those without a religious affiliation, the data tells a clear story: trying to convert atheists is going to end in failure ninety-nine times out of a hundred. The success rate for evangelizing agnostics is higher but still not great, succeeding just one in thirty times. However, that rate goes up dramatically for nothing in particulars. The data indicates that one in six of them will move back toward a Christian tradition over a four-year period.

The Religious Continuum in the United States

FIGURE 4.12

Data from Stephen Ansolabehere, Brian F. Schaffner, and Sam Luks, Cooperative Congressional Election Study, Cambridge, MA: Harvard University, http://cces.gov.harvard.edu.

When I conceptualize what American religion looks like, I think a simple continuum can be very helpful without being overly reductive. Atheists occupy the far left of the landscape in figure 4.12 and make up about 6 percent of the American population. The data indicates that they are almost completely dismissive of religion. Nine in ten never attend church, and 95 percent say that religion is "not at all important." They are the hardest to convert.

Just to the right of atheists are agnostics, who also make up 6 percent of Americans. They are still fairly averse to religious behaviors and beliefs. For instance, seven in ten of them never attend church, and the same share say that the religion is "not at all important." Many of them become atheists over a four-year period, but almost an equal number become nothing in particular as well. They are somewhat more likely to become Christians than atheists, but the probability of conversion is very low.

However, the next group over is the nothing in particulars, which appears to be somewhat of a transfer station between religious groups on one side and atheists and agnostics on the other side. They are clearly warmer and more welcoming to religion than atheists and agnostics, but half of them never attend church services. Yet where they end up over a four-year period is much more diverse and equally distributed. While 8 percent become agnostics and 5 percent become atheists, another 8 percent move into a non-Christian faith tradition, and 16 percent affiliate with a Christian tradition. For those 13 percent who move from nothing in particular to atheist or agnostic, the likelihood of them ever joining a Christian tradition is remote. If one wants to identify the harvest for new religious converts, it can be found among the one in five Americans who say that they are nothing in particular.

CONCLUSION

While it still seems useful to refer to atheists, agnostics, and nothing in particulars as religious nones, I hope this chapter serves as a word of caution to anyone who tries to paint this group with a broad brush. Atheists are some of the most educated individuals in the United States, and many of them have above-average incomes. They are also very male dominated. They describe themselves as liberals and often vote for Democratic candidates. They are incredibly politically active, engaging in behaviors of all types to help their preferred candidates and advocate for their policy positions. They are also far from organized religion and are incredibly unlikely to become Christians.

It seems that agnostics are a somewhat more restrained version of atheists. They too have high levels of education and enjoy high incomes. They are slightly less liberal than their atheist counterparts but also lean toward the Democrat side of the political spectrum. They engage in politics a great deal more than the average American but somewhat less than atheists. They do participate in church activities more than atheists but not very often, and very few of them are open to a Christian message.

Nothing in particulars are the largest group and share little in common with atheists or agnostics. While their gender distribution reflects that of the United States as a whole, they have incredibly low levels of educational attainment, and many of them make below-average incomes. Socially and politically, they are isolated. They don't attend rallies, they don't go to political meetings, and they are less likely to give blood. However, they are not as far from religion as atheists or agnostics. A minority of them attend church at least once a month, and just four in ten say that religion is "not at all important" to them. About one in six of them becomes affiliated with a Christian tradition over a four-year period.

However, nothing in particulars represent the fastest-growing religious group in the United States today. Their numbers have increased a full five percentage points in just the past decade. The group also seems by and large to be struggling in American society. Nearly six in ten of them are making less than $50,000 per year. They seem isolated as well. These are the people who may be the most receptive to faith and the most likely to gain real social and economic benefits from being part of a religious community. If religious groups want to reverse the growth of the nones, they should look no further than the nothing in particulars in their midst.

CHAPTER 5

What We Can Change and What We Cannot

ONE OF THE THINGS THAT I TRY TO DO IN THE COLLEGE POLITICAL science classes I teach is to get my students to understand and think deeply about the big picture. Often, educators at all levels can get stuck in the rut of having students memorize esoteric facts that are quickly forgotten once the next exam is handed in. Giving them a view through a wider lens will give them a framework to process information for the rest of their lives. Having seen the value of big-picture thinking for my students, I invite you to take a deep dive with me as I conclude this book.

TWO UNSTOPPABLE FORCES

Globalization

I believe the most important force in American life today is globalization. Not a single person alive does not feel the effects of the increasingly globalized economy. Simply put, this is why most computers, automobile parts, and clothing are now made in the developing world. Capital is now mobile, and when the biggest expense a company faces is labor, business leaders naturally seek places where their products can be cheaply and effectively made. That is not in the United States.

Sensing that major manufacturers were on the lookout for places to build factories on a grand scale in the 1970s, countries primarily in Southeast Asia began to pour hundreds of billions of dollars into infrastructure, transportation, and technology, making access to cheap foreign labor even easier for Fortune 500 companies. Countries made these investments to transform their local economy, but the result has been to change the entire planet.

These shifts have sent shockwaves across the United States. In 1949, nearly one-third of all American adults worked in a factory. But by 2019, that number had dropped to just 8.5 percent.[1] In the wake of massive offshoring, America has often struggled to find its footing in the new globalized economy. One of the ramifications of this process has been wage stagnation for those in the middle class. According to the Pew Research Center, the peak of American earnings was in the early 1970s.[2] American workers are more productive than at any point in history, yet they have the same purchasing power they did four decades ago.

Almost every economist who studies globalization says that it would be nearly impossible to meaningfully reverse the offshoring of American manufacturing without spending millions of dollars that would never be recovered through jobs coming back to the United States. Trying to stop the flow of jobs out of the United States is the equivalent of trying to contain a forest fire that is engulfing millions of acres by bringing in larger fire hoses. No matter how much water is dumped on the flames, it will likely have very little impact on the outcome.

Not that the impossibility of the challenge has stopped politicians from trying, however. Candidates from both parties make the promise that they will bring back manufacturing jobs to the United States a central part of their platforms. In February 2016, then presidential candidate Donald Trump made the offshoring of over two thousand jobs from a Carrier air-conditioning plant in Indiana a centerpiece of his stump speech. After being offered tens of millions of dollars in subsidies from the federal government to stay in the United States, Carrier agreed to keep about seven hundred jobs in Indiana. (Note that the company said it would use the government subsidies to invest in automation, which will eventually lead to the elimination of even more positions.[3])

In addition to brokering these types of incentive packages for American manufacturers, Donald Trump has also tried to combat globalization with tariffs. Early in his negotiations with Carrier, Trump threatened to institute a 35 percent tariff on any Carrier air conditioner imported into the United States. He has also levied tariffs on billions of dollars of goods flowing in from China as a means of pressuring that country into honoring prior trade agreements. These efforts to implement a protectionist economic policy have aimed to stem the tide of globalization, but by almost all accounts, they have been unsuccessful.

Globalization has also led disaffected American workers to look for someone to blame for their economic misfortunes, and US leaders have been quick to find scapegoats. Donald Trump not only likes to blame the Chinese for the ills of the American working class but also continues to pin many of the problems of American society on undocumented immigrants to the United States. This has led to an increase in hate crimes against racial minorities and the construction of billions of dollars of fencing around the southern border.

That's not to say that politicians on the left have not found a place to direct their ire about wage stagnation as well. Senator Bernie Sanders ran two high-profile campaigns for president of the United States focusing on the issue as well. In his view, the reason that most Americans are not getting ahead is that rich and powerful business leaders in the United States are capturing billions of dollars in newly created wealth rather than sharing it with the average American. The solution for Sanders, and others on the left side of the political spectrum, is to heavily tax the richest Americans and provide more government services to the American populace.

The sad reality of human nature is that when things go wrong, we look for someone to blame. For those on the right, it's China and immigrants. For liberals, it's economic elites. But casting blame on any of these groups sidesteps the reality that globalization is only going to accelerate, and the problem facing American workers in a decade won't be foreigners taking their jobs or the concentration of wealth in the hands of a few; it will be automation. In short, no matter what any politician or business leader says, there is very little they can do to truly reverse the changes to American society brought about by technology and globalization.

Secularization

I think it's helpful for people of faith to think about the rise of the nones in much the same way as globalization. In both cases, the same cold, hard fact is true: we cannot stop it. Both waves are only continuing to build in strength and speed. Any efforts to impede them will be futile. To try to stop globalization by imposing tariffs on imported goods is the functional equivalent of attempts to stop secularization by posting the Ten Commandments in more American courthouses.

Globalization and secularization followed much the same course. The changes were gradual, happening so slowly that by the time many people realized the significance of the shift in American society, it was already too late. Millions of people born in the 1960s and 1970s were content to follow the life course their parents had. They assumed they would graduate from high school, go work in the factory, and live a good and fulfilling life. Then it all went up in smoke. When their jobs moved overseas, many of them were too old, or too set in their ways, to learn a new skill or accept the shifting reality. They fell through the cracks of the American economy—casualties of globalization. Government and business were unwilling or unable to reach out to them in effective ways to retrain them for this new reality.

In the same way, churches happily glided along during the 1950s and 1960s, spending massive amounts of time and money on programs and buildings. The pews were packed and offering plates were filled. Then in the early 1990s, the American religious landscape began a tectonic shift. Many prayed for a day when the young people who grew up in their churches would get married and return with their own children, but that never happened. Churches kept using the same old methods of evangelism and church growth. They bought LED signs and printed more tracts. They redoubled their efforts on "Invite a Friend" Sunday and put on more elaborate productions for Easter and Christmas. As the 1990s gave way to the new millennium, the pews got a little emptier and the collection plates a bit lighter. Many churches began using their endowment funds to make up for budget shortfalls. Now, a few decades later, many of them are closing up shop—casualties of secularization.

All these changes can seem so depressing. How do people of faith deal with some of the statistics presented in this book when they are left with the overwhelming fact that the America of tomorrow will look nothing like the America of thirty years ago? I am reminded of a conversation between two characters in the 2014 movie *Wish I Was Here*. Aidan, played by Zach Braff, is racked with grief that his father, Gabe, has had a reoccurrence of cancer.

Aidan exclaims, "There's so much bad news all at once. What do we do?"

And Gabe calmly responds, "What do you mean, 'What do we do?' We move forward. It's the only direction God gave us."

HOW DO WE MOVE FORWARD?

Reinhold Niebuhr succinctly captures the advice I would give the modern church about how to respond to the rise of the nones: "God, grant me the serenity to accept the things I cannot change, the courage to change the things I can, and the wisdom to know the difference."

Let me make one small amendment: ". . . and the data to know the difference."

Let's begin with the things that cannot be changed. I think that no matter how effective the church was at evangelism or missions or community service over the past four decades, those efforts would have been only slightly effective at stopping the rise of the nones. The best apologists, the most charismatic speakers, or the catchiest praise and worship bands would not have held secularization at bay. There's no way to know for certain, but it's fair to say that a significant chunk of the increase in the unaffiliated was due to shifts in American culture away from religion. Recall that Max Weber believed that as educational levels increased, people would begin to look toward science, not God, to explain the world. It is foolhardy to think that what happened in Europe, which was also experiencing a dramatic rise in educational levels, would not, to some extent, come to American shores. The reality is simply this: Americans used to be Christians simply by default, not because of their belief in the words of the Apostles' Creed. Secularization merely gave permission for a lot of people to express who they truly are—religiously unaffiliated.

But I must make one more data-driven observation. While I have shared dozens of data points across these pages about the tremendous number of Americans who no longer affiliate with a religion, I have intentionally left out a crucial piece of information: religious belief in this country is still surprisingly robust. In 1988, 1.8 percent of respondents to the General Social Survey said that God didn't exist, and another 3.8 percent said that God might exist but there's no way to find out. In 2018, just 4.7 percent of people said that there was no God, and 6.5 percent said there was no way to know for sure. While nearly one in four Americans no longer affiliates with religion, just one in ten Americans does not believe God exists. The issue is not that interest in spiritual matters has declined; it's that people do not want to label themselves as a Christian, Mormon, or Buddhist.

So what gives? If almost all Americans still believe in the divine, we should not be seeing the number of nones continue to slowly and steadily grow every passing year. But we are. So how do we respond? To return to Niebuhr's prayer, it's crucial for the church to focus on what can be changed. I'll discuss two possible avenues for change. One is related to how we have not listened to the nones' stories, and the other to how Christians, specifically white Protestants and Catholics, have made Democrats feel more and more marginalized with every passing election.

Behind Every Survey Respondent Is a Story

One of the things I constantly have to remind myself when I do data analysis is that every single row on my spreadsheet represents a human being who has a story to tell. People who grew up in faith communities but left them when they moved into adulthood all have a story to tell. Some of those stories are not that enlightening. The church just didn't work for them, and they saw no benefit in regular attendance. Others left for reasons that are much more instructive. Whatever their motives, we should be seeking out people willing to tell their stories, inviting them to tell us, and listening—*really* listening—to them.

What sort of stories might we hear? Many people have been abused at the hands of people who claim to act in the name of

Jesus Christ. For decades, parents have told their LGBT children that they are no longer allowed in their house. Some have been made to feel unwelcome when they've asked too many questions about why God acted so terribly in the Old Testament or how an all-powerful force could allow children to die of cancer. Others have been raised in such a controlling environment that rebellion has become their motivating force in adulthood. Because of some of the previously mentioned effects of globalization, many have been forced to work two or three jobs to make ends meet, and church is a luxury these people feel they can't afford. Some felt ostracized for marrying someone of a different faith or getting pregnant out of wedlock. These stories, and many more, are completely legitimate reasons to walk away from any institution—regardless of whether it embodies the Truth or not.

A phrase I often repeat to my students when we talk about respecting other people's political viewpoints is "Your world is not their world." I might also say, "Your story is not their story." I think many Christians have a hard time putting themselves in the shoes of the person who left church and never came back or those who never made the connection in the first place. They don't recognize that to belittle, minimize, or try to explain away the stories of those who walked away or never connected to a church home is to fail to understand that not everyone comes to faith the same way we did, and people do not stay (or leave, or stay away) for the same reasons we do either.

Beyond Every Survey Respondent Is Politics

One aspect of people's stories that we often do not attend to is their politics. I know this observation has become an overwrought cliché, but God is not a Republican or a Democrat. But if someone walked into most Christian houses of worship this upcoming weekend, they would not find much evidence to support that conclusion. In 1972, half of all white weekly churchgoers were Democrats; now just a quarter are. Of the twenty largest predominantly white Protestant traditions in the United States, sixteen became more Republican between 2008 and 2018. Four in five white evangelical Protestants voted for Donald Trump for president in 2016. The totality of that shift is absolutely staggering, and for many people whose politics lean left but who still want to be part of a Christian community, there are no options for them locally. And some churches seem to go out of their way to make that reality known.

I'm friends with a number of pastors on Facebook, acquaintances I have picked up over the past fifteen years in ministry. Often, I feel like scrolling my newsfeed is a type of social science experiment. I'm just flabbergasted by how often that these pastors post things that belittle, demean, or misrepresent the views of their political opposition. In my mind, what they are doing is no different from placing a sign on the front door of their church every Sunday morning that says, "No Democrats Allowed." If Christians want to seek and save the lost, why would some of them go out of their way to alienate a third of the population of the United States? There are already enough hurdles for someone who might want to come back to church. Why add another?

I have arrived at two conclusions about their words and deeds. The first is that these pastors don't realize there are Democrats who could potentially want to visit their church next Sunday. The second is that these pastors are convinced that no other political beliefs are compatible with the Gospel. And I see my liberal Christian friend fall into this trap as well. There are lots of people who voted for Donald Trump for well-considered reasons, and maligning these Republican voters does Christianity no favors. Either conclusion shows such an unbelievable lack of awareness and leaves no doubt in my mind as to why so many people have become or remain religiously unaffiliated.

Now, that's not to say that all pastors engage in such behavior on social media. I know what many of those who are reading this may be thinking right now: *I don't preach politics on my Facebook feed or from the pulpit!* I agree with you, and so does the data.[4] Very few pastors are expressly political in their preaching. But pastors need to recognize that their members are absorbing political messages from other aspects of their church involvement. They might pick up clues from a conversation they had before church about property taxes or a Wednesday evening small group discussion about abortion or gay marriage. There are no truly apolitical churches.[5]

I understand the conundrum that pastors face. Most of them realize that speaking about politics from the pulpit might engender support from a majority of congregants but might drive others away, so they know it's prudent for them to steer clear. That's a natural response, and I think it comes from a good place. However, church members are always on the lookout for people to help them think about how to respond to current events or government policies. When pastors do not apply the Gospel to the very real concerns of modern society, they are opening the door for others to influence church members. Those "others" might be friends, family, pastors of other churches—almost anyone, really. But a pastor once mentioned to me that while he has a captive audience for one hour once a week, the cable news networks are piped into members' homes for eight hours a day, seven days a week. That's a sobering thought. If pastors don't give congregations guidance on how to think about politics, then they will get it from somewhere else. And unfortunately, what drives clicks, eyeballs, and ad revenue are media personalities who do their best to not only make their political party look good but make the other side of the aisle look ignorant, out of touch, and immoral.

So here's my suggestion: speak Truth to them. Preach sound biblical doctrine that cuts across the political spectrum. One of the theological principles that shapes the way I view the world dates back to the Old Testament. It's the concept of *imago Dei*—the understanding that every human being is created in the image and likeness of God, and because of that, every person on Earth is deserving of love and respect. It sounds so simple, yet it can have a profound impact on how we think, act, and vote.

The political implications of *imago Dei* are tremendous and should give pause to both Republicans and Democrats. This worldview rises above partisanship. It teaches that neglecting the poor is a violation of *imago Dei*, and it also teaches us that we should value the lives of the unborn. *Imago Dei* means that the disabled bear the image of the Creator, just like all of us. But *imago Dei* also teaches us that no matter someone's immigration status or the color of their skin, they were fearfully and wonderfully made. Those who follow *imago Dei* should fight for the concept of religious liberty not just for Christians but for all people of any faith tradition.

FEELING HOPELESS? JUST KEEP THROWING OUT SEED

If I were a younger man, this is the part of the book where I would try to offer some sage wisdom and practical advice to fill the pews back up. However, experience tells me that there is no easy answer. I became a senior pastor at the tender age of twenty-three. I had just started a graduate program and honestly needed to make some money to pay the rent. Luckily, the older congregants of a small church welcomed me with open arms. I thought that if I just preached really well and did a lot of visits, people would come to church. After a year, I left. I think that the church expected me to be a miracle worker, and I did nothing to downplay those expectations. I learned that just last year, the church officially closed its doors, and the building was razed a few weeks later.

The church I currently serve had fifty regular worshippers when I assumed the pulpit thirteen years ago. Today, we are down to about fifteen most Sundays. We've had weeks when the total attendance was in the single digits. Again, I thought that if I set myself on fire, people would come to watch me burn. That's not what happened. About five years into my ministry, I became listless and angry. Why wasn't the church growing? Why can't we bring in some young people? I thought of myself as a failure. I felt like one of those factory workers who got laid off after twenty years of hard work and dedication, wondering why my efforts weren't being rewarded.

I kept thinking about what the church used to be—nearly three hundred members with activities almost every day of the week and a tremendous influence on the community. Now we were struggling to keep the lights on. I was no different from the guys who meet for coffee at fast-food restaurants and talk about life before the factory closed. The word *nostalgia* can be translated "an ache for home." It seems that I, the coffee-shop crew, and frankly, a lot of people are consumed by this pining for a bygone era.

But after a period of wallowing, I realized that our church must move forward. So we stepped out in faith and began packing brown paper sacks filled with food for schoolchildren who were struggling with poverty in our community. We started with thirty bags per weekend. We had no idea if it would work or if we could actually afford it. Nearly a decade later, we pack nearly three hundred bags of food each weekend and serve three local schools. Every time we think that the money is going to run out, a check shows up. Like the factory worker who sees the plant closure as an opportunity to go back to school and retrain for a different career, our food program was the avenue we took to keep moving forward.

When we first started organizing our brown bag program, some members of the congregation thought that we should drop a tract into the bags, but I refused. For me, the purpose of those bags was not to try to bring people to Christ. It was to show those kids that someone they don't even know loves them and wants to help. So we just include a simple note saying who we are and what we are doing. We make sure to let them know that if they need help, they can just give us a call.

Well, one Friday, the phone rang. It was a grandmother of one of the children who had received a bag. The temperature had begun to drop, and her grandson didn't have a warm coat. She asked for help. It just so happened that we were having a rummage sale that weekend and had a fellowship hall full of clothes. We invited her to come down and take whatever she needed. Just an hour later, she and her grandson stuffed two armloads of clothes into her trunk and drove away.

I have no idea if that young man or his grandmother will ever come to know Christ. But here's what I do know: they left our church that day knowing that they were born in the image and likeness of God and that people who they had never met cared deeply about them. When that young man is sitting around as an adult one day, talking about spiritual things, he might have some bad things to say about the church, but I hope that when he tells his story of faith, he at least makes mention of the one time when he needed help and a church came to his rescue. That young man's story of faith will be just a bit different because of what our little church did for him. But there are millions of people who can't say the same thing, because for them, church did not make their lives better. It just made them feel worse.

One of my favorite parables from the Gospel of Matthew involves a farmer who is trying to plant seed. Jesus notes that some of the seed falls on inhospitable soil and never takes root, while other seed manages to find fertile ground, takes root, and creates a bountiful harvest. I firmly believe that the church needs to stop trying to control where the seed lands. The winds of secularization and polarization are swirling like never before. Most of that seed is going to fall on rocky soil, never to reap a harvest. And it seems that there are fewer people to spread it every year. It's easy to give up hope. But we must recall the words of the apostle Paul to the church in Galatia: "So let us not grow weary in doing what is right, for we will reap at harvest time, if we do not give up" (Gal 6:9). Seed that expresses the love and grace and hope of Jesus Christ is never truly lost. Don't give up!

Notes

CHAPTER 1: WHAT DOES THE AMERICAN RELIGIOUS LANDSCAPE LOOK LIKE?

1 Sarah Kaplan, "It's Official: The Definition of a Kilogram Has Changed," Science Alert, November 16, 2018, https://tinyurl.com/ycb2xvbo.

2 Stacey Vanek Smith, "The Santa Suit," NPR, December 20, 2017, https://tinyurl.com/y2pmzvth.

3 Christopher H. Achen and Larry M. Bartels, *Democracy for Realists: Why Elections Do Not Produce Responsive Government* (Princeton and Oxford: Princeton University Press, 2017), 266.

4 In fact, historian Thomas Kidd wrote two hundred pages on the concept for his 2019 book, *Who Is an Evangelical?* (New Haven, CT: Yale University Press).

5 "Fast Facts about the SBC," Southern Baptist Convention, accessed August 24, 2020, https://tinyurl.com/y2xjw6g5.

6 Sarah Pulliam Bailey, "White Evangelicals Voted Overwhelmingly for Donald Trump, Exit Polls Show," *Washington Post*, November 9, 2016, https://tinyurl.com/qfx2394.

7 Mary Newton Stanard, *Colonial Virginia: Its People and Customs* (Philadelphia: Lippincott, 1917).

8 "Marriage Equality," United Church of Christ, accessed August 24, 2020, https://tinyurl.com/y2ut3hzd.

9 Ryan P. Burge, "Are Mainline Protestants Democrats?," Religion in Public, September 10, 2019, https://tinyurl.com/yy4gon48.

10 Kenneth D. Wald, "The Puzzling Politics of American Jewry (ARDA Guiding Paper Series)," Association of Religion Data Archives at the Pennsylvania State University, accessed August 24, 2020, https://tinyurl.com/yx9oo3os.

11 Jana Riess, "Mormon Growth Continues to Slow, Especially in the US," Religion News Service, April 13, 2018, https://tinyurl.com/y3qgeglg.

CHAPTER 2: A SOCIAL SCIENTIST TRIES
TO EXPLAIN RELIGIOUS DISAFFILIATION

1 Heather Pringle, "The Slow Birth of Agriculture," *Science* 282, no. 5393 (1998): 1446–47.

2 See Deuteronomy 11 for evidence of this among the Hebrews.

3 Max Weber, *From Max Weber: Essays in Sociology*, trans. and ed. H. H. Gerth and C. Wright Mills (New York: Oxford University Press, 1946), 129–16.

4 Karl Marx, "Introduction to a Contribution of the Critique of Hegel's Philosophy of Right," in *The Marx Engels Reader*, trans. T.B. Bottomore (New York: W. W. Norton, 1972), 12.

5 Naftali Bendavid, "Europe's Empty Churches Go on Sale," *Wall Street Journal*, January 2, 2015, https://tinyurl.com/hux7x7q.

6 Fenggang Yang, *Religion in China: Survival and Revival under Communist Rule* (New York: Oxford University Press, 2011).

7 Seymour M. Lipset and Stein Rokkan, eds., *Party Systems and Voter Alignments: Cross-National Perspectives*, vol. 7 (New York: Free Press, 1967).

8 Alexis de Tocqueville, *Democracy in America*, trans. Arthur Goldhammer (New York: Library of America, 2004), 343.

9 Kenneth D. Wald and Allison Calhoun-Brown, *Religion and Politics in the United States* (Lanham, MD: Rowman & Littlefield, 2014), 21.

10 Robert N. Bellah, "Civil Religion in America," *Daedalus* 96, no. 1 (1967): 1–21.

11 Sarah Pulliam Bailey, "Christianity Is Declining at a Rapid Pace, but Americans Still Hold Positive Views about Religion's Role in Society," *Washington Post*, November 15, 2019, https://tinyurl.com/y2h38smw.

12 C. Kirk Hadaway, Penny L. Marler, and Mark Chaves, "What the Polls Don't Show: A Closer Look at US Church Attendance," *American Sociological Review* 58, no. 6 (1993): 741–52.

13 Elisabeth Noelle-Neumann, "The Spiral of Silence a Theory of Public Opinion," *Journal of Communication* 24, no. 2 (1974): 43–51.

14 Pablo Porten-Cheé and Christiane Eilders, "Spiral of Silence Online: How Online Communication Affects Opinion Climate Perception and Opinion Expression regarding the Climate Change

Debate," *Studies in Communication Sciences* 15, no. 1 (2015): 143–50.

15 Sherice Gearhart and Weiwu Zhang, "'Was It Something I Said?' 'No, It Was Something You Posted!' A Study of the Spiral of Silence Theory in Social Media Contexts," *Cyberpsychology, Behavior, and Social Networking* 18, no. 4 (2015): 208–13.

16 Sarah Pulliam Bailey, "White Evangelicals Voted Overwhelmingly for Donald Trump, Exit Polls Show," *Washington Post*, November 9, 2016, https://tinyurl.com/qfx2394.

17 Ryan Burge (@Ryanburge), "I am kind of shocked by how little the vote choice of white Christians changed across the last three elections," Twitter, October 27, 2019, https://tinyurl.com/y2n6sg8t.

18 Ryan Burge, "Why Politics May Kill White Churches," Religion News Service, May 29, 2019, https://tinyurl.com/y5uoctwc.

19 Wald and Calhoun-Brown, *Religion and Politics*, chap. 8.

20 Randall Balmer, "The Real Origins of the Religious Right," *Politico Magazine*, May 27, 2014, https://tinyurl.com/y3x46nzj.

21 Kevin M. Kruse, *One Nation under God: How Corporate America Invented Christian America* (New York: Basic Books, 2015).

22 Ryan Burge, "Democratic Party Is at an Inflection Point When It Comes to Courting Religious Voters," Religion News Service, October 1, 2019, https://tinyurl.com/y5kk5zeu.

23 Michael Hout and Claude S. Fischer, "Why More Americans Have No Religious Preference: Politics and Generations," *American Sociological Review* 67, no. 2 (2002): 165–90.

24 Michele F. Margolis, *From Politics to the Pews: How Partisanship and the Political Environment Shape Religious Identity* (Chicago: University of Chicago Press, 2018).

25 Robert D. Putnam, *Bowling Alone: America's Declining Social Capital* (New York: Palgrave Macmillan, 2000), 178.

26 Matthew Pressman, "Ambivalent Accomplices: How the Press Handled FDR's Disability and How FDR Handled the Press," *Journal of the Historical Society* 13, no. 3 (2013): 325–59.

27 James P. Pfiffner, "Sexual Probity and Presidential Character," *Presidential Studies Quarterly* 28, no. 4 (1998): 881–86.

28 Virginia A. Chanley, Thomas J. Rudolph, and Wendy M. Rahn, "The Origins and Consequences of Public Trust in Government:

A Time Series Analysis," *Public Opinion Quarterly* 64, no. 3 (2000): 239–56.

29 "Public Trust in Government: 1958–2019," Pew Research Center, April 11, 2019, https://tinyurl.com/yxc4g5ok.

30 "Church Allowed Abuse by Priest for Years," *Boston Globe*, January 6, 2002, https://tinyurl.com/j5vpm6y.

31 Lyle E. Larson and Walter Goltz, "Religious Participation and Marital Commitment," *Review of Religious Research* 30, no. 4 (1989): 387–400.

32 Arland Thornton, William G. Axinn, and Daniel H. Hill, "Reciprocal Effects of Religiosity, Cohabitation, and Marriage," *American Journal of Sociology* 98, no. 3 (1992): 628–51.

33 Stan L. Albrecht and Marie Cornwall, "Life Events and Religious Change," in *Latter-day Saint Social Life: Social Research on the LDS Church and Its Members* (Provo, UT: Religious Studies Center, Brigham Young University, 1998), 231–52.

CHAPTER 3: THE DEMOGRAPHICS
OF DISAFFILIATION

1 "Figure MS-2 Median Age at First Marriage: 1890 to Present," United States Census Bureau, accessed August 25, 2020, https://tinyurl.com/y9gonr3p.

2 Robert S. Erikson and Laura Stoker, "Caught in the Draft: The Effects of Vietnam Draft Lottery Status on Political Attitudes," *American Political Science Review* 105, no. 2 (2011): 221–237, https://tinyurl.com/yxtdqxeu.

3 Gary C. Jacobson, "The 1994 House Elections in Perspective," *Political Science Quarterly* 111, no. 2 (1996): 203–223, https://tinyurl.com/y5bo99z4.

4 Mark J. Perry, "Table of the Day: Bachelor's Degrees for the Class of 2016 by Field and Gender. Oh, and the Overall 25.6% Degree Gap for Men!," AEIdeas, June 18, 2018, https://tinyurl.com/y6625xsy.

5 Nikki Graf, Anna Brown, and Eileen Patten, "The Narrowing, but Persistent, Gender Gap in Pay," Fact Tank, Pew Research Center, March 22, 2019, https://tinyurl.com/y49w5sjg.

6 Gretchen Livingston, "The Rise of Single Fathers," Pew Research Center, Social & Demographic Trends, July 2, 2013, https://tinyurl.com/yxvm9lr2.

7 Megan Brenan, "Record-High 56% of U.S. Women Prefer Working to Homemaking," Gallup, October 24, 2019, https://tinyurl.com/y2s2rpje.

8 Ryan P. Jordan, "Race and Religion in the United States," Oxford Research Encyclopedias, published online April 2017, https://tinyurl.com/y6z4y6nm.

9 Larry L. Hunt, "Hispanic Protestantism in the United States: Trends by Decade and Generation," *Social Forces* 77, no. 4 (1999): 1601–24.

10 Jason E. Shelton and Michael O. Emerson, *Blacks and Whites in Christian America: How Racial Discrimination Shapes Religious Convictions* (New York: NYU Press, 2012).

11 Janelle S. Wong, *Immigrants, Evangelicals, and Politics in an Era of Demographic Change* (New York: Russell Sage Foundation, 2018).

CHAPTER 4: NONES ARE
NOT ALL CREATED EQUAL

1 Thomas Henry Huxley, letter to Charles A. Watts (publisher of the *Agnostic Annual*), 1883, in *Life and Letters of Thomas Henry Huxley* (London: Macmillan, 1913), 3:97.

CHAPTER 5: WHAT WE CAN
CHANGE AND WHAT WE CANNOT

1 Steve Goldstein, "U.S. Enjoys Best Manufacturing Jobs Growth of the Last 30 Years," Market Watch, January 4, 2019, https://tinyurl.com/y4jlprwp.

2 Drew Desilver, "For Most U.S. Workers, Real Wages Have Barely Budged in Decades," Fact Tank, Pew Research Center, August 7, 2018, https://tinyurl.com/y2ok8x9z.

3 Chris Isidore, "Carrier to Ultimately Cut Some of Jobs Trump Saved," CNN, December 9, 2016, https://tinyurl.com/y3a4fpym.

4 Paul A. Djupe and Christopher P. Gilbert, *The Prophetic Pulpit: Clergy, Churches, and Communities in American Politics* (Lanham, MD: Rowman & Littlefield, 2003).

5 Kenneth D. Wald, David E. Owen, and Samuel S. Hill, "Churches as Political Communities," *American Political Science Review* 82, no. 2 (1988): 531–48.

Recommended Resources

Armstrong, Karen. *The Case for God*. New York: Knopf, 2009.

This book has stuck with me ever since I first read it a decade ago. *The Case for God* does a tremendous job of packing thousands of years of religious history into a very accessible and well-researched text. I find great value in thinking about God in a way that differs from my Protestant upbringing, and Karen Armstrong is unmatched in her ability to make the reader think about the concept of the divine from the perspectives of different cultures. Her work has also helped me understand why some people find no benefit in believing in God. Every once in a while, I include an anecdote from this book in my Sunday sermon, which is a testament to her work.

Bellah, Robert N., Richard Madsen, William M. Sullivan, Ann Swidler, and Stephen M. Tipton. *Habits of the Heart: Individualism and Commitment in American Life*. With a new preface. Berkeley: University of California, 2007.

If one were to take a graduate-level survey course on American religion, I am certain that *Habits of the Heart* would be on the syllabus. Robert Bellah and his colleagues conducted in-depth interviews with two hundred research subjects to try to get a sense of what spirituality means in contemporary America. The authors confront a unique facet of American life: our rugged individualism. Their research tries to understand how that predisposition toward personal satisfaction either hinders or enhances the spiritual life of the average citizen. The authors believe that as American society has become fractured, so has religion in the country. As Americans have disconnected from other people, they have drifted away from a belief in the divine. Or, said another way, social isolation and spiritual isolation are deeply related.

Putnam, Robert D. *Bowling Alone: The Collapse and Revival of American Community.* Revised and updated. New York: Simon & Schuster, 2020.

This book is the one I bring up most often in interviews, speeches, and presentations when talking about the changes in American society since the 1950s. *Bowling Alone* may be the most widely read political science book published in my lifetime—and for good reason. In astonishing detail, Robert Putnam notes how American society has become fractured and disjointed. People don't meet for social gatherings—for example, by joining bowling leagues—as much as they used to. The book was published two decades ago, so Putnam's assertion that cable television has led to a lot of the social isolation we are experiencing seems quaint now, but the general thesis of the book still rings true today: technology can drive people apart.

Putnam, Robert D., and David E. Campbell. *American Grace: How Religion Divides and Unites Us.* New York: Simon & Schuster, 2010.

Robert Putnam might be the most widely read political scientist alive today, and when he teamed up with one of the preeminent scholars of American religion, David Campbell, they put together a book that is essential reading for those who are interested in long-term trends in American religion. This book excels in weaving together survey data with case studies that focus on interesting ways in which religion has shaped American society. I often assign this text to bring my students up to speed on what has happened in American evangelicalism since the 1970s.

White, James Emery. *The Rise of the Nones: Understanding and Reaching the Religiously Unaffiliated.* Grand Rapids, MI: Baker, 2014.

This book is one of the earliest to describe the rise of the religiously unaffiliated. James Emery White is a full-time pastor, and therefore, this book is written with a tone and purpose different from many academic books. White does a terrific job of helping fellow religious leaders understand the broad contours of the nones in American society. His book is practical in its approach and includes resources such as discussion questions at the end of each chapter as well as concrete advice for those who are interested in evangelizing the religiously unaffiliated.

Wuthnow, Robert. *Inventing American Religion: Polls, Surveys, and the Tenuous Quest for a Nation's Faith.* Oxford: Oxford University Press, 2015.

Robert Wuthnow is one of the giants in the field of the sociology of religion, having authored a number of the seminal pieces in the field. In his later years, he has taken a more reflective tone, and *Inventing American Religion* made me think deeply about a central question: What if all quantitative attempts to study American religion are inaccurate? Obviously, I don't buy Wuthnow's entire argument, but he goes to great lengths to point out some of the issues with the polling industry. If academia has taught me anything, it's to second-guess myself, and this book does a good job of sowing seeds of doubt.

"John Ortberg in *Who Is This Man?* pr... ...eyond a shadow of a doubt what James A. Francis wrote about more than eighty years ago in *One Solitary Life*: 'All the armies that have ever marched, All the navies that have ever sailed, All the parliaments that have ever sat, All the kings that have ever reigned, put together have not affected the life of mankind on this earth as much as Jesus.' Read this book and realize that regardless of your religious persuasion, if you long to make a difference — and down deep, I think we all do — the example set by Jesus can guide your way. He demonstrated that we don't need fame, money, and connections to live a life that really matters. Thanks, John, for reminding us."

— KEN BLANCHARD, Coauthor of
The One Minute Manager and *Lead Like Jesus*

"We live in a Jesus-shaped world in ways many people may not imagine. Find out why people still ask 'who is this man?' after two thousand years."

— CHRISTINE CAINE, Founder, The A21 Campaign

"Brilliantly and inspiringly written, this book overwhelms the reader with the dominating role that Jesus has played in creating our history and culture. John Ortberg leaves little doubt that the man Jesus is not just a man, but 'that in Him the fullness of God is revealed.'"

— TONY CAMPOLO, Author, professor at Eastern University

"John Ortberg is one of my favorite Bible teachers. He has wit, wisdom, and imagination. He is easy to read but not fluffy, and he speaks with authority but isn't arrogant. There's nothing more beautiful to write about than Jesus. And there are few writers more eloquent than John. Whether you are a Christian or suspicious of Christians, John invites you to dream about this man named Jesus who somehow has survived all the embarrassing things we Christians have done in his name. Enjoy this book like a wonderful feast."

— SHANE CLAIBORNE, Author, activist, and lover of Jesus

"Sometimes in the clutter and noise of 'religion,' we lose sight of who Jesus is. Once again, John Ortberg helps us do what he does best: he helps us see God as he really is and connect with him amid all the noise. This book is a gift."

— DR. HENRY CLOUD, Psychologist,
coauthor of the *Boundaries* books

"This is the most compelling and thought-provoking book on Jesus I have ever read! Whether you are a believer or a skeptic, this book brings to light all the fascinating ways this man changed the world forever. This book goes on my shelf of all-time favorite books."

— JEFF FOXWORTHY, Comedian, actor,
funny guy who loves Jesus

"The first thing I noticed about John Ortberg's latest work was the title —not who WAS this man, but who IS this man, Jesus. While John does a masterful job of explaining the 'biblical Jesus,' where he's at his absolute best is the way he shows us who Jesus is this year ... this day ... this hour ... this moment. The book will encourage, inspire, and flat-out blow you away."

— ERNIE JOHNSON JR., Sportscaster, TNT/TBS

"We live in a period where the divide between the secular and the sacred has never been greater. John Ortberg's book *Who Is This Man?* bridges this gap by sharing in his inimitable and entertaining style the undeniable and profound impact of Jesus Christ on our world. It is incredible to comprehend the impact that one person, leading a small group of twelve people for three short years, has had on our world. His impact, over two thousand years later, is more profound on the day-to-day lives of people—believers or not—than the impact of any other person at any point in history. John shows how Christ came to teach us how to live and in the process changed the world forever and for good."

— RON JOHNSON, CEO, J. C. Penney

"The third step in a Twelve Step recovery program asks us to 'turn our will and our lives over to the care of God as we understand Him.' But who is God, really, and can we understand Him well enough to trust Him? Without Jesus, we can only guess. Jesus, the Son of God, came to show us God's character. Pastor John Ortberg brings fresh insight into the life of Jesus on earth, through which we can better grasp the nature of God in heaven."

— RICH KARLGAARD, Publisher, *Forbes Magazine*

"A wonderful and timely reminder for our forgetful world that Jesus continues to be more than just another voice, another man, in history. He is *the* voice, *the* man of history, and of course, He is more. John Ortberg brings Christ's humanity to light in a way that makes us better able to ponder His divinity. A powerful read for skeptics and believers alike."

— PATRICK LENCIONI, President, The Table Group; author, *The Five Dysfunctions of a Team* and *The Advantage*

"Enlightening and highly readable, Ortberg's book thoughtfully explores the paradox of Jesus. He was the villager who outlasted empires, the carpenter who inspired universities, the most posthumously successful person of all time. Ortberg rightly challenges us to ask, 'Who is this man?'"

— D. MICHAEL LINDSAY, President, Gordon College

"The arrival of this book is good news! Anytime John Ortberg writes, we, the readers, benefit. And this time he has taken his creative pen and clear thinking to the grandest topic: Jesus Christ. Make room on your shelf for this book. Make room in your heart for its subject."

— MAX LUCADO, Pastor and bestselling author

"John Ortberg is one of my favorite authors, and this book took me to a new level in admiring him as a wonderful writer. More importantly, it took me to a new level in worshiping Jesus as a wonderful Savior!"

— RICHARD MOUW, Author, president of Fuller Theological Seminary

"We seek the wisdom of business gurus, health experts, and battlefield greats. But one person, more than anyone else in history, radically changed the world we live in. Discover that person and be changed by him through John Ortberg's captivating book."

—RICHARD STEARNS, President of World Vision US,
and author of *The Hole in Our Gospel*

"Here is a book by one of America's most dynamic and powerful preachers that is destined to become as influential and widely read as *The Purpose Driven Life*. Jesus has seldom been written about with such penetrating insight and illuminating clarity."

—NEIL CLARK WARREN, Founder and chairman,
eHarmony.com

"The constant human task is to come to terms with reality. What is *there* for us? What can we count on for direction and strength? Currently what we are most likely to miss is the reality of Jesus Christ and the kingdom of God, over which he presides. A complex and powerful historical drift has deprived him of historical substance and of moment-by-moment relevance—even for most of those who would hope to be his friends. *Who Is This Man?* mounts a powerful counterattack. It helps us see how much of what is good and best in the world is due to what Jesus has done and is doing, through his continuing presence and through his people. Everyone who hopes to stand with and for him in current society should carefully study this book and make the Jesus it teaches the framework of all they do and say. If we do that, the reality of Christ and his kingdom will flood into our lives and our communities. There will be a battle, but things will increasingly go as they ought. The reality of God will validate itself through lives lived in God. Simply put it to the test and you will see."

—DALLAS WILLARD, Author, professor
at the University of Southern California

"John Ortberg has nailed one of the Big Lies of Our Time, the assertion that Christianity has been part of the problem rather than the source of the solution. Most people today don't realize that things we now take for granted, like education and health care, were reserved for the rich elite in the ancient world until the Christians insisted on providing them for everyone within reach. Many imagine that Christianity was bad for women, whereas early Christianity provided the biggest transformation of attitudes to women the world has ever seen. Ortberg tracks these and much, much more back to Jesus himself. As a pastor, he knows very well that the church often gets it badly wrong. But the impact of Jesus on the whole world, even when his followers have been muddled or misguided, towers breathtakingly over all human achievements. This book provides enormous encouragement both to celebrate what Jesus' followers have done in the past and to stimulate a fresh vision of our mission in the future. And, above all, to be amazed and awed once more at Jesus himself, who lived, died, and rose to launch such a transformative vision."

—N.T. WRIGHT, Professor at the University of
St Andrews, author of *Jesus and the Victory of God*

"With 1,500 books about Jesus published each year, where does a reader start? I recommend John Ortberg's latest offering, which gives a clear and heartfelt introduction to the most important person who has ever lived."

—PHILIP YANCEY, Author of *The Jesus I Never Knew*

Resources by John Ortberg

An Ordinary Day with Jesus
(curriculum with Ruth Haley Barton)

Everybody's Normal Till You Get to Know Them
(book, audio)

God Is Closer Than You Think
(book, audio, curriculum with Stephen and Amanda Sorenson)

*If You Want to Walk on Water,
You've Got to Get Out of the Boat*
(book, audio, curriculum with Stephen and Amanda Sorenson)

Know Doubt
(book, formerly entitled *Faith and Doubt*)

The Life You've Always Wanted
(book, audio, curriculum with Stephen and Amanda Sorenson)

Living the God Life

Love Beyond Reason

The Me I Want to Be
(book, audio, curriculum with Scott Rubin)

Teaching the Heart of the Old Testament and
Truth for Today from the Old Testament
(book, curriculum with Kevin and Sherry Harney)

When the Game Is Over, It All Goes Back in the Box
(book, audio, curriculum with Stephen and Amanda Sorenson)

WHO IS THIS MAN?

The Unpredictable Impact *of the* Inescapable Jesus

JOHN ORTBERG

ZONDERVAN®

ZONDERVAN.com/
AUTHORTRACKER
follow your favorite authors

ZONDERVAN

Who Is this Man?
Copyright © 2012 by John Ortberg

This title is also available as a Zondervan ebook. Visit www.zondervan.com/ebooks.

This title is also available in a Zondervan audio edition. Visit www.zondervan.fm.

Requests for information should be addressed to:

Zondervan, *Grand Rapids, Michigan 49530*

ISBN 978-0-310-27595-4

International Trade Paper Edition

Published in association with Yates & Yates, www.yates2.com.

Cover design: *Extra Credit Projects*
Cover photography: *Jupiter Images®*
Interior design: *Beth Shagene*

Printed in the United States of America

Contents

Foreword

So much has been written about our Lord that one is tempted to ask if there is anything more to say. As the daughter and granddaughter of Presbyterian ministers, I have been a follower of Christ since birth. And yet when I heard John Ortberg's sermons in the series "Who was this Guy?" as a parishioner at Menlo Park Presbyterian Church, I turned to my cousin (also a Presbyterian minister's daughter) and said, "I never thought of it that way." Thankfully, our Lord's story continues to be revealed by inspired teachers who tell it in language that brings it to life for our modern, troubled times. In *Who Is This Man?* John has written a powerful testament to the impact that Jesus has had on human history, on the human condition, and on our understanding of the obligations of one human being to another.

This book reminds us first and foremost that Christ was a revolutionary figure. The apostle Paul's summary statement of the faith was a thunderbolt in the ancient world: "In Christ Jesus you are *all* children of God through faith.... There is neither Jew nor Gentile, neither slave nor free, nor is there male and female, for you are all one in Christ Jesus." Before that revelation, one's status from birth defined one's life until the grave. But with the coming of Christ, who humbled himself to enter our world as a helpless baby and die like a common criminal, it is now and forever clear that every life is worthy before God. It is from this belief that we conclude, "all men (and women) are created equal."

Through countless biblical stories we are led to understand that Christ did not just say these things; he lived them. He dined with outcasts, touched the unclean, recruited women into his ministry, revealed himself after the resurrection to these "second-class citizens," and chastised hypocrites who piously kept the letter of the law but cared little for their brethren. In the end, he would refuse to save himself from death on the cross in order to fulfill the promise of the resurrection — and in doing so, save mankind.

Those who followed him would begin to act as if every life is worthy. The community of people called Christians would minister to the sick and disabled and build hospitals, pursue universal education, spread teaching through universities, and lift up the poor in faraway places, "for they would inherit the earth."

John Ortberg has demonstrated that nothing in our human existence has been quite the same since that fateful Sunday so long ago. We join Johann Sebastian Bach in saying (as he wrote at the beginning of his compositions), "God help me." And we glory in the belief that our Lord answers. But we too often fail to say, as Bach did at the end of his magnificent works, "(Everything) To the Glory of God."

So the real power of this book is in its exploration of the paradox of our faith: that acceptance of the Lord Christ Jesus is not a pathway to an easy life but a call to do hard things if we are to live in the image of our Lord. "Love my enemies?" "Give my riches to the poor and take up the cross?" "Die so that I might live?"

Jesus emerges from this book as a complex figure with a disruptive set of teachings — sometimes "cranky" with those who don't get it, often tough on his followers, and yet compassionate with those in need. At the end, we want to know him even better.

In *Who Is This Man?* John Ortberg gives those who believe and those who are perhaps not so certain a compelling reason to seek answers. And he reminds us that seek we must, because there has never been a more important question in the history of humankind.

CONDOLEEZZA RICE
Former U.S. Secretary of State

Acknowledgments

The New Testament tells about a group of ten lepers who were cleansed by Jesus; only one came back to say thank you, and that one was a Samaritan. Thus, in a single story, the message of compassion to all who suffer, the inclusion of the outcast, and the beauty of gratitude were unforgettably passed on to the human race.

So this is a "Samaritan moment"—a chance to pause and say thank you to a group of people to whom I owe a very pleasant debt of gratitude. I am most grateful to the church I serve for making time available for me to write. This book grew more than most out of our life together, and I'm thankful for more discussions and feedback around this material than I could count.

Glenn Lucke and the Docent Research group—particularly Sharon Miller—were invaluable partners at helping to locate sources and stories worth exploring. An unforgettable breakfast with historian David Kennedy at the home of Bob and Dottie King (who were generous with their home in many ways) was wonderfully instructive about how historians approach their craft.

My friend Gary Moon is much responsible for this book going the direction that it did rather than down a far different path. Scot McKnight and Mark Nelson gave wise counsel at several junctures. Dallas Willard points to Jesus like no one else I know and helped me in a number of conversations to know where to look for the Jesus "wake" left in the sea of human history.

Chuck Bergstrom and Rick Blackmon were, as always, sounding boards and feedback-givers and, mostly, lifelong friends.

Linda Barker with whom I work is a treasure of both organization and creativity. Blues Baker is not only a great friend but also a teammate in ministry; it's an honor to serve as a cupbearer. Nancy Duarte has been generous in thinking about the message of this book and how it might be communicated in compelling ways; merely entering the space of the Duarte Group can't help but make the enterer more creative.

John Sloan has been more than an editor—a partner and fellow dreamer and lover of thoughts and words. Jim Ruark and Laura Weller gave care and precision to the crafting of each sentence.

Sealy and Curtis Yates came into this journey partway through and made it much more fun and energized than it otherwise would have been.

My daughter, Laura Turner, is gifted as a writer herself and has been a fountain of ideas and feedback for this book.

N. T. Wright was so surprisingly generous with his scholarship and observations and encouragement that I feel compelled to add the time-honored caveat that he is not responsible for any remaining errors but saved me from a number of others.

Sam and Betsy Reeves generously allowed me to use their house for writing. Sam interrupts a lot and is probably responsible for many errors here.

Nancy, after nearly thirty years of marriage, is with me in the thinking and the writing always.

S.D.G.

CHAPTER 1

The Man Who Won't Go Away

On the day after Jesus' death, it looked as if whatever small mark he left on the world would rapidly disappear. Instead, his impact on human history has been unparalleled.

After his disappearance from earth, the days of his unusual influence began. That influence is what this book is about. Rightly seen, this effect on past and current history will cause any thoughtful person —apart from their religious ideas about Christianity—to ask, "Who was this man?"

You can miss him in historical lists for many reasons, perhaps the most obvious being the way he lived his life. Jesus did not loudly and demonstrably defend his movement in the spirit of a rising political or military leader. He did not lay out a case that history would judge his brand of belief superior in all future books. He did not start by telling his disciples, "Here are proofs of my divinity; affirm them and I'll accept you."

Normally when someone dies, their impact on the world immediately begins to recede. As I write this, our world marks the passing of digital innovator Steve Jobs. Someone wrote that ten years ago our world had Bob Hope, Johnny Cash, and Steve Jobs; now we have no Jobs, no Cash, and no Hope. But Jesus inverted this normal human trajectory, as he did so many others. Jesus' impact was greater a hundred years after his death than during his life; it was greater still after five hundred years; after a thousand years his legacy laid the foundation for much of Europe; after two thousand years he has more followers in more places than ever.

If someone's legacy will outlast their life, it usually becomes apparent when they die. On the day when Alexander the Great or Caesar Augustus or Napoleon or Socrates or Mohammed died, their reputations were immense. When Jesus died, his tiny failed movement appeared clearly at an end. If there were a kind of "Most Likely to Posthumously Succeed" award given on the day of death to history's most influential people, Jesus would have come in dead last.

His life and teaching simply drew people to follow him. He made history by starting in a humble place, in a spirit of love and acceptance, and allowing each person space to respond. He deliberately placed himself on a collision course with Rome, where he would have been crushed like a gnat. And he was crushed.

And yet . . .

Jesus' vision of life continues to haunt and challenge humanity. His influence has swept over history like the tail of a comet, bringing his inspiration to influence art, science, government, medicine, and education; he has taught humans about dignity, compassion, forgiveness, and hope.

Since the day he did come—as G. K. Chesterton put it—"It has never been quite enough to say that God is in his heaven and all is right with the world; since the rumor is that God had left his heavens to set it right."

———•———

Jesus is history's most familiar figure. His impact on the world is immense and non-accidental.

Great men have sometimes tried to secure immortality by having cities named after them; the ancient world was littered with cities that Alexander named Alexandria and Caesar named Caesarea. While Jesus was alive, he had no place to live. Yet today I live in the San Francisco Bay area, which has its name because a man named Francis was once a follower of this man Jesus. Our state capital is named Sacramento, because Jesus once had a meal with his followers—the Last Supper—that became known as a Sacrament. You cannot look at a map without being reminded of this man.

Powerful regimes have often tried to establish their importance by dating the calendar around their existence. Roman emperors would date events according to the years of their reign; they marked past history by the founding of Rome itself. The French Revolution tried to enlighten everyone with a calendar that marked the reign of Reason. The USSR dated time from the deposing of the tsar and theoretically giving power to the people. It formed the "League of the Militant Godless" in the twenties to stamp out faith; a 1929 magazine cover showed two workers dumping Jesus out of a wheelbarrow. But the League's leader, Yemelian Yaroslavsky, grew frustrated at the stubbornness of faith. "Christianity is like a nail," he said. "The harder you strike it, the deeper it goes."

The idea of Jesus trying to impose a calendar on anyone was laughable. The beginning of his ministry was carefully noted by Luke according to the Roman calendar: "In the fifteenth year of the reign of Tiberius Caesar — when Pontius Pilate was governor of Judea, Herod tetrarch of Galilee, his brother Philip tetrarch of Iturea and Traconitis, and Lysanius tetrarch of Abilene." From complete obscurity, Jesus came to public attention for the blink of an eye — maybe three years, maybe as few as one. Yet today, every time we glance at a calendar or date a check, we are reminded that chronologically at least, this incredibly brief life has become somehow the dividing line of history.

> *Jesus is history's most familiar figure. His impact on the world is immense and non-accidental.*

Famous people often seek to preserve their legacy by having others named for them. The Bible mentions various characters named Herod or even Herodias who were intended to remind us of Herod the Great. On the day after Jesus' death, no one in the tiny circle that knew his identity was naming their new baby after him. But today the names of Caesar and Nero are used, if at all, for pizza parlors, dogs, and casinos, while the names in Jesus' book live on and on.

The quickest and most basic mental health assessment checks to see if people are "oriented times three": whether they know who they are, where they are, and what day it is. I was given the name of Jesus' friend John; I live in the Bay area named for Jesus' friend Francis; I was born 1,957 years after Jesus. How could orientation depend so heavily on one life?

No one knows what Jesus looked like. We have no paintings or sculptures. We do not even have any physical descriptions. Yet Jesus and his followers became the most frequent subjects for art in the world. His image settled on in Byzantine art by around AD 400 is the most recognized in history.

He has been portrayed in movies by Frank Russell (1898), H. B. Warner, Jeffrey Hunter, Max von Sydow, Donald Sutherland, John Hurt, Willem Dafoe, Christian Bale, and Jim Caviezel as well as countless others. Songs about him have been sung by too many too count, from the first known song listed by the apostle Paul in the letter to the Philippians to an album ("Under the Mistletoe") released last Christmas by Justin Bieber.

Even in the field of mental health, if patients have grandiose identity disorders, it is Jesus they imagine themselves to be. (Milton Rokeach's *Three Christs of Ypsilanti* is a classic in its field.) Do grandiose Buddhists imagine themselves to be the Buddha?

It is in Jesus' name that desperate people pray, grateful people worship, and angry people swear. From christenings to weddings to sickrooms to funerals, it is in Jesus' name that people are hatched, matched, patched, and dispatched.

From the Dark Ages to postmodernity, he is the man who won't go away.

But it's not just that ...

———•———

Yale historian Jaroslav Pelikan wrote, "Regardless of what anyone may personally think or believe about him, Jesus of Nazareth has been the dominant figure in the history of Western Culture for almost twenty centuries. If it were possible, with some sort of super magnet, to pull up out of the history every scrap of metal bearing at least a trace of his name, how much would be left?

We live in a world where Jesus' impact is immense even if his name goes unmentioned. In some ways, our biggest challenge in gauging his influence is that we take for granted the ways in which our world has been shaped by him. G. K. Chesterton said that if you want to gauge the impact of his life, "The next best thing to being really inside Christendom is to be really outside it."

Children would be thought of differently because of Jesus. Historian O. M. Bakke wrote a study called *When Children Became People: The Birth of Childhood in Early Christianity*, in which he noted that in the ancient world, children usually didn't get named until the eighth day or so. Up until then there was a chance that the infant would be killed or left to die of exposure—particularly if it was deformed or of the unpreferred gender. This custom changed because of a group of people who remembered that they were followers of a man who said, "Let the little children come to me."

> *We live in a world where Jesus' impact is immense even if his name goes unmentioned.*

Jesus never married. But his treatment of women led to the formation of a community that was so congenial to women that they would join it in record numbers. In fact, the church was disparaged by its opponents for precisely that reason. Jesus' teachings about sexuality would lead to the dissolution of a sexual double standard that was actually encoded in Roman law.

Jesus never wrote a book. Yet his call to love God with all one's mind would lead to a community with such a reverence for learning that when the classical world was destroyed in what are sometimes called the Dark Ages, that little community would preserve what was left of its learning. In time, the movement he started would give rise to libraries and then guilds of learning. Eventually Oxford and Cambridge and Harvard and Yale and virtually the entire Western system of education and scholarship would arise because of his followers. The insistence on universal literacy would grow out of an understanding that this Jesus, who was himself a teacher who highly praised truth, told his followers to enable every person in the world to learn.

He never held an office or led an army. He said that his kingdom was "not from this world." He was on the wrong side of the law at the beginning of his life and at its end. And yet the movement he started would eventually mean the end of emperor worship, be cited in documents like the Magna Carta, begin a tradition of common law and limited government, and undermine the power of the state rather than reinforce it as other religions in the empire had done. It is because of his movement that language such as "We hold these truths to be self-evident, that all men are created equal; that they are endowed by their Creator with certain unalienable rights" entered history.

The Roman Empire into which Jesus was born could be splendid but also cruel, especially for the malformed and diseased and enslaved. This one teacher had said, "Whatever you did for one of the least of these …, you did for me." An idea slowly emerged that the suffering of every single individual human being matters and that those who are able to help ought to do so. Hospitals and relief efforts of all kinds emerged from this movement; even today they often carry names that remind us of him and his teachings.

Humility, which was scorned in the ancient world, became enshrined in a cross and was eventually championed as a virtue.

Enemies, who were thought to be worthy of vengeance ("help your friends and punish your enemies"), came to be seen as worthy of love. Forgiveness moved from weakness to an act of moral beauty.

Even in death, Jesus' influence is hard to escape. The practice of burial in graveyards or cemeteries was taken from his followers; *cemetery* itself comes from a Greek word meaning "sleeping place." It expressed the hope of resurrection. If there is a tombstone, it will often have the date of birth and the date of death with a dash in between, the length of that human life measured by its distance from Jesus' lifetime. In many cases, if a tombstone is unaffordable, a grave is marked with a cross, a reminder of Jesus' death. To this day, if a cartoonist wants a shorthand way of referring to the afterlife, a simple sketch of Saint Peter in the clouds by a pearly gate will be understood. Whatever it did or did not do to his existence, death did not end Jesus' influence. In many ways, it just started it.

He is the man who would not give up.

But it's not just that.

— ·•· —

Jesus is deeply mysterious, not only because he lived long ago in a world strange to us. Jesus is mysterious not just because of what we *don't* know about him. He is mysterious because of what we *do* know about him.

As N. T. Wright observed, what we do know about him "is so unlike what we know about anybody else that we are forced to ask, as people evidently did at the time: who, then *is* this? Who does he think he is, and who is he in fact?" From the time on the cusp of manhood when he began discussing God, we are told that people were amazed and his own parents were astonished (Luke 2:47–48).

When he began to teach, people were some-times delighted and sometimes infuriated but always astounded. Pilate couldn't under-stand him, Herod plied him with questions, and his own disciples were often as con-fused as anybody. As Wright said: "People who listened to him at the time said things

> *Jesus is mysterious not just because of what we don't know about him, but because of what we do know about him.*

like, 'We've never heard anyone talking like this' and they didn't just mean his tone of voice or his skillful public speaking. *Jesus puzzled people then, and he puzzles us still.*"

Jesus' impact on history is a puzzle. When we turn to look at his short life, it has this same puzzling quality. No one knew quite what to make of him.

But it's not a random, absurd, meaningless puzzle.

Understanding his life is like trying to wake up from a dream. It's like listening to an answer which—when you get it—you'll realize you always somehow knew. Like light on a strange path that, when you fol-low it, turns out to lead you home.

Jesus is as hard to nail down as Jell-O. Kings think that if they name his name, they can co-opt his authority. But Jesus the liberator keeps breaking through. When people claim his authority for slavery, a Wil-liam Wilberforce or Jonathan Blanchard sees in him the call to freedom. He inspires Leo Tolstoy, who in turn inspires Mohandas Gandhi, who in turn inspires Martin Luther King Jr. He inspires Desmond Tutu to dream up and pray up a Truth and Reconciliation Commission.

The number of groups claiming to be "for" Jesus are inexhaustible; to name a few: Jews for Jesus, Muslims for Jesus, Ex-Masons for Jesus, Road Riders for Jesus, Cowboys for Jesus, Wrestlers for Jesus, Clowns for Jesus, Puppets for Jesus, even Atheists for Jesus.

Labor leader Eugene Debs claimed him as the friend of socialism:

"Jesus Christ belongs to the working class. I have always felt that he was my friend and comrade," while Henry Ford said his capitalism was Christian idealism. The Quakers found in him the command for pacifism ("when Christ dis-armed Peter, he dis-armed us all"), while Constantine was converted by the promise of battlefield victory through the cross ("In this sign you will conquer").

Look at the people Jesus brings together: Jesse Jackson and Jerry Falwell; Jim Wallis and Jim Dobson; Anne Lamott and Thomas Kincaide; Billy Graham and Billy Sunday and Bill Clinton and "Bill" Shakespeare; Bono and Bach and Bev Shea; Galileo and Isaac Newton and Johannes Kepler; Thomas Aquinas and Thomas à Kempis; T. S. Eliot and C. S. Lewis and J. R. R. Tolkien; George Washington and Denzel Washington and George Washington Carver; Sojourner Truth and Robert E. Lee; Constantine and Charlemagne; Sarah Palin and Barack Obama; John Milton and Paul Bunyan and Mr. Rogers and Jimmy Carter and Peter the Great.

Something about Jesus keeps prodding people to do what they would rather not: Francis of Assisi gives up his possessions, Augustine gives up his mistress, John Newton gives up his slave trade, and Father Damien gives up his health.

A secular British curmudgeon named Malcolm Muggeridge was brought up short while visiting an Indian leprosarium run by the Missionaries of Charity. As he saw Mother Teresa in action, he realized with the force of sudden insight that humanists do not run leprosariums.

He is the man nobody knows.

But not just that.

———— ·•· ————

The first person to write about him—who would become known as Paul —said that Jesus appeared to him unbidden and unwanted. And he had a strange way of continuing to show up where he was not always sought or even welcome.

Novelist Mary Karr was a lifelong agnostic, daughter of a mother who married seven times, set Mary's toys on fire, and tried to stab her to death. Karr was the celebrated author of *The Liars' Club* and a chronic alcoholic. Jesus was the last person in the world she was expecting. She said: "If you'd told me a year before ... that I'd wind up whispering my sins in the confessional or on my knees saying the rosary, I would've laughed myself cock-eyed. More likely pastime? Pole dancer. International spy. Drug Mule. Assassin."

Jesus was a teacher, but somehow not just a teacher. He was claiming to have announced something or discovered something or inaugurated something in a way teachers never did. As Pelikan said: "It is not merely in the name of a great teacher, not even the greatest teacher who ever lived, that Justinian built Hagia Sophia in Constantinople or Johan Sebastian Bach composed the Mass in B-Minor. There are no cathedrals in honor of Socrates."

How does Jesus survive his followers? The Inquisition and witch hunts and Crusades and defense of slavery and imperialism and resistance to science and wars of religion come and go and return. Judgmentalism and intolerance and bigotry infect continents and centuries, scandals of money and sex among church leaders never seem to cease, and Jesus' followers cause him far more trouble than his enemies. Maybe that's why he seems to move around a lot.

Andrew Walls noted that most religions remain centered in their original homes. But with the Jesus movement things are different. It began in Jerusalem, but was embraced by unwashed Gentiles with such zeal that it began to move across the ancient Mediterranean to North Africa and Alexandria and Rome. Then more barbarians took it to heart, and it began to expand to northern Europe and eventually to North America. In the past century, it has dramatically shifted again: the majority of Christians now live in the global South and the East. When asked why, Walls said that "there is a certain vulnerability, a fragility, at the heart of Christianity. You might say it is the vulnerability of the cross." Where the faith has too much money and too much power for too long it begins to spoil, and the center moves on.

Ralph Waldo Emerson said once that the name of Jesus was "not so much written as ploughed into the history of this world."

H. G. Wells marveled that after two millennia,

> a historian like myself, who doesn't even call himself a Christian, finds the picture centering irresistibly around the life and character

of this most significant man.... The historian's test of an individual's greatness is "What did he leave to grow?" Did he start men to thinking along fresh lines with a vigor that persisted after him? By this test Jesus stands first.

Why?

Maybe because of its timing. Maybe Jesus was just a sympathetic figure who happened to come along when Roman infrastructure was good and Greek philosophy was undermining the gods, when paganism was dying and social systems were collapsing, when stability was down and anxiety was up and gullibility was strong and ... it was just dumb luck. Maybe Jesus was a kind, simple, innocent soul with a good mom and a knack for catchy sayings who showed up in the right place at the right time. Jesus Gump. Maybe his place in history is a remarkable accident.

But maybe it isn't.

CHAPTER 2

The Collapse
of Dignity

He entered the world with no dignity.

He would have been known as a *mamzer,* a child whose parents were not married. All languages have a word for *mamzer,* and all of them are ugly. His cradle was a feeding trough. His nursery mates had four legs. He was wrapped in rags. He was born in a cave, targeted for death, raised on the run.

He would die with even less dignity: convicted, beaten, bleeding, abandoned, naked, shamed. He had no status. Dignity on the level of a king is the last word you would associate with Jesus.

There is a king in the story, though. Jesus was born "during the time of King Herod."

To an ancient reader, Herod—not Jesus—would have been the picture of greatness. Born of noble birth, leader of armies, Herod was so highly regarded by the Roman Senate that they gave him the title "King of the Jews" when he was only thirty-three years old. He was so politically skilled that he held on to his throne for forty years, even persuading Caesar Augustus to retain him after he had backed Caesar's mortal enemy, Mark Antony. He was the greatest builder of his day. "No one in Herod's period built so extensively with projects that shed such a bright light on that world." The massive stones of the temple he built are visible two thousand years later.

Jesus was a builder. A carpenter. He likely did construction in a town called Sepphoris for one of Herod's sons. Nothing he built is known to endure.

In the ancient world, all sympathies would have rested with Herod. He was nearer to the gods, guardian of the *Pax Romana*, adviser to Caesar. The definitive biography of him is called: *Herod: King of the Jews, Friend of the Romans*. The two phrases are connected: if Herod were not a friend of the Romans, he would not be king of the Jews.

Jesus would be called "friend of sinners." It was not a compliment. He would be arrested as an enemy of the Romans.

Herod ruled in a time when only the ruthless survived. He cowered before no one. He had ten or eleven wives. He suspected the ambitions of the only one he ever truly loved, so he had her executed. He also had his mother-in-law, two of his brothers-in-law, and two of his own sons by his favorite wife executed. When his old barber tried to stick up for his sons, he had his barber executed. Caesar remarked that (given the Jewish refusal to eat pork) it was better to be Herod's pig than his son. Herod rewarded his friends and punished his enemies, the sign of a great-souled man in his day.

No one would bear that title "King of the Jews" after Herod, except for a crucifixion victim impaled one Friday afternoon.

Jesus, when he was a man, would be nearly as silent and passive before Herod's successor as he was when he was a baby before Herod.

Herod clung to his title to the end. While he was dying, he had a group of protestors arrested, the ringleaders burned alive, and the rest executed. Five days before his death, he had another son executed for trying to grab power prematurely. His will instructed scores of prominent Israelites be executed on the day he died so there would be weeping in Israel.

Herod was considered by Rome the most effective ruler over Israel the empire ever had. No one would bear that title "King of the Jews" again, except for a crucifixion victim impaled for a few hours one Friday afternoon.

We are used to thinking of Herod as the cardboard villain of the Christmas pageant, but he would have been considered great by many in his day, especially those whose opinion would have mattered most. How greatness came to look different to the world is part of what this story is about. No one knew it yet, but an ancient system of Dignity was about to collapse. Human dignity itself would descend from its Herod-protecting perch and go universal.

The lives of Herod and Jesus intersected when magi from the East asked where they could find the one born (notice the title) "king of the Jews." Herod claimed to follow the religion of Israel, but it was the pagan magi who sought truth with respect and humility. There is something about this Jesus, even on his first day, that had a way of forcing people to declare where they stand.

"When King Herod heard this he was disturbed" (major understatement here), "... and all Jerusalem with him." Now it's clear why.

Herod "was furious, and he gave orders to kill all the boys in Bethlehem and its vicinity who were two years old and under ... Then what was said through the prophet Jeremiah was fulfilled: 'A voice is heard in Ramah, weeping and great mourning, Rachel weeping for her children and refusing to be comforted, because they are no more.'"

I grew up in a church that did Christmas pageants every year. We would dress up in bathrobes and pretend to be Joseph and Mary and the shepherds and the wise men. Somehow that Herodian part of the story never made it into those pageants. It became known as the *slaughter of the innocents.*

This is not the kind of story you would write songs about. The night Jesus is born, all is not calm, all is not bright. That little baby does not "sleep in heavenly peace."

Herod sends soldiers to Bethlehem into the homes of peasant families who are powerless to stop them. They break in, and when they find an infant boy, they take out a sword and plunge it into that baby's body. Then they leave. Someone wrote a song centuries later: "O little town of Bethlehem, how still we see thee lie." Bethlehem was not still when Herod came for Jesus.

Matthew underlined the pain of the gap between peasant and king: "*Rachel weeping for her children.*" The rabbis said that centuries earlier, the Jewish matriarch Rachel had been buried in Bethlehem near the major road leading out of Israel so that she could weep for the helpless exiles leaving their home.

—◆—

Soon some more people would leave. Jesus' parents would flee to Egypt. Meanwhile, Jesus lay helpless and unaware. Herod, who built cities and ruled armies, was called Herod the Great.

No one called Jesus "the Great." Jesus is repeatedly given a different title by Matthew: "'Go and search carefully for *the child*' … the place where *the child* was … they saw *the child* with his mother … 'take *the child* … and escape to Egypt' … 'take *the child* … and go to the land of Israel' … so he got up, took *the child*.'"

The title "child," especially in that day, would be a vivid contrast with "king" or "great." In the ancient, status-ordered world, children were at the bottom of the ladder. In both Greek and Latin, the words for children meant "not speaking'; children lacked the dignity of reason.

Plato wrote about the "mob of motley appetites pains and pleasures" one would find in children, along with slaves and women. Children were noted for fear, weakness, and helplessness. "None among all the animals is so prone to tears," wrote Pliny the Elder. To be a child was to be dependent, defenseless, fragile, vulnerable, at risk.

Those were not qualities associated with heroism in the ancient world. A hero was someone who made things happen. A child was someone things happened to. In old stories about Hercules, he grabbed two poisonous snakes while he was still in the cradle and killed them with his bare, chubby little hands. By the second and third century AD, people made up stories about Jesus having great power as a child: in one of them he makes clay birds come alive; in another he magically causes the death of a child. But they are the kind of stories the Greeks made up to give their heroes dignity as children. The four Gospels have no stories like this about Jesus as a child.

Herod the Great made things happen. Things happened to the child Jesus.

———•—•———

There is a reversal going on in this story. The next season of Jesus' life is introduced with the phrase "After Herod died…."

In fact, three times in chapter 2 alone, Matthew mentions the fact that Herod is dead. Matthew wants the reader to know: Herod the Great, with all his wealth, glory, power, and crown, is now Herod the Dead.

Herod died. This is a subtle reminder of a great leveler. Who else is going to die?

Herod died. This is a subtle reminder of a great leveler. Who else is going to die?

A friend of mine gave me a watch I still wear. One hand says *Remember*, and the other hand says *You will die*. Every time somebody asks me, "What time is it?" I look at this watch. Every time I look at my wrist, what I see is, "Remember you will die." A *friend* gave me this watch. Not a good friend really ... but it helps me remember.

A new time had come with Jesus, a time when thinking about kings and children would begin to shift. You might say there was an idea lying there in the manger along with a baby. An idea that had mostly been confined to a little country called Israel, but which was waiting for the right time to crawl out into the wider world—an idea which that wider world would be unable to wholly resist.

All peoples in the ancient world had gods. Their gods had different names, but what they shared was a hierarchal way of ordering life. At the top of creation were the gods; under them was the king. Under the king were members of the court and the priests, who reported to the king. Below them were artisans, merchants, and craftspeople, and below them was a large group of peasants and slaves—the dregs of humanity.

The king was divine, or semi-divine. The king was understood to be made in the image of the god who created him. Only the king was made in the image of the god. This was a dividing line between the king and the rest of the human race. Peasants and slaves were not made in the image of *the* god; they were created by inferior gods.

This is the Dignity Gap. The farther down the ladder, the wider the gap.

But that gap was challenged by an idea that lay there in the manger, an idea that had been guarded by Israel for centuries: *There is one God. He is good. And every human being has been made in his image.*

Because God is Creator of all, the earth is full of creatures. But human beings reflect the image of God in a way no other creature can, with the capacity to reason, choose, communicate, and invent. Man is a critter who can Twitter.

Imagine what it did to the hearts of the dregs of humanity to be told that not just the king but they too were created in the image of the one great God. Male and female, slaves and peasants, made in God's image.

God said that these human beings are to exercise "dominion." That's a royal word. But it is no longer reserved for the few. Every human being has royal dignity. When Jesus looked at people, he saw the image of God. He saw this in everyone. It caused him to treat each person with dignity. This was the idea to which that little baby in a manger was heir, which had been given to Israel, which would be clarified and incarnated in his life in a way not seen before.

———•⊶•———

The belief that all people are made in God's image has woven its way into our world in a manner we often do not see. The United States' Declaration of Independence begins, "We hold these truths to be self-evident: That all men are created equal; that they are endowed by their Creator with certain inalienable rights; that among these rights are life, liberty, and the pursuit of happiness."

There is a raft of ideas here: that people are created, not accidents; that their Creator gives them certain endowments and confers worth on them. This worth means that they come with certain rights that ought to be respected for a society to be considered good. This is true for all human beings—all are created equal.

The idea of the equality of all human beings was not "self-evident" to the ancient world. Aristotle did not think all men were created equal. He wrote that inequality—masters and slavery—was the natural order of things: "For that some should rule and others be ruled is a thing not only necessary, but expedient; from the hour of their birth, some are marked out for subjection, others for rule."

Who came in between Aristotle and Thomas Jefferson to change this?

Yale philosopher Nicholas Wolterstorff observes that throughout world history, human beings by nature tend to be tribal. We don't think of "outsiders" as having the same worth or rights. What accounts for the emergence of this moral subculture that says every human being has rights?

Wolterstorff gives an amazing answer: the teaching of the Scriptures, clarified and made available to all the world through Jesus, that every human being is made in the image of God, and loved by God.

— • ◦ • —

There are gradations of talent, strength, intelligence, and beauty. Martin Luther King Jr. said, "There are no gradations of the image of God."

The reason every person has great worth, for Jesus, is that every person is loved by God. Each person has what might be called "bestowed worth."

When one of our daughters was tiny, she had one doll she loved above all others; a doll that initially belonged to her sister. She loved that doll so much, she commandeered her and we had to buy her sister another one. She called her doll Baby Tweezers. That doll got loved so much that her dress fell apart, and all she had was her little plastic head and limbs and squishy soft inner body. She then was renamed "Naked Baby Tweezers." She was not loved for her beauty. She set a new standard for ugly. She was loved: "Because." Just "because."

> *The reason every person has great worth, for Jesus, is that every person is loved by God and has "bestowed worth."*

We could never throw out Baby Tweezers. Our daughter loved Baby Tweezers—and we loved our daughter. Baby Tweezers has "bestowed worth."

We all know this kind of love: Get a pet, live in a house twenty years, raise your kids there. You come to love it—not because it's more excellent; just "because."

Novelist George MacDonald delighted in writing about princesses and princes. Someone asked him why he always wrote about princesses. "Because every girl is a princess," he said.

When the questioner was confused, MacDonald asked what a princess is. "The daughter of a king," the man answered.

"Very well, then every little girl is a princess."

Every human being is the child of a King.

— • ◦ • —

The ancient world did not teach this. Ordinary children did not share the king's image. They were not created by the same god. And so they grew up in a different world.

In the Roman Empire, some babies grew up to be women, who were generally shut off from education and public life. Some grew up to be slaves, who were needed for their labor but regarded as inferior to those who were free.

Many babies did not grow up at all. In the ancient world, unwanted children were often simply left to die, a practice called "exposure." The head of the household had the legal right to decide the life or death of other members of the family. This decision was usually made during the first eight or so days of life. (Plutarch wrote that until that time the child was "more like a plant than a human being.")

The most common reasons to expose a child would be if the family lived in poverty, or if a wealthy family did not want the estate divided up, or if the child was the wrong gender (meaning a girl—more on this in another chapter), or if the child were illegitimate.

The Jews were opposed to exposure because of their faith. Since Jesus was regarded as a *mamzer*—the descendant of a forbidden relationship between two Jews—he would likely not have survived had Joseph been Roman. Abandoned children were often left on a dump or a dung hill. They most often died; sometimes they were rescued, but usually this was to become enslaved. This happened often enough that hundreds of ancient names are variations of the word *kopros*, which was Greek for "dung."

Babies that were disabled or appeared weak were often disposed of by drowning. An ancient Roman law said that a boy who was "strikingly deformed" had to be disposed of quickly. One archaeological dig found "a gruesome discovery," the bones of "nearly 100 little babies apparently murdered and thrown into the sewer."

Ancient parents could be as tender and loving as moderns. But children had value to the extent that they could serve the state. And the state was embodied by Herod. In themselves, children were disposable.

Then the child born in Bethlehem grew up. He began to say things about children no one else thought of.

One day Jesus was asked the question, "Who . . . is the greatest in the kingdom of heaven?" Matthew wrote, "He called a little child to him, and placed the child among them. [Maybe a child named *Kopros*.] And he said: '... Unless you change and become like little children, you will never enter the kingdom of heaven. Therefore, whoever takes the lowly position of this child is the greatest in the kingdom of heaven.'"

Jesus said it wasn't the child's job to become like Herod. It was Herod's job to become like the child. Greatness comes to people who die to appearing great. No one else in the ancient world—not even the rabbis—used children as an example of conversion.

Then Jesus said the kind of thing that would literally never enter the mind of another human being to say: "And whoever welcomes one such child in my name welcomes me."

Kopros has a new name.

There were many clubs and associations in the ancient world. None of the qualities associated with children—weakness, helplessness, lowliness—qualified one to join any of them. There were no clubs for children. Until Jesus.

> *Jesus said it wasn't the child's job to become like Herod. It was Herod's job to become like the child.*

Another time Jesus acted out a little parable of this teaching. Children "were brought" to Jesus. The language says they could not even come themselves: passive, dependent. The disciples rebuked the parents. Jesus rebuked the disciples. "Let the little children come to me, and do not hinder them, for the kingdom of heaven belongs to such as these."

A kingdom for children. Before Walt Disney. And the little children came.

As the movement that Jesus started spread, it created an alternative community for children. Early instructions among his followers, such as the *Didache* in the second century, prohibit the widespread practices of abortion, exposure, and infanticide.

There is an old joke that the most basic of the Ten Commandments for parents is "Thou shalt not kill." In some ways, that is a new joke; in the ancient world it was the basis of a revolution. Exposure was forbidden—not because the state needed more workers (Caesar Augustus would try to limit it on this basis), but because as the Shepherd of Hermas put it, "All babies are glorious before God." Saint Ambrose of Milan said that the church must care not only for babies, but also for the poor, because poverty often destroys their ability to care for children.

Homer did not say that Zeus or Apollo or Pan valued all human beings equally. G. K. Chesterton wrote that the elevation of the dignity of childhood would have made no sense to the ancients. It came into the world through Jesus, and even where belief in him has eroded the elevation of childhood, Jesus' thought remains: "The pagan world, as such, would not have understood any such thing as a serious suggestion that a child is higher or holier than a man. It would have seemed like the suggestion that a tadpole is higher or holier than a frog.... Peter Pan does not belong to the world of Pan but the world of Peter."

An average life expectancy of thirty or so meant the ancient world was full of orphans. Now for the first time, a community began to collect money to care for them indiscriminately. At baptism children would receive "god parents," who would promise to care for them if their parents died.

By the late fourth century, a Christian emperor outlawed the practice of exposure for the entire empire. Over time, instead of leaving unwanted babies on a dung hill, people began to leave them outside a monastic community or a church. The beginnings of what would be known as orphanages began to rise, usually associated with monasteries or cathedrals.

Merely claiming a religious label is no more a guarantee of family health now than it was for Adam and Eve. But those who live in a culture truly touched and changed by Christianity view individuals differently because of Jesus, whatever they might think of him. The ordinary and the lowly have great dignity. All children should live. All human beings are created equal.

A few years ago I spoke at an event where the hero was a dad named Dick Hoyt. When Dick's son Richard was born, the umbilical cord was wrapped around his neck. He was brain-damaged; he would never be able to walk or speak. In ancient Rome, both by custom and by law, he would have had to be discarded.

Dick and his wife brought Richard home to care for him. When he was eleven, they took him to the engineering department at Tufts University to see if a device could be invented to help him communicate. They were told that his brain was incapable of comprehension.

"Tell him a joke," Dick said. When they did, Richard laughed. The department constructed a computer that allowed Richard to laboriously type out a sentence by hitting a button with the side of his head—the only part of his body he could move.

When Richard heard one day about a benefit race being run to help a young man who had been paralyzed, he typed out a sentence: *Dad, I want to run.* By this time Dick was forty, a self-described porker who had never run over a mile. He somehow pushed his son in a wheelchair over the course. Afterward, Richard wrote the sentence that changed Dick's life: *When I ran, I didn't feel disabled.* Dick began to run.

We watched videos of this strong father pushing and pulling and carrying his son over two hundred triathlons. Not a dry eye in the room. More than eighty-five times Dick has pushed Richard's wheelchair the 26.2 miles that make up a marathon. Dick's best time is a little over two and a half hours—within thirty minutes of the world's record, which was not set, as sports columnist Rick Reilly observed, by a guy pushing his son in a wheelchair.

I said earlier that the hero in the room was Dick. That's not quite right. Dick said that his hero—his inspiration, his courage, his reason for running—is the 110-pound motionless, speechless body of the man in the chair.

The Greeks loved physical excellence and perfection, the nobility of striving. They gave us the Olympics, through which mortals strove to be like the gods of Olympus. They gave us the marathon, the ultimate test of human will and strength. They did not give us the story of a marathon being run by a man carrying his crippled son.

I recently read an article that speaks of a "theology of disability," which explores how the divine is present in limitation and suffering and handicap. It is a phrase that would have been senseless in Rome.

———•◦•———

The child in Bethlehem would grow up to be a friend of sinners, not a friend of Rome. He would spend his life with the ordinary and the unimpressive. He would pay deep attention to lepers and cripples, to the blind and the beggar, to prostitutes and fishermen, to women and children. He would announce the availability of a kingdom different from Herod's, a kingdom where blessing — of full value and worth with God — was now conferred on the poor in spirit and the meek and the persecuted.

People would not understand what all this meant. We still do not.

But a revolution was starting — a slow, quiet movement that began at the bottom of society and would undermine the pretensions of the Herods. It was a movement that was largely underground, like a cave around Bethlehem where a dangerous baby might be born and hidden from a king.

Since that birth, babies and kings and everybody else look different to us now — as in the poignant list of David Bentley Hart: " the autistic or Down syndrome or otherwise disabled child ... the derelict or wretched or broken man or woman who has wasted his or her life away; the homeless, the utterly impoverished, the diseased, the mentally ill, the physically disabled; exiles, refugees, fugitives; even criminals and reprobates." These were viewed by our ancient ancestors as burdens to be discarded. To see them instead as bearers of divine glory who can touch our conscience and still our selfishness — this is what Jesus saw that Herod could not see.

> *A revolution was starting — a slow, quiet movement that began at the bottom of society and would undermine the pretensions of the Herods.*

Strange reversal. Men who wear purple robes and glittering crowns and gaudy titles begin to look ridiculous — (when is the last time a politician attached "the Great" to his name?) — and yet the figure of the child born in a manger seems only to grow in stature. "We see the glory of God in a crucified slave, and [consequently] ... we see the forsaken of the earth as the very children of heaven."

He came into the world with no dignity.

CHAPTER 3

A Revolution
in Humanity

Jesus could be a very irritating person to be around.

We are going to look at a dinner where he deliberately picked arguments four times running.

I say this because compassion is a quality Jesus might be most famous for. When a leper asked for healing, Jesus was "filled with compassion." When a widow cried out to him, "his heart went out to her, and he said, 'Don't cry.'" Adulterers and tax collectors and prodigals and Samaritans all evoked his compassion. A compassion makeover was coming to the world.

There is a general perception that Jesus was one of those extremely tender feelers who just couldn't stand pain. Elaine Aron has written a book called *Highly Sensitive People* about folks who startle easily, who are easily affected by others' mood or pain, who care deeply about others' opinions. There is nothing wrong with being a Highly Sensitive Person. I am one myself. What's it to you?

But other parts of Jesus' story do not make him look like an HSP. In a story told in all four Gospels, he saw people exploiting the poor in the temple; he took out a whip and drove them away, scattering their money and overturning their tables and saying, "How dare you."

Most of us Highly Sensitive People do not throw furniture.

Jesus said to another group: "You snakes! You brood of vipers! How will you escape being condemned to hell?" That's not typical HSP language. Jesus was as militant as he was compassionate.

How can *this* man be *that* man?

— ·•· —

There was a day when he exhibited both qualities together.

It was one of the most awkward dinner parties of all time. Jesus had been invited to eat in the house of a prominent Pharisee, and Jesus was being carefully watched. A man with edema—a painful, unattractive, sometimes dangerous condition in which parts of the body fill with fluid —was present.

It was a Sabbath. In that Jewish society, no medical treatment was to be offered on the Sabbath unless someone's life was in jeopardy. If Jesus had been an affable guest, he would have pretended not to notice the man.

But Jesus was not affable. He called everyone's attention to the man.

Jesus was sensitive to suffering. He asked if it was permissible to heal this man on the Sabbath. This was not an abstract discussion; the man was listening. Making religious leaders have this discussion with the man looking right at them, seems insensitive on Jesus' part.

No one said a word. Jesus touched the man and healed him. The diners were not happy about this. The host did not invite the man to stay for dinner, so Jesus did what the host should have done and bade the man farewell.

The diners had nothing to say. This was not a comfortable silence. A storm was about to break.

This was awkward. If Jesus had smooth social radar, he would have recognized that now was the time to change the subject.

Jesus did not have smooth social radar. He asked, "If one of you has a child or an ox that falls into a well on the Sabbath day, will you not immediately pull it out?" And they had nothing to say.

This was not a comfortable silence. A storm was about to break.

The issue was not that Judaism was a religion of legalism and Jesus came to start a new religion called Christianity. Jesus was thoroughly Jewish. He was a rabbi, and you can't be a rabbi and not love the Torah.

The issue was what was the worth of a human being?

— ·•· —

Jesus insisted that the whole law pointed toward love, and love meant seeing and valuing the worth God had placed in human life.

We are obsessed with worth. We want to know the worth of everything. If we want to know the worth of a car, we can find it in a source called the *Blue Book,* because if we really want the car and we find out how much it costs, we will feel blue.

Jesus talked about the value of humans quite a lot:

> "If any of you has a sheep and it falls into a pit on the Sabbath, will you not take hold of it and lift it out? How much more valuable is a person than a sheep!"

> "Look at the birds of the air; they do not sow or reap or store away in barns, and yet your heavenly Father feeds them. Are you not much more valuable than they?"

> "Are not sparrows sold two for a penny? Yet not one of them will fall to the ground outside your Father's care. And even the very hairs of your head are all numbered. So don't be afraid; you are worth more than many sparrows."

God values sparrows—more than you know. He feeds them, gives them trees and twigs for nests, and gives them other sparrows to mate with. God cares so much about them that he has a running inventory.

Now how about you? "The hairs on your head are all numbered." When you care about someone, you notice details. When a baby is born, what do parents do when they look at their fingers and toes for the first time? They count them. For years afterward, every time that kid comes home, if they are missing one of those ten fingers or toes, the parents notice. Even mediocre parents do this.

Jesus was saying, "God doesn't just number your fingers and toes. God loves you so much that he numbers the hairs on your head. He notices their quantity. He mourns when they go away. He notices their color." Proverbs 16:31 tells us, "Gray hair is a crown of splendor; it is attained by a righteous life." When you see a person with gray hair, stop in wonder and admiration, because you're looking at a spiritual giant. It says so in the Bible.

The child Jesus is praising is God's child. God's people matter to

God more than anything else. Jesus in effect is saying, "Does anybody here have the moral clarity and spiritual courage to speak up on God's disabled child?" Nobody does. There is another silence. This is brutal.

This makes Jesus mad. In the face of deliberately ignored suffering, he is not a highly sensitive compassionate person. He is a highly irritated compassionate person.

The Jewish leaders thought they were going to watch Jesus. It turned out that Jesus was watching them. They thought they were going to judge Jesus. It turned out that Jesus was judging them. This was *really* awkward. The host who convened the dinner thought, *I hope whoever talks next picks a safer topic.* Jesus talked next. He did not pick a safer topic.

———·◆·———

Jesus noticed how the leaders picked places of honor at the table. This is simply one more way we value some people over others. We violate God's Blue Book.

So Jesus gave some tongue-in-cheek advice: When somebody invites you to a feast, don't go for the seat of honor. Go sit in the kitchen. Humble yourself.

Jesus was essentially saying to the host, "Hey, host! Let me give you some advice. Your seating chart is all wrong. You think healing the sick on the Sabbath is wrong and that competing with people for status is right. Let me redo your table assignment. Exalt somebody else."

The leaders were all embarrassed; they were all furious. For sure, now they didn't know where they should sit.

The host was thinking, *I hope Jesus doesn't have any more advice.*

Jesus turned to the host and said, "Let me give you some more advice." Jesus was on a roll now. "When you give a luncheon or dinner, do not invite your friends, your brothers or sisters, your relatives, or your rich neighbors; if you do, they may invite you back and so you will be repaid. But when you give a banquet, invite the poor, the crippled, the lame, the blind, and you will be blessed. Although they cannot repay you, you will be repaid at the resurrection of the righteous."

(If Jesus was saying you should never invite your relatives for dinner, you may have been looking for this verse your whole life long.)

Jesus was not giving a law here. He was contrasting God's Blue Book with ours. Inviting the poor for dinner might be a possibility, if unusual. But the crippled, the lame, and the blind—that's another matter.

Anything malformed or defective was considered by Pharisees to be unable to reflect the perfect holiness of God. Therefore, nothing malformed was allowed within the precincts of the temple.

The Pharisees generally took great pride in following perfectly in their homes the regulations that were supposed to govern the temple. They believed the temple had been corrupted by Rome, so they could honor God by treating their homes as miniature temples. All the regulations that should be observed in the temple would be observed in their homes.

For Jesus to tell this prominent Pharisee to deliberately invite malformed, defective human beings into his holy little temple was a deliberate slap in the face. Jesus was telling him to put on his guest list people whose defects offended him.

We are never told that Jesus had compassion on someone because they deserved it. It was only because they were in need.

Jesus' crankiness and compassion came from the same source: his outrageous love for every individual, and his pain when anyone is undervalued. In all the stories of Jesus' compassion, we are never told that he had compassion on someone because they deserved it. It was only because they were in need.

———◆———

By this time at the gathering, everybody's blood pressure was going off the charts. A Highly Sensitive Guest tried to distract Jesus with a little platitude: "Blessed is anyone who will eat at the feast in the kingdom of God."

Jesus would not be distracted. He began a story about who is on the guest list for the feast in the kingdom.

The host was thinking, *Here we go again.*

In Jesus' story, the man who threw the feast was insulted by expected guests who rejected him at the last minute with lame excuses.

As we would expect, the master was angry. As we would not expect, he turned his anger into grace. He told his servant to go to the streets and alleys of the town and bring in "the poor, the crippled, the blind and the lame."

Them again! What was it with Jesus? He just couldn't let it go!

The servant did what his master said but informed him that empty spaces remained around the table. The master sent him on a second sweep — this time to the "roads and country lanes." Nonvillagers. Outsiders.

According to Nicholas Wolterstorff, "Jesus' understanding of who are the downtrodden has been expanded well beyond the Old Testament understanding, to include not just the victims of social structures and practices — widows, orphans, aliens, the poor, the imprisoned — but also those excluded from full participation in society because they are defective, malformed, or seen as religiously inferior. The coming of God's just reign requires that these too be lifted up."

After Jesus died, some of his followers remembered his words.

Sociologist Rodney Stark argued that one of the primary reasons for the spread of Jesus' movement was the way his followers responded to sick people.

During the reign of Marcus Aurelius around AD 165, an epidemic of what may have been smallpox killed somewhere between a third and a fourth of the population, including Marcus Aurelius himself. A little less than a century later came a second epidemic, in which at its height five thousand people were reported dying daily in the city of Rome alone.

For the most part, people responded in panic. There was no guidance in the writings of Homer, no commands from the Greek god Zeus to care for dying people you do not know while putting your own life at risk. Greek historian Thucydides wrote about how people in Athens responded during an earlier plague: "They died with no one to look after them. Indeed there were many houses in which all the inhabitants perished through lack of any intention for care. The bodies of the dying were heaped up, one on top of the other.... No fear of god or law of man had a restraining influence." Now what had happened in Greece was happening in Rome: "At the first onset of the disease, they pushed the sufferers away and fled from their dearest, throwing them into the roads before they were dead and treated unburied corpses as dirt, hoping thereby to avert the spread and contagion of the fatal disease."

But there was in that world a community that remembered they followed a man who would touch lepers while they were unclean; who told his disciples to go heal the sick, who got in arguments at dinners that embarrassed whole tables. Dionysius, a third-century bishop of Alexandria, wrote about their actions during the plagues: "Heedless of the danger, they took charge of the sick, attending to their every need, and ministering to them in Christ. And with them departed this life serenely happy, for they were infected by others with the disease, drawing on themselves the sickness of their neighbors, and cheerfully accepting their pains."

Read now what might be familiar words: "I was hungry and you gave me something to eat, I was thirsty and you gave me something to drink, I was a stranger and you invited me in, I needed clothes and you clothed me, I was sick and you looked after me.... Truly I tell you, whatever you did for one of the least of these brothers and sisters of mine, you did for me."

The idea that "the least of these" were to be treasured—that somehow the Jesus that they followed was present in despised suffering—was essentially a Copernican revolution of humanity. It created a new vision of the human being. People actually took Jesus at his word.

> *The idea that "the least of these" were to be treasured created a new vision of the human being. People actually took Jesus at his word.*

As Christian communities responded to the hungry and the sick, even outsiders took notice. By the late fourth century, an opponent of the faith, Emperor Julian the Apostate, chastised pagan priests for not keeping up: "I think that when the poor happened to be neglected and overlooked by the priests, the impious Galileans observed this and devoted themselves to benevolence.... The impious Galileans support not only their poor, but ours as well, everyone can see that our people lack aid from us."

———•———

In the early centuries of the church, leprosy meant isolation, uncleanness, and death.

A church father named Basil had an idea: "What if we build a place to love and care for lepers? They don't have money. They don't even have to pay for it. We'll raise the money."

One of the most famous sermons in that century was by his brother, Gregory of Nyssa (also a church father), and it was to raise money for this place to take care of leprosy. This is what Gregory said: "Lepers have been made in the image of God. In the same way you and I have, and perhaps preserve that image better than we, let us take care of Christ while there is still time. Let us minister to Christ's needs. Let us give Christ nourishment. Let us clothe Christ. Let us gather Christ in. Let us show Christ honor."

That was the beginning of what would come to be known as hospitals. The Council of Nyssa (the same council that affirmed the Nicene Creed) decreed that wherever a cathedral existed, there must be a hospice, a place of caring for the sick and poor. That is why even today many hospitals have names such as "Good Samaritan" or "Good Shepherd" or "Saint Anthony." They were the world's first voluntary, charitable institutions.

Another follower of Jesus named Jean Henri Dunant couldn't stand the sound of soldiers crying out on a battlefield after they had been wounded, so this Swiss philanthropist said he would devote his life to helping them in Jesus' name. That started an organization in the 1860s that became known as the Red Cross. Every time you see the Red Cross, you are seeing a thumbprint of Jesus.

A Lutheran pastor in Germany named Theodor Fliedner trained a group of mostly peasant women to nurse the sick. This led to a movement of hospitals all over Europe, and this inspired a young woman named Florence Nightingale to give her life to care for the sick. She asked that after she died she wanted her grave to be marked with simply a cross with her initials; she wanted to serve with no acclaim.

Another follower of Jesus became known as Father Damien. A Belgian priest, he worked in Hawaii in the nineteenth century and created a place where lepers could be loved and cared for. He used to tell them every week, "God loves you lepers." And then one week he got up and he said, "God loves *us* lepers." He died from leprosy.

Centuries ago the church father Tertullian said, "It is our care of the helpless, our practice of loving kindness that brands us in the eyes of our opponents." It's not that the Romans knew nothing of compassion, but compassion was not connected to the gods. The gods demanded sacrificial offerings, not acts of charity.

Nevertheless, compassion became the "brand" of this new religious movement, not because it attracted such wonderful people, but because they understood from their founder it was not an optional piece of equipment.

———•◦•———

In the ancient world, slavery was universal. Unlike later slavery in America, it had virtually nothing to do with one's race. It could happen to anyone—and often did. Although conditions varied somewhat, slaves generally had little dignity or worth. A slave was *non habens personam* before Roman law, literally "not having a person" or even "not having a face." Roman masters literally held the power of life and death over slaves. The slaves had no court of appeal. The slaves' pain was so lightly regarded that when they were called to testify, torture could be applied as a matter of course. Beatings and kickings were usually not given to free children precisely because such forms of punishment were reserved for slaves.

In the early church, a slave might wander in and have one of the masters—one of the rich and powerful—get down on his knees, take a basin and a towel, and wash the feet of one regarded as a non-person by the law. The *Didascalia Apostolorum*, an early church order, instructed bishops *not* to interrupt a service to greet a wealthy person of high rank who entered late. But if a poor man or woman entered the assembly, the bishop was to do whatever was needed to welcome them in, even if it meant the bishop were to end up sitting on the floor.

Historian Thomas Cahill says that Galatians 3:28 was the first statement of egalitarianism in human literature.

The seating chart was changing.

The apostle Paul said, "There is neither Jew nor Gentile, neither slave nor free, nor is there male and female, for you are all one in Christ Jesus." Historian Thomas Cahill says that this was the first statement of egalitarianism in human literature.

During Lent in AD 379, Gregory of Nyssa criticized slavery as an institution and scolded Christians who owned slaves: "You condemn to slavery the human being, whose nature is free ... upon the one who was created to be lord of the earth and appointed to rule the creation, upon this one you impose the yoke of slavery."

The church father cited the teaching of Jesus that the whole world cannot equal the worth of one soul: "How can you who have equality in everything have superiority in any particular, as you say, supposing yourself as a human being to be master of a human being?"

John Newton was forced to serve at sea as a young boy. He made his money buying and selling captured human beings, and he wrote that there was no method of getting money—not even robbing for it on the highway—that was so morally destructive. He said that if seamen were cruel, it was because there was no trade with which people were treated with so little humanity. His life was marked by gambling, profanity, and drinking; he contemplated suicide. Then he experienced a spiritual conversion. He became an Anglican vicar. He wrote the song "Amazing grace, how sweet the sound that saved a wretch like me."

A British politician named William Wilberforce got converted. He came to John Newton for career advice. He wanted to leave politics, but Newton told him he should stay and devote his life to the abolition of slavery. It became Wilberforce's consuming passion. He introduced his first bill to oppose slavery in 1787, and it was defeated. But he and his friends fought for decades through what became known as the Clapham Sect. The Parliament finally outlawed slavery in 1833, one month after Wilberforce's death.

The length of time it took the church to realize the implications of Paul's teaching "neither slave nor free" should help any Christian avoid triumphalism. Worse yet was the addition of racism to slavery in the West. (Mark Noll observed that in all the biblical debates about slavery, no one suggested that slavery was a good biblical system for *white* people.) Jesus' life and teachings were sometimes more disregarded inside the church than out.

Historically, prisons were hellholes. But his followers remembered how Jesus had said, "I was in prison and you came to visit me," and they would visit. A pagan second-century Greek writer named Lucian wrote about how when a Christian was put into prison, other Christians would bring him food.

· Years ago I was in Ethiopia when it was under a Marxist regime and the church was mostly underground. One or another of the leaders of the Christian group would frequently be arrested and put into prison, which was horribly over-crowded and unspeakably foul. Other prisoners used to long for a Christian to get put in prison, because if a Christian was jailed, his Christian friends would bring him food — actually, far more food than that one person could eat, and there would be leftovers for everybody. It became the "prisoner's prayer": "God, send a Christian to prison."

Two centuries ago a seventeen-year-old English girl named Elizabeth Gurney, who wrote in her diary that she had "no religion," met a Quaker who instilled in her a sense of God's presence. Her faith grew more serious, she became recognized as a Quaker "minister" at the age of thirty (by that time married to Joseph Fry ten years), and three years later she visited a jail near London named Newgate. Prisons then were often filthy and dark; women would often be jailed after falling in debt when their husbands ran away or died. Elizabeth was so struck by what Jesus said that she organized teams to visit women in prison to read the Bible to them and teach them to sew. She began a reform movement that led to Parliament passing the Prison Act of 1823. Elizabeth Fry became known as the Angel of Prison. Leaders from all over Europe would come to learn what she was doing.

In shopping malls, we still hear people ringing bells, part of an organization called the Salvation Army that flowed from the faith of William Booth. Whenever you say the words "World Vision" or "YMCA" or "Samaritan's Purse" or "Compassion International," you are speaking — know it or not — of the movement of Jesus.

———•·•———

This is not to say that there would be no compassion in the world without Christianity. Christians often fall short. In Jesus' story known as "the Good Samaritan," it is the *least* religiously orthodox person who shows the *greatest* compassion. Few people show less compassion than those who try to argue that Christians have a corner on compassion.

But philosopher Mark Nelson put it like this:

> If you ask what is Jesus' influence on medicine and compassion, I would suggest that wherever you have an institution of self-giving for the lonely (and for practical welfare of the lonely), schools, hospitals, hospices, orphanages for those who will never be able to repay, this probably has its roots in the movement of Jesus.

Jesus once said that "the poor you will always have with you." So it is with all human suffering. Contemporary slavery expert Kevin Bales said it endures today with one major difference—a complete collapse in price. Historically, slaves were worth around $40,000 in today's money; today the average slave costs around $90. They have become disposable units.

Few people show less compassion than those who try to argue that Christians have a corner on compassion.

In desperately poor Haiti, child slaves are often called *restaveks*, a Creole word meaning "stay with" for children who live with families that are not their own.

Nonna Harrison wrote about a young *restavek* named Bill Nathan. His father died of malaria after his birth. His mother died when he was seven. He was an orphan who ended up a slave. He had to quit school. When he made a mistake, he was beaten by the mistress. He was once given money to shop for the family and told to do so quickly. He ran all the way to town, and when he got there, exhausted, he was tricked out of his money.

The mistress found out. "You lost the money?"

He tried to speak but choked on tears instead. She kicked him to his knees. She handed him two rocks and told him to hold them out with extended arms. If he dropped them, she would kill him.

She took out a whip and began to lash him. As he screamed, she whipped him everywhere—his head, his eyes. After twenty minutes, his blood lay in pools on the ground. He still held the rocks.

Haitians have a word for *restaveks* who lose their sense of identity and their will to live: zombified. As if he did not have a will. As if he was not a person: *non habens personam*. Bill could not remember what it was like to be free.

When he was eleven, a group of Christians working to eradicate slavery rescued Bill. Today he is a drummer in a band that tours internationally. He tells his story and speaks out against slavery; he has grown into a man of strong and gentle faith in a God who works to free slaves.

I wonder how mad Jesus would be about *restaveks* and zombies?

Whatever you do for the least of these....

CHAPTER 4

What Does
a Woman Want?

More than twenty years ago Nancy and I went to a church campout. We had a two-year-old and a tiny baby. Nancy said to me, "You've got to help me watch these girls. I know that because this is a church event you will be tempted to be preoccupied with other matters, but I need your help."

On the second day, Nancy was in town with the baby and a few other moms. She got back to the campground in the early afternoon. It was over a hundred degrees outdoors.

I had to meet a couple at a coffee shop off the campground about ten miles away to discuss a very sensitive counseling matter. I saw that our car was back in the parking area, so I hopped in and drove off. You'd think it might have occurred to me to check with Nancy before I left, to tell her where I was going, but I did not.

I didn't know that the baby had fallen asleep in the car seat or that Nancy had asked someone to watch the car for a second while she got our two-year-old settled.

When I was almost to the coffee shop, I heard a tiny little sigh coming from the back seat. I looked back, and there was the baby in her car seat.

If I hadn't heard that sigh, I would have left her in the car for the afternoon in hundred-degree heat with the windows rolled up. It was unthinkable.

I started to shake at what a close call it had been. I picked that little baby up and hugged her as tight as I could and told her, "I'm so grateful you're alive. I'm so grateful you made that sigh. I'm so grateful you're so tiny and won't remember this. I'm so grateful you can't talk yet and won't tell mommy. I'll tell her some day. In twenty years. In a safe vehicle. Like a book."

There is not a parent I know who does not tremble at a story like that. Every parent has something close to an obsessive compulsive disorder (or perhaps "order") about the safety of their children.

And yet . . .

Our perceptions of our obligations to children are shaped much more by our world and our culture than most of us know.

———•◦•———

In the ancient Greco-Roman world, there was a huge shortage of women —about 140 men for every 100 women. What happened to the other women?

They were left to die when they got born the wrong sex.

A first-century letter from a husband to his pregnant wife shows the (to us) severe contrast of his tender regard for his wife and hoped-for son versus his disregard for a possible daughter: "I ask and beg of you to take good care of our baby son. . . . If you are delivered of a child [before I come home] if it is a boy, keep it; if a girl, discard it. You have sent me word, 'don't forget you.' How can I forget you? Do not worry."

By the Law of Romulus in Rome, a father was required to raise all healthy male children, but only the firstborn female; any others were disposable. According to the Greek poet Posidippus (third century BC), "Everyone raises a son even if he is poor but exposes a daughter even if he is rich."

In the city of Delphi, out of six hundred known families, six of them raised more than one daughter. The rest were apparently abandoned to die.

The undervaluing of a life because it is female is not confined to the ancient world. In 1990 Amartya Sen wrote a much-noticed essay entitled "More than 100 Million Women Are Missing," about the gender imbalance in China, India, and elsewhere. Twenty years later it was far worse: Mara Hvstendahl published *Unnatural Selection: Choosing Boys over Girls and the Consequences in a World Full of Men.* Asia alone has an imbalance of 163 million more males than females; once a fetus has been identified as a female, it is more likely to be unwanted. This imbalance in turn has consequences for women: rich families cannot find brides for their sons, so poor families are more likely to sell their daughters, which leads to a rise in sex trafficking and the marriages of girls sometimes younger than twelve years old.

In the ancient world, over a period of centuries the gender imbalance began to change. Could it possibly have had something to do with a carpenter who lived two thousand years ago? Forget what you believe about his divinity. He was a man. He lived a brief life in an obscure, provincial, male-dominated culture. Is it possible that ripples went out from that one life that have affected and still speak to women today?

———•—

The longest conversation recorded between Jesus and one other person is in John 4. Jesus sat down by a well to rest, "tired as he was from the journey." (It is striking how casually the Gospel writers note Jesus' limitations—that he got tired from walking.) A Samaritan woman came by for water, and Jesus asked her for a drink. When the disciples met up with him, they were surprised by what they saw. Something very unusual was going on there: "Just then his disciples returned and were surprised to find him talking with a woman."

> *Over centuries the gender imbalance began to change. Did it have something to do with a carpenter who lived two thousand years ago?*

At one point Jesus said to this woman she had had five husbands and was now living with a man to whom she was not married. Lynn Cohick notes a long line of interpreters who assume this means she was sexually immoral or unfaithful.

In reality, divorces were rare in Jesus' day. We don't know how many of this woman's marriages ended in divorce or death. There are apparently no records of a woman being the one to initiate divorce. In other words, she was no Elizabeth Taylor. She was a woman who had been rejected.

Her current arrangement was probably not about casual sexuality. If a man wanted a woman of lower class, he could bring her into his preexisting marriage as a concubine or second wife; this was very possibly her only means of survival.

Interestingly, the woman's marital history interests Bible scholars much more than it interested Jesus. While his culture (and ours) so often identified women in terms of shame — body shame, character shame, sexual shame — Jesus did not begin by identifying her shame.

Often the church's interpretations of biblical females say more about the church's (usually male) interpreters than about the characters. (For instance, Mary Magdalene was often assumed to be a prostitute, although there is nothing in the Bible to support this.) In modern-day telling of this story, it is often assumed that the Samaritan was a scandalized woman — a social outcast among her own people. But in the text she was actually listened to in her community: "many of the Samaritans from that town believed in him because of the woman's testimony."

This woman was poor; she had to draw her own water. Jesus was saying: "I know you. I know you're a woman, a Samaritan. Your life is very hard. I know your story. I care about you." This rabbi sat at a well and engaged in a deep, theological, personal discussion about this woman's relationship with God. He took seriously her mind and opinions and questions.

Is it any wonder she could not stop talking about this man?

Jesus was doing something very subversive.

He was treating a woman like someone who had her own identity.

Men in Jesus' day had this tendency to define women's identities in terms of the men in their lives.

Hard to imagine.

There is an old story where a chief executive officer and his wife are traveling and stop to get gas. The CEO goes inside, and when he comes out, he notices that his wife is talking to the service station attendant. He asks her why; it turns out she knew the attendant and used to date him. Feeling smug, he says: "I'll bet you're thinking you're glad you married me, a CEO, not a service station attendant."

She said: "No, I'm thinking if I'd married him, he'd be a CEO and you'd be a service station attendant."

The problem with that story is, how come *she* can't be the CEO?

Better yet, how come she can't work with freedom and joy and love with dignity and honor instead of finding identity in a husband or a title?

———•◦•———

The story had changed. Jesus offered women a new community.

> After this, Jesus traveled about from one town and village to another, proclaiming the good news of the kingdom of God. The Twelve were with him, and also some women...: Mary (called Magdalene) ...; Joanna the wife of Chuza, the manager of Herod's household; Susanna; and many others. These women were helping to support them out of their own means.

We can overlook how shocking this arrangement would have been in the ancient world. Women did not travel with men. They often were encouraged to simply remain indoors.

In Greece, Hellenistic plays were mostly populated by slave girls and prostitutes because they were set outdoors, and respectable urban women and young unmarried girls were expected to remain home, out of sight.

Jesus had women and men travel and study and learn and do ministry together. Imagine what kind of rumors flew around.

Women were paying the bills — including, you may have noticed, a woman named Joanna, whose husband worked for Herod. The Herod who was trying to kill Jesus.

Not only did Jesus not consider it demeaning or threatening, but he welcomed it.

———•◦•———

Jesus was, in a sense, planting seeds of subversion that would take centuries to grow. He was not a champion of twenty-first-century (or any other century) Western social structure. He did not try to talk a woman into running for Caesar. He was a man of his time.

He was also thoroughly Jewish. Far too often Christians have been guilty of a form of anti-Semitism by picking selective texts to make it look as if Jesus was liberating women from oppressive Judaism. This would offend both Jesus and Judaism.

Israel was at least as diverse in Jesus' day as Christianity is in ours. It is possible to find extreme rabbinic statements ("better that Torah should be burned than taught to a woman"); it is also possible to find examples of women being taught. There is an infamous rabbinic prayer thanking God for not being made a Greek, a boor, or a woman. This was actually borrowed from Socrates, only in his case he *was* grateful for being Greek. Judaism was actually unusual in teaching that women as well as men fully bear the image of God.

> *Jesus was not a champion of twenty-first-century Western social structure. He was a man of his time.*

What is remarkable about Jesus — one of those seeds he planted that keeps producing surprising growth — is his amazing inclusivity of all people. It is as if he turned Socrates' idea on its head: "Blessed art Thou, O God, whose image I see in every person I meet." There was an inclusivity to Jesus' spirit that is part of what drew people to him — and still draws them — and it marked his relationships with women. Dietrich Bonhoeffer wrote, "Jesus gave women human dignity.... Prior to Jesus, women were regarded as inferior beings, religiously speaking."

In ancient Athens, girls received little or no education. They were legally classified as a "child" no matter how old they were or how high their IQ was. Therefore they were always the property of some man. They were often married by the onset of puberty or even before. If a woman was seduced or raped, her husband was legally obligated to divorce her. Seduction was punished more severely than rape, because if you seduced a married woman, she might give you some of her husband's money. Laws about women were largely laws about property.

In our world, if your car is damaged, compensation goes to you, because you are the owner. In the ancient world, if a woman was violated, compensation went to her husband or her father — not her — on the same principle. It was the owner who got compensated.

———•———

In the community that followed Jesus, women would be given a different place. Paul expresses this when he talks about who will be "adopted" into Jesus' family. "In Christ Jesus you are *all* children of God through faith.... There is neither Jew nor Greek, neither slave nor free, nor is there male and female, for you are all one in Christ Jesus."

In the ancient world, adoption was very different from today. An orphan might be taken in to serve as a slave but was not adopted. Adoption existed to create an heir who could be *paterfamilias*—head of the household. A girl could not grow up to be a *paterfamilias*. In Greece, girls could not even have an inheritance. If a father died with a daughter but no son, his estate would pass to the nearest male relative.

But Paul says that what earthly fathers only gave to *sons*, God—through Jesus—is now giving to *women* as well: "You are no longer a slave but a son; and since you are a son, God has made you also an heir" —Gentile as well as Jew, slave as well as free; female as well as male.

———•••———

Moreover, in the ancient world, a woman's highest calling was to bear children—particularly male children (as in *The Godfather* movie, the supplicant's wedding day wish: "may her first born child be a *masculine* child").

In ancient Sparta, a mother who gave birth to a son would receive twice the food rations as a mother who gave birth to a daughter. The only women who got their names on their tombstones were women who died in childbirth.

For much of Rome's history, even freeborn girls (unlike boys) lived under guardians throughout their lives. Caesar Augustus decreed that a woman could be liberated from her guardian after the birth of her fourth child.

One day Jesus was teaching. "As Jesus was saying these things, a woman in the crowd called out, 'Blessed is the mother who gave you birth and nursed you.'"

Someone was complimenting Jesus' mother. We could expect a polite reply: "Thank you. My mom's the best ever. She was a virgin, you know."

Instead, Jesus offered a sharp rebuttal: "Blessed *rather* are those who hear the word of God and obey it."

Jesus deliberately gave an edgy response: "No; you're wrong." For Jesus, the highest calling of a woman was no longer to bear a child.

Motherhood, like fatherhood, is a noble calling. But it's not the ultimate calling. If you don't have children, you have not missed out.

Not on Jesus' call. And by the way, if you do have children, you are not defined by how they "turn out."

Because they share a common humanity, the highest calling of a woman is also the highest calling of a man: The glorious adventure of coming to know and do the will of the God in whose image they are created. Through Jesus, this calling is now available to any woman regardless of her age, marital status, or child-bearing capacity.

> *Because they share a common humanity, the highest calling of a woman is also the highest calling of a man.*

In Rome, a woman lived under the life-or-death power of the head of the family — the previously mentioned *paterfamilias*. He was also chief priest of the family. So he was to determine her religion.

We actually have a remnant of Roman customs in our language tradition: the phrase to "give one's hand in marriage." In Rome marriage could involve something called *manus* — Latin for "hand." (That is why a *manuscript* was handwritten.) A wife could be given into "hand" of her husband (he got control of her) or could be given "*without hand*," which meant her father retained control of her.

She was in somebody's hands. If she was given into her husband's hand, she was expected to renounce her father's religion and worship at her husband's altar.

In Jesus' movement, women had a God who is higher than the state or their husband. They defied custom and sometimes risked their lives by following this Jesus. This was the source of serious concern in the ancient world. This faith was not simply a different religion to Rome; it involved a different *idea* of religion, one that might threaten social structures rather than strengthen them.

— ◆ —

One day Jesus was teaching in the home of Mary and Martha. Martha was doing all the work of preparation and hosting. "She had a sister called Mary, who sat at the Lord's feet listening to what he said." Martha got ticked off and complained to Jesus about this. "'Martha, Martha,' the Lord answered. 'You are worried and upset about many things, but few things are needed—or indeed only one. Mary has chosen what is better, and it will not be taken away from her.'"

(When Jesus says your name twice—watch out!)

Many people in our day turn this into a little story about busy-ness: it is better to be the quiet contemplative Mary than the busy activist Martha. No one in the first century would have read this that way. The phrase "to sit at someone's feet" is a technical term meaning to be someone's disciple. Paul used it when he was defending himself after being arrested at the temple in Jerusalem: "I am a Jew ... brought up in this city at the feet of Gamaliel, educated strictly according to our ancestral law."

Stereotypes die hard. While attending a Marriage Weekend, a husband and wife I will call Max and Esther listened to the instructor declare, "It is essential that husbands and wives know the things that are important to each other."

He then addressed the men. "Can you name and describe your wife's favorite flower?"

Max leaned over, gently touched Esther's arm, and lovingly whispered, "Betty Crocker's Gold Medal, isn't it?"

In our day, we have seen this a thousand times: men gathered around the grill or the television set, and women in the kitchen. These patterns are strong in our day; they were stronger in Jesus' day. For a woman to join the men around the grill was unheard of back then.

Mary came to the grill. Jesus smiled. Martha did what the culture valued in women: cleaned the house and cooked the food. Mary did what the culture valued in men: became a disciple.

Jesus said Mary got it right. Jesus was inviting women to be his disciples.

———•◦•———

In the Gospels, it was women who followed Jesus to the cross when all the men were afraid and ran away. The early church father John Chrysostom wrote that here is where womanhood "most shows its courage. When the disciples had fled, these were present."

In all four Gospels, the task of being witnesses who proclaim the resurrection is given to women. This is remarkable, because in the ancient world a woman's testimony was generally disregarded.

When a Greek philosopher named Celsus wanted to argue that there are not good grounds for believing that Jesus was resurrected, he noted, "But who saw this? A hysterical female, as you say, and perhaps some one other of those who were deluded by this same sorcery."

In Israel, receiving testimony from women might be something like receiving legal testimony from minors in our day. Under special circumstances, if no other testimony were available, it might be admissible, but there would be a bias against it and a more favorable receptivity to the witness of an adult man. It is true that the testimony of women like Deborah and Miriam and Huldah are received with joy in the Hebrew Scriptures. And there are accounts of women giving legal testimony, but rarely.

We see a little of this dynamic in Luke: "When they came back from the tomb, they told all these things to the Eleven and to all the others.... But they did not believe the women, because their words seemed to them like nonsense."

Can you imagine the frustration of the women?

Then Jesus appeared to the disciples. I would love to have been there the next time the women saw the disciples: "Jesus Christ is risen. Told you so."

—·•·—

This radical value of women meant that they began to take on unusually prominent roles of leadership in the early church. Roughly half of the households Paul mentions that form the infrastructure for the early church are headed by women. Women began to find value in a new community for which they would devote their lives. Pliny the Younger noted in a letter to the emperor that in order to learn about the faith, "I judged it all the more necessary to find out what the truth was by torturing two female slaves who were called deaconesses."

In Rome a widow was fined if she didn't remarry in two years. It was considered bad form to outlive your husband; you were a drag on the economy.

But one community remembered that when Jesus was on the cross, he told one of his followers to look after his widowed mother when he was gone. Followers of Jesus spread to a broader world the tradition of Israel in which widowhood was honored; care of widows was part of the community.

According to journalist Tim Miller Dyck, it is highly likely that women were a clear majority in the early church. One church in Cirta, North Africa, was seized during persecution in AD 303. Archaeologists have found there sixteen male tunics—meaning that at least sixteen men were part of that church—but also found eighty-two women's tunics, thirty-eight veils, and forty-seven pairs of female slippers.

———•◦•———

Jesus is why an aged woman named Apollonia—when she was taken by the Romans, was beaten, had her jaws beaten and her teeth broken, and was offered her freedom if she would renounce Christ—instead chose to spring into the fire and be consumed.

Jesus is why mystic Julian of Norwich in 1393 wrote the first book in English written by a woman—*The Sixteen Revelations of Divine Love*—which is so profound that it is studied to this day.

Jesus is why women have traveled continents, spent decades learning a strange language so they could translate the gospel, planting churches, caring for the sick, educating the illiterate, and marching for the oppressed.

Is it possible that our world has still not caught up to Jesus?

The binding of the feet of women in China, the suicide by funeral pyre of widows in India, the practice of female genital mutilation in Africa, polygamy, lack of education, lack of opportunity... Perhaps our world needs to meet Jesus once more at the well.

———•◦•———

I was speaking on this in Chicago recently when a man approached me who runs a ministry called As Our Own in India. They rescue orphaned girls—usually from sex trafficking—to raise them "as our own," a reference to the notion that in Christ all are to be one family.

One story involved a girl I will call Rani, who lost her childhood when she was eleven years old. She and a friend were drugged, abducted, and transported three thousand miles away from home (equal to the distance between New York and Los Angeles), and the captors coerced her into sex trafficking through sexual torture en route. The combination of poverty, threats, and beatings made it clear that for Rani there was no escape.

Eventually Rani became pregnant and gave birth to a little daughter she named Preema. Soon her captors wanted to use Preema as well. They offered money and then made threats to be able to do to the daughter what they had done to her mother.

The staff of As Our Own heard about Preema's situation and intervened, although it took much time to gain Rani's trust. They have rescued Preema from this world at some risk; Rani herself remains a captive. She now works from inside the slave world to help other daughters gain freedom. Rani's statement when handing her daughter over to the staff was, "I will not live many more years; please take care of Preema when I am gone."

The Mediterranean world into which Jesus was born was a world where (outside Israel) the sexual use of enslaved illiterate children was neither uncommon nor illegal nor considered particularly scandalous. As O. M. Bakke has documented, it was where the church spread in the early centuries after Jesus that girls ceased as a matter of routine being disposed of at birth and being enslaved and sexually exploited in childhood.

——— ·◆· ———

Is it possible that the church has still not caught up to Jesus? Sigmund Freud once famously (or infamously) wrote, "The great question that has never been answered, and which I have not yet been able to answer, despite my thirty years of research into the feminine soul, is 'What does a woman want?'"

Freud's stock has not been rising for the last fifty years or so; and his views on women have not helped. How striking that Jesus, although he lived nineteen hundred years earlier, seemed remarkably absent of condescension toward women. He seemed, in his life and interactions, to somehow know what eluded Freud.

A contemporary of Freud's, a brilliant scholar-writer who happened to be a woman, was quite clear on what it was she wanted.

Dorothy Sayers was the first woman to receive a degree from Oxford (which she did with first class honors). She became a devoted follower of Jesus; here she tells a little about why:

> I think I have never heard a sermon preached on the story of Martha and Mary that did not attempt, somehow, to explain away its text. Mary's, of course, was the better part — the Lord said so, and we must not precisely contradict him. But ... Martha was doing a really feminine job, whereas Mary was just behaving like any other disciple, male or female; and that is a hard pill to swallow.
>
> Perhaps it is no wonder that the women were first at the Cradle and last at the Cross. They had never known a man like this Man — there never has been such another. A prophet and teacher who never nagged at them, never flattered or coaxed or patronized; who never made arch jokes about them; who never treated them either as 'The women, God help us!' or "The ladies, God bless them!"; who rebuked without [demeaning] and praised without condescension; who took their questions and arguments seriously; who never mapped out their sphere for them, never urged them to be feminine or jeered at them for being female; who had no axe to grind and no uneasy male dignity to defend.

What are the odds that a brilliant Oxford-educated scholar would say, in the twentieth century after Jesus' birth, that the reason Mary was so drawn to this young, itinerant rabbi is that to this day there still has not been another man like him?

CHAPTER 5

An Undistinguished
Visiting Scholar

Jesus spent most of his adult life as a blue-collar worker, crafting benches and tables. Then one day he decided to change jobs.

I write these words on a plane, sitting next to a man named Timothy whom I just met, a distinguished visiting scholar at Stanford University. Timothy's father grew up an illiterate untouchable in India, who learned to read and write because Jesus changed jobs. But that's getting ahead of the story.

We do not know what prompted Jesus to change occupations, or how long the idea had been in his mind, or what his family thought when he told them. One Sabbath he went to the synagogue in his hometown, picked up a scroll and read a passage in Isaiah, and then sat down.

Sitting down is the traditional teaching posture of a rabbi — the scholar-teachers of Israel. When Jesus sat down, he was proclaiming his new occupation. He claimed in his first message that God is a Gentile-lover ready to embrace anybody. Jesus claimed to *know* this. By the end of his sermon the congregation was so furious that they drove him out of town and attempted to throw him off a cliff. They resisted his knowledge.

If this were me, at the end of my first sermon I would be tempted to feel discouraged. Jesus began his new career — to put it mildly — as an *un*distinguished visiting scholar.

Jesus was a teacher. He had a quality — generally restricted to either a genius or a psychotic — of being so convinced that he was right that even intense opposition did not sway him.

He was a rabbi, like other rabbis, yet not like other rabbis. This is affirmed at the end of the Sermon on the Mount: "When Jesus had finished saying these things, the crowds were amazed at his teaching, because he taught as one who had authority, and not as their teachers of the law."

———— .•. ————

Jesus was called "Rabbi" some eleven times in the Gospels. So we have to understand rabbis to understand Jesus.

There are no rabbis in the Hebrew Scriptures. The word does not occur. There is an important reason for this. When a nation dreams of national greatness, her heroes are often kings and soldiers. As Israel's dreams withered in exile, kings and soldiers were replaced by a new kind of hero.

A teacher. An educator.

Israelites had no army, no wealth, no power. What did they have?

They had a book. Nobody else had a book like this one. It spoke to the great questions of human existence and guidance for life. It kept them together when they lost everything else. Rome had armies; Greece had culture; Egypt had wealth; Phoenicia had ships. Israel was *the people of the book*.

As Israel's dreams withered in exile, kings and soldiers were replaced by a new kind of hero. A teacher. An educator.

Rabbis knew the book. When they taught it, they would cite great rabbis for the correct interpretation of the Scriptures. "Rabbi Shammai says ... but Rabbi Hillel says...." That wasn't a sign of bad teaching. It is very much like in our day when a judge is going to make a ruling. We expect a good judge to cite precedents.

Jesus was a rabbi like other rabbis but not like *any other* rabbi. He didn't cite others; he said, "*Truly*, I say to you...." In the gospel of John, he doubled down and said it twice: " '*Truly, truly*, I say to you....' " These words appear seventy-five times in the Gospels.

What Jesus was saying is, "I know how things are. I know. I know about money. I know all about economics. I know 'it is more blessed to give than to receive.' I have watched both options play out. I have thought it through. I will spare you the heartache of the wrong path if *you will keep your elbow in.* I know how resentment festers. I know the human heart. I know forgiveness is superior."

Jesus did not cite anybody. He was very different from other rabbis. He was very different from other great teachers. G. K. Chesterton wrote about how normally the greatest teachers often emphasize what they don't know: "Socrates, the wisest man, knows that he knows nothing." Socrates said that what marked him as wise is that he knew better than other people that he didn't know that. Jesus never said anything like that; he never said, "I don't know." Not because Jesus was arrogant. Rather, Jesus was supremely *humble* in his relationships yet supremely *confident* in his convictions.

People often picture Jesus as a well-meaning but naïve guru who wandered around tossing off catchy sayings of simple folk wisdom and happened to spark a movement he could never have predicted.

But no one who knew him thought that.

———◆———

Paul, by all accounts, was one of the most brilliant people who ever lived. He studied under the person who may have been the greatest rabbi of that day, Gamaliel. People sometimes think of Jesus as an amiable sage, while they think of Paul as the genius theologian who invented Christianity. One person who would not have thought that way was Paul himself. Paul said that Jesus is "Christ, in whom are hidden all the treasures of wisdom and knowledge." Paul did not say that about Gamaliel; nor did he say that about himself.

Brilliant intellects do not matriculate to study under someone dumber than themselves. Paul recognized Jesus as master of the intellect, above him in every way. Jesus' ability to help the simplest person while still challenging the smartest was understood as one sign of his mastery. Early church fathers had a favorite saying that the Gospels are a river in which a gnat can swim and an elephant can drown.

The historical impact of Jesus' thinking is so pervasive that it is often taken for granted. The record of his life and teaching, the Gospels, have impacted the world so much that they have been translated into 2,527 languages. The second-most-translated book, *Don Quixote*, has been translated into about 60 languages.

The Bible is the bestselling book of all time, according to the *Guinness Book of World Records*. The second bestselling book of all time, according to the *Guinness Book of World Records*, is the *Guinness Book of World Records*.

In the academic world, scholars keep score by how often an article they write is cited by other scholars. By this sheer secular score, Jesus' intellectual impact is unprecedented. According to Harvard professor Harvey Cox, "the words [of the Sermon on the Mount] are the most luminous, most quoted, most analyzed, most contested, most influential moral and religious discourse in all of human history. This may sound like an overstatement, but it is not."

> *The historical impact of Jesus' thinking is so pervasive that it is often taken for granted.*

Jesus, as Dallas Willard often says, is a really smart guy. He may be thought of as more than this, but you will never trust somebody if you don't believe they know what they're talking about.

One reason this is sometimes missed is the *method* of Jesus' teaching: Jesus taught to change lives. In the educational system of our day, we tend to think of *teaching* as the transfer of information. The teacher pours information into the student like pouring water into an empty jug, and the student is evaluated by one thing only: can he parrot back what the teacher said?

The number one question in any class is (if you're a teacher, you know this), "Will this be on the final?" We all take notes so we can remember until the final exam.

No one took notes when Jesus taught. Why? Because it is natural to automatically remember what changes our lives. If you were around on 9/11 or when President John Kennedy was assassinated or when Pearl Harbor got attacked, you remember.

I went surfing recently in a lonely section of ocean when a few feet from me a large, dark fin rippled by. It was gone too quickly for me to be sure what it was, but I had a religious experience. I had a little talk with Jesus right there. I effortlessly remembered that moment. I did not have to write it down.

—◦—

Another reason we miss Jesus' brilliance is that we think of *education* differently in our day than the ancient world did. The president of an Ivy League university once welcomed incoming students by saying: "We cannot supply you with a philosophy of education anymore than we can supply you with a philosophy of life. This has got to come from your own active learning, your own choices, your own decisions. Think for yourself."

If a student says that Columbus discovered America in 1493, or that $e = mc^2$, then the university will supply knowledge. But when it comes to values and wisdom, it's every man for himself. There is no major in "becoming a good person."

The people of Israel could not have had a more counter-cultural message. The primary text of Israel, recited twice every day, was called the *shema* from its first word: "Hear, O Israel: The LORD our God, the LORD is one. Love the LORD your God with all your heart and with all your soul and with all your strength."

The text did not read, "O Israel, think for yourselves. Go with your gut. Maximize your bliss. You are the autonomous center of the universe."

Hear. Listen. Be quiet. Here is Torah. Wisdom. Strap it on your arms, tie it to your head, put it on the door, paint it on the gate, say it first thing in the morning and last thing at night, talk about it with your kids. Miss everything else in life, but not this: Love God with all you've got.

Jesus began to teach anyone who would listen regardless of gender status or age.

Whatever anyone might think of the answers that he gave, the education of the world would begin to change.

The final command Jesus is recorded as giving his followers is this: "All authority in heaven and on earth has been given to me. Therefore go and make disciples of all nations ... teaching them to obey everything I have commanded you." (That would be a lot of authority. Nobody else ever said that. Socrates never said that. Neither Confucius nor the Buddha ever said that. Only Jesus said that.)

Jesus' followers took this seriously. "Day after day, in the temple courts and from house to house, they never stopped teaching." They began a process of education called *catechesis*. They would teach both men and women for years.

About AD 150, a man named Justin Martyr formed schools in Ephesus and Rome. Rome and Greece valued learning. All human beings love to learn, and a large task for the church over many centuries was to try to integrate what Jesus taught with the depth of classical learning.

But there was a new development. In the Greco-Roman world, formal education was reserved for male children of wealthy families. Yet the leaders of the church remembered that they followed a man who taught everyone, who commanded them to teach *all* peoples. So they did. They began to teach both men and women, both slaves and free.

——•·——

Somebody asked Jesus, "Which is the greatest commandment?" Jesus quoted the *shema*, which every devout Israelite knew: "Love the Lord your God …"

But Jesus made a profound emendation in the Matthew version of this statement: "Love the Lord your God with all your heart and with all your soul and with all your mind." He added the word *mind*.

To love God with your mind begins with being curious about God. We may go weeks, months, or even years without ever wondering, *Is there Somebody who made this world? What's he like?*

But for followers of Jesus, loving God with "all your mind" meant even more. They believed Jesus taught that God created everything, that God thought everything up. Therefore, anytime we learn something that's true, anytime we learn about how creation works or even about math or logic, we are actually thinking God's thoughts after him. We're getting to know God, and we do that because we love him.

> *To love God with your mind begins with being curious about God. . . . But loving God with "all your mind" means even more.*

Learning can become an act of worship. Jesus' followers said that learning about anything is actually helping us to know and love God better. They loved truth.

Some prominent Christians have felt that this means that we should not read secular philosophers. Tertullian asked, "What does Jerusalem have to do with Athens?" Saint Jerome was afraid he might receive divine punishment for reading Cicero.

But others reasoned that if God could speak through Balaam's donkey, there's no telling where truth might be found. They would read not just the Bible, but pagan Greek and Roman writings and look for wisdom anywhere they could find it because, as Augustine, said, "All truth is God's truth."

Rome collapsed and barbarians — Huns, Goths, and Visigoths — overwhelmed Roman civilization. There were few books and no printing presses. There were scrolls that decayed easily and quickly. By the sixth century, an illiterate Europe had no libraries left.

Thomas Cahill relates in *How the Irish Saved Civilization* about how monastic communities copied every ancient text they could get their hands on. For many centuries, monasteries were the only institutions in Europe for the acquisition, preserving, and transmitting of knowledge.

The single greatest preserver of pagan classical documents was followers of Jesus. According to Jaroslav Pelikan, "one may perhaps begin to comprehend how completely Christ the Monk conquered the scholarly world of the Middle Ages by checking, in the standard modern editions, how many works of antiquity even exist for us today only because they were copied by monks in some medieval scriptorium ... [works of] not only Christian saints but of classical and pagan authors."

—— • ——

The great intellectual challenge of the early church was integrating Christian truths with pagan learning.

Monasteries became places of great learning. A Jesus-follower named Benedict collected so many ancient manuscripts that he became known as "the godfather of libraries." Education included integrating classical learning with Christian faith. George Marsden wrote, "Education was not conceivable without the pagans. Latin and Greek were the very languages of education. All the practical elements (the trivium of grammar, rhetoric, and logic and the quadrivium of arithmetic, music, geometry and astronomy) had been established by the ancients."

From monasteries came universities. The beginnings of today's faculty system were scholars who formed self-governing guilds, licensed by the pope to have sole authority to grant degrees. The first university was established in Paris around the twelfth century, and Oxford and

Cambridge began in the thirteenth. (The motto of Oxford University is from Psalm 27:1: "The LORD is my light.") Then came universities in Rome, Naples, Vienna, and Heidelberg. These were all begun by followers of Jesus so people could love God with all their minds. They came to be called *universities* because they reflected the idea that in the beginning, God created all things. Reality is not just this random cyclical accident. God is supremely rational, so that means there is a reality that can be studied to a large extent known to the glory of God. So these were made not multiversities, not random chaos, but rather a *university* to study a *universe*.

People who teach in universities came to be called *professors*. Why? Because they were thought to have something to *profess*. To "profess" means there is something I believe to be true and it is of value and needs to be known. I have a *profession* to make. ("upon your profession of faith ...," a traditional baptismal formula states.) Those people are the wise ones who are to teach us.

———•·•———

Education changed again when Martin Luther emphasized from the New Testament the priesthood of all believers. Luther said it means that every person needs to be able to read and write so they can study the Scriptures for themselves because we are all to be priests now. This led to a goal of universal literacy for everybody in a society.

Luther said he would write a book about parents who neglect the education of their children: "I shall really go after the shameful, despicable, damnable parents who are not parents at all but despicable hogs and venomous beasts devouring their own young." (Luther apparently did not have a hard time expressing his emotion.)

In America, the first law to require mass universal education was declared in Massachusetts in 1647. It was called, believe it or not, "The Old Deluder Satan Act." "It being one chief product of that Old Deluder, Satan, to keep men from the knowledge of the Scriptures...; and to the end that learning may not be buried in the graves of our forefathers."

This is a beautiful vision that everyone should learn: that ignorance is the devil's tool, that God is the God of truth.

George Marsden noted that "one of the remarkable facts about

American history is that within six years of landing in the Massachusetts wilderness, Puritans established what would soon become a reputable college." This is from its student handbook: "Let every student be plainly instructed and earnestly pressed to consider well, the main end of his life and studies is, to know God and Jesus Christ, which is eternal life, (John 17:3), and therefore to lay Christ ... as the only foundation of all sound knowledge and learning."

Martin Luther emphasized the priesthood of all believers.... This led to a goal of universal literacy for everybody.

That was Harvard University. Then educators began Yale and William & Mary and Princeton and Brown with the same founding purpose, that the main end of one's life and studies is to know God and Jesus Christ. All but one school started before the American Revolution was begun to serve the Jesus movement.

Ninety-two percent of the first 138 colleges and universities founded in America were begun for followers of this uneducated, itinerant, never-wrote-a-book Carpenter.

Many people have heard of Sunday school. Most have no idea where it came from. In 1780 a Jesus-follower in Great Britain named Robert Raikes could not stand the cycle of poverty and ignorance that was destroying little children, a whole generation. He said, "The world marches forward on the feet of little children." So he took children who had to work six days a week in squalor. Sunday was their free day. He said, "I'm going to start a school for free to teach them to read and write and learn about God." He did, and he called it "Sunday school."

Within fifty years, there were 1.5 million children being taught by 160,000 volunteer teachers who had a vision for the education of a generation. Sunday school was not a privatized, optional program for church kids. It was one of the great educational volunteer triumphs of the world.

The alphabet of the Slavic peoples is called Cyrillic. It was named for Saint Cyril, who was a missionary to the Slavs and discovered they had no written alphabet. Thus he created one for them so they would be able to read about Jesus in their own language.

In nation after nation, Christian missionaries found languages had not been committed to writing. So in acts of remarkable sacrifice, they devoted their lives to this task. In many cases, the first efforts of the scientific study of a language were done by Christian missionaries. They compiled the first dictionaries. They wrote the first grammars. They developed the first alphabets. The first important proper name written in many languages was the name *Jesus*.

A Methodist missionary, Frank Laubach, cited an extraordinary encounter with God about a century ago that put him on a mission to lift the world out of ignorance. He began a worldwide literacy movement. The phrase "Each one teach one" flows out of the extraordinary life of this man. He traveled to more than a hundred countries and led to the development of primers in 313 languages. He became known as "the Apostle to the Illiterates."

———•———

The worldview of Jesus is part of how science came about in our world. In our day, many people think science and faith are enemies. But Princeton professor Diogenes Allen writes, "We have begun to realize from its very birth, science owed a great deal to Christianity."

According to Allen, there are attitudes Christianity has that were indispensable for science to be able to rise. Christians, unlike Plato, believe that matter is good, since God created it. So to study it would be good. The world was created by an orderly and rational God, and therefore there is reason to expect not chaos, but order and reason, law, and regularity in creation, in nature. On the other hand, since God is free and omniscient, we could never predict ahead of time what it is he would do, so we'll have to investigate. We'll have to experiment to find out.

A number of historians argue that certain ideas about how the world must work if it was created by a good, rational God were crucial in leading to the creation of science. In March 2009, NASA sent out a telescope named after Johannes Kepler, the great mathematician and astronomer of about AD 1600. Here is what Kepler wrote: "God, like a Master Builder, has laid the foundation of the world according to law and order. God wanted us to recognize those laws by creating us after His image so we could share in His own thought."

"Love the Lord your God ... with all your mind"—and people did.

The vast majority of the pioneers of science — William of Ockham, Francis Bacon, Galileo, Copernicus, Blaise Pascal, Joseph Priestley, Louis Pasteur, Isaac Newton (who ended up writing commentaries on Revelation) — viewed their work as learning to think God's thoughts. George Washington Carver said he started his studies by holding up a peanut and saying, "God, what's in a peanut?"

Alfred North Whitehead, one of the dominant thinkers of the twentieth century, asked, "What is it that made it possible for science to emerge in the human race?" His answer was fascinating: "It's the medieval insistence on the rationality of God." Because if you believe creation was made by a rational God, it will lead to fundamentally different assumptions than if you started with the idea that it's just a random accident.

> *The vast majority of the pioneers of science viewed their work as learning to think God's thoughts.*

This is not to say that science could not have arisen otherwise, but Dinesh D'Souza put it this way: "Science as an organized, sustained enterprise arose only once in human history ... in Europe, in the civilization then called Christendom."

———•·•———

A unique flowering of technology grew out of Jesus-oriented communities in the Middle Ages. Stanford University professor Lynn White wrote, "The humanitarian technology that our modern world has inherited from the Middle Ages was not rooted in economic necessity; for this necessity is inherent in every society.... the labor-saving power-machines of the later Middle Ages were produced by the implicit theological assumption of the infinite worth of even the most degraded human personality."

Vishal Mangalwadi noted that while the technology for many inventions was observed around the world across centuries, it was developed and harnessed most often by Christian monks. The theological factor that drove technology was that the Bible distinguished "work" (to work is to be like God) from "toil" (which is the curse of sin). Therefore, using creative reason to liberate people from toil is part of the redemptive work of Jesus.

This is why, even though the horse was not native to Europe, it was European peasants who leveraged the horse through the invention of the horseshoe, the tandem harness, and the horse collar. The first recorded use of a windmill to grind grain was by Abbot Gregory of Tours in the sixth century, to free his monks to pray.

Mechanical clocks were invented by monks because they needed to know when to pray. Communal prayer after dark meant everyone needed to share the same time. The clock became a religious as well as a practical necessity. For centuries it was the church from which villages learned the time.

We first learn about the invention of eyeglasses in a sermon around 1300. It was monks who required them so they were able to pore over texts. Jaroslav Pelikan argued that contrary to a common assumption that the Renaissance arose when thinkers rejected faith and returned to classical Greco-Roman skepticism, the renewal was actually stimulated by the desire to read the New Testament in Greek by thinkers like Erasmus. " 'The Renaissance,' wrote Konrad Burdach, 'which establishes a new concept of humanity, of art, and of literary and scholarly life [arose] not in opposition to the Christian religions but out of the full vitality of a religious revival.' "

—— ·•· ——

Sometimes the church has gotten a bum rap about its openness to learning. Most people nowadays think that folks in medieval times believed in a flat earth. The reality is that all educated people in the Middle Ages knew it is spherical. The myth of flatlanders was actually penned by American novelist Washington Irving, who made up a trial where church leaders charged Christopher Columbus with heresy for teaching that the world is round. Irving's myth caught on, partly because it reinforces the stereotype that the church has always been anti-science.

But other times the rap is deserved. "Love the Lord your God with *all* your mind," Jesus said, and often his followers have shrunk back from that little word *all*. To love God with *all* my mind means following truth ruthlessly wherever it leads. It means cherishing truth whether it comes from the Bible or from science or from an atheist. It means anti-intellectualism is anti-Christian.

I grew up in an evangelical tradition for which I am grateful, but the life of the mind was not always prized. "The scandal of the evangelical mind," wrote Mark Noll in a book with that title, "is that there is not much of an evangelical mind." When I began my studies for a PhD in clinical psychology, a woman from my church said, "What do you need to go study Freud for? Don't we have the Bible?"

I said, "Have you ever actually read anything Freud wrote? Have you ever read a single one of his books? Do you understand him? Do you know the difference between projection and reaction formation? Do you see what the difference is between the conscience and the ego ideal? Can you distinguish between repression and suppression?

"Freud, whatever you think of him, was one of the dominant minds of the twentieth century. A brilliant neurologist, he won the Goethe Prize for influencing the German language. One of the shapers of the modern mind, and you tell me he can be dismissed and you can't even come up with a title of a single book he wrote?"

It was the last time my mother ever talked to me about psychology.

Mark Noll wrote that often Christians have too quickly passed judgment on areas such as science based on wrong assumptions. For instance, the early reformers rejected the idea of a heliocentric solar system because they assumed it contradicted Scripture. (Luther called Copernicus an "upstart astrologer"; he may have been a little cranky that Copernicus dedicated his work to the pope.) Within two generations, all leaders of the Reformation church accepted the new solar system picture. The overwhelming evidenced for it forced them to re-examine old assumptions about what the Bible is really saying. Moving slowly before we pass theological judgments on scientific theories is one of the ways we can love God with *all* our mind.

> *Moving slowly before we pass theological judgments on scientific theories is one way we can love God with all our mind.*

Robert Wilkins wrote a wonderful book about the writings of early critics who did not believe in Christianity: *The Christians as the Romans Saw Them*. He noted how having to answer difficult questions and objections of critics helped early Christians to sharpen their thinking: "They helped Christians to find their authentic voice, and without them

Christianity would be much the poorer." Intellectual muscles, like physical ones, grow stronger when they face resistance.

But Christians have often not received the gift of critics with the grace of Jesus. The works of Christianity's earliest critics — Roman thinkers named Celsus and Porphyry, a physician named Galen, an emperor named Julian the Apostate — have to be pieced together from quotes and scraps. After the fourth century, when the church got enough power, it simply burned these authors' works. Until the fourth century, the church was not in the book-burning business; only barbarians did that.

Loving God with all your mind means answering the works of people you disagree with, rather than burning the works. Loving God with all your mind means you don't have to be nervous about where a book might lead if its reader is sincerely seeking truth.

At the beginning of this chapter I mentioned Timothy, who was sitting next to me on a plane. He told me how his father, David, was brought up in a Dalit (outcaste) family in Maharashtra, India; he knew that his generations were cursed by the gods of Hindu pantheon to be left in this state of rejection both by religion and by citizens of upper castes. As an illiterate, untouchable Dalit, David could not enter the temple of his village, so he set out on a forty-five-mile pilgrimage by foot to get a glimpse of the nearest Hindu temple of any significance. He had to wait in line three weeks. Standing in line, not knowing if he would be allowed in, he met a missionary, who told him that Jesus taught he had not been cursed by God but was loved by God. David had grown up forbidden to enter a temple or bathe in a river on an auspicious day to keep them undefiled for higher castes. It took six months for David to absorb the notion that God loved him.

When David decided to follow this Jesus, he was beaten by his family and thrown out of his village. He returned to the missionary, who gave him shelter and taught him to read and write. He eventually graduated from Union Biblical Seminary in Maharashtra, and then he planted churches as well as ran a boarding school for little girls rescued from temple prostitution. For his seventieth birthday, David decided to adopt a leper colony outside of Poona, India, and build a crèche and church among the lepers. Every Thursday he and his wife would go to Yarvada prison in Poona (where Mohandas Gandhi was once confined) and pray with inmates on death row.

Timothy graduated with an engineering degree, an MBA from Duke University, and an advanced degree from Moore College Sydney, and he currently serves as distinguished visiting scholar at Stanford University. He explained that vast amounts of higher education in India have their roots in the Jesus movement.

The Stanford family who began that university where Timothy is now a scholar also supported in its early days the church in Menlo Park that I now serve. The ripples do not stop.

—— •◆• ——

One day a carpenter left his shop and began to teach.

What would the history of our world be if Jesus had not changed careers? Imagine that he stays in the shop: there is no teaching ministry, no crucifixion, no rise of the church, no New Testament scriptures, no monastic communities. The reason for which Oxford and Cambridge and Harvard and Yale got founded does not exist.

It is a mark of Jesus' impact that the scenario is simply, literally, unimaginable.

CHAPTER 6

Jesus Was Not
a Great Man

Jesus was not a great man.

There are two ways to think about a meaningful life, says Georgetown University professor Francis Ambrosio. One is the way of the hero; the other is the way of the saint. In the Greco-Roman world, what was admired was a hero. A hero is somebody who overcame obstacles to achieve his full potential of excellence and therefore to receive status, honor, and recognition. Life is a striving for this recognition.

That is why for the Greeks, the Olympics were not just games; they were a religious ceremony. They were a microcosm of what makes for a worthy life. The word for that contest is the Greek word *agon.* We get our English word *agony* from that: "the thrill of victory and the *agony* of defeat."

This concept and attitude led to a society where status—the pecking order—was absolutely fundamental. Cicero wrote, "Rank must be preserved." Identity is determined by ladder rung. Descent is tragedy.

The Greeks knew what greatness is, and for them, greatness did not involve humility. Philosopher Alasdair MacIntyre noted that humility was not considered a virtue in that world. Aristotle's "'great-souled man' is extremely proud. He despises honors offered by the common people.... He indulges in conspicuous consumption, for 'he likes to own beautiful and useless things, since they are better marks of his independence.' Incidentally, he walks slowly, has a deep voice, and a deliberate mode of utterance."

Imagine living in a world obsessed with status. (It may not require all that much effort.)

The Roman Empire organized its occupants the way most airlines organize their customers, the most basic distinction being "first class" and "coach." Airlines work hard to reinforce this distinction: First-class passengers get to board first; they get to walk through a separate gate featuring a glorious *red carpet* upon which the rest of us may not tread; they sit nearest the front; they eat on fine china and drink free wine. Airlines basically try to re-create middle school society: a small clique of the privileged few envied by everyone on the outside.

Roman society was roughly divided between first class (maybe 2 percent of the population) and coach—those whom Tacitus called "the rabble." The rabble served an important purpose; as one ancient writer put it, "... the existence of inferiors is an advantage to superiors since they will be able to point out those over whom they are superior."

But there are further subdivisions. Airlines have 100K club members: Executive Premiers, Gold premiers, Silver premiers, Straw premiers, Just Barely premiers, and so on down to people who have no "status" at all. No matter what status category you are in, there is always one above you. The goal is to accumulate enough points to achieve the next-highest status.

> *Imagine living in a world obsessed with status. (It may not require all that much effort.)*

In Rome, the highest flyers were the six hundred or so senators who ran things under Caesar. Under them came the equestrians—originally a class wealthy enough to own horses for military affairs (the idea being that a mode of transportation could be a status symbol). Then were the decurians—wealthy citizens who occupied government offices and priesthoods.

These were the Romans who flew first class. They walked the red carpet. They each had a series of honors within their own class that they would vie for. This was called the *cursus honorum*—the "race for honors." Running this race defined life. Winning was heroic.

Underneath these elite Romans were the other 98 percent of people who flew coach. They were the "nobodies"—a *personis mediocribus*, for whom greatness was out of the question. But they too had their own set of status categories.

Some of the "nobodies" were citizens of the empire, which meant they enjoyed certain legal protections and rights. Others were freedmen who did not have the rights of citizens but had personal liberty. At the bottom of the pecking order were slaves. Conditions of slaves varied widely, but they had no rights, and they lived at the mercy of the *paterfamilias*, the head of the household they served.

Even nonelite categories would create voluntary associations and clubs where they could imitate the status-seeking of the elite. The president of the chess club may not win girls the way the quarterback of the football team would, but being alpha dog of the chess club is better than not being alpha at all.

———•–•·—

Airlines use seat size, red carpets, crockery, and entry order to reinforce status. In Rome, every conceivable aspect of life was used to reflect the race for honor.

Clothes were, literally, status symbols. If you were not a slave, you could wear what was called a "freedman's cap." That showed at least you were not on the bottom rung.

A male citizen from the age of about fourteen was allowed to wear the *toga virilis*, the garment of manhood. Ironically, the toga was "a remarkably incommodious garment." Drafty in winter, sticky hot in summer, keeping one hand covered and unusable, difficult to arrange (the rich employed slaves specially trained in toga-draping), it had only one value: the proclamation of status.

A senator could wear a purple stripe on his toga, purple being associated with nobility. An equestrian couldn't wear the stripe, but was allowed to wear both an expensive toga and gold rings. The equestrian class was sometimes called, "The Order of the Rings." During those days James the brother of Jesus warned believers not to favor a visitor "wearing a gold ring and fine clothes" over a shabbily dressed man. Jesus was giving the same worth to slaves as to equestrians. Jocks and nerds would begin eating at the same table.

—·•·—

Occupations were ordered around rank. The most honorable was to own vast tracts of land and have slaves that work on it. The elite would never do manual labor. Cicero wrote, "Vulgar are the means of livelihood of all hired workmen whom we pay for mere manual labor."

Legal condition reflected social status. A second-century AD legal saying said, "One law for the more honorable, another law for the more humble." Or, as a British proverb put it in the nineteenth century: "One law for the rich and another for the poor."

For example, a Roman citizen could never be crucified. The other official means of execution — decapitation and burning alive — were equally terminal but less shameful. Crucifixion was reserved particularly for slaves; it was informally known as the "slave's punishment."

So when the apostle Paul started a letter to people in Rome by describing himself not as a citizen of the Rome Empire (which he was), not as a wearer of the toga, but as "a slave of Christ Jesus," he was committing social suicide. No one talked that way. Might as well mark your Facebook status "Loser" and hope for a date.

> *When Paul described himself in a letter to Rome as "a slave of Christ Jesus," he was committing social suicide.*

This race for honor was the backdrop for Paul's words to the church at Corinth, "... we preach Christ crucified: a stumbling block to Jews and foolishness to Gentiles." He did not pick words out of the air; he was being surgically precise here. The Old Testament says, "Anyone hung on a tree is under God's curse," so the Jews thought that someone who was crucified was cursed by God.

To have a group of people say, "We serve a crucified slave named Jesus; we consider ourselves slaves to a slave," was incomprehensible. Paul named it precisely.

—·•·—

Seating at public events reinforced status. At theaters, seats were arranged not by ticket cost, but by rank. The higher rank, the closer to the stage. The college I attended required chapel attendance. One semester, to aid the attendance-spies, we were secretly seated based on SAT scores. When the secret got out, the students revolted (especially those of us in the balcony).

In the ancient world, such revolt was not contemplated. At a private party, guests were seated according to their social status. Hosts would sometimes invite guests of inferior rank just to highlight their own status. If you were a guest of inferior rank, you would actually be served inferior food to reinforce your inferiority. (Imagine getting Spam — a Latin acronym for "Status-Preserving Alternative Meat" — while your betters dine on filet mignon.)

Low-status people were not allowed to interrupt high-status people, but high-status folks could interrupt low-status talkers any time. Similarly, a boss who interrupts an employee a lot is called an extrovert, whereas an employee who interrupts a boss too often is called an ex-employee.

Even the giving of gifts reinforced status in Roman days. Rich people might build public baths or parks or buildings, but this was done to benefit citizens, not the poor, and to display status for the giver. This is sometimes called *monumentalism*: "I will leave a monument to me."

The French sociologist Marcel Mauss observed that a wealthy person might give away possessions as a sign of wealth, but there was a string attached. The receiver was expected to reciprocate. In fact, sometimes just to show off, a rich man might deliberately ruin someone by inviting him to a banquet and then give him a gift that was so expensive that the recipient would go bankrupt trying to reciprocate.

Plutarch wrote, "Most people think that to be deprived of a chance to display their wealth is to be deprived of wealth itself."

Titles were an indicator of status. Eventually, when an emperor replaced the senate as the real power of Rome, offices carried little functional meaning; they were simply labels of honor.

Because everyone was expected to claim their honor, learning to toot your own horn was compulsory. Plutarch wrote a self-help book that might crack bestseller lists in our day: *How to Praise Yourself Inoffensively*. A classic example of the genre is *The Achievements of the Divine Augustus*, written by Emperor Caesar Augustus himself, inscribed on bronze tablets, with copies distributed throughout the empire. Some excerpts:

Three times I triumphed at oration. Twenty-one times I was named emperor. The Senate voted yet more triumphs for me which I declined because of victories won by me. The Senate voted thanks [for me] to the immortal gods. Fifty-five times in my triumphs, nine kings or children of kings were led before my chariot. I have been consul 13 times. I was highest-ranking senator for 40 years. I held the office of Pontific Maximums. All citizens with one accord unceasingly prayed in every holy place for my well-being.

[A] golden shield was ... given me by the senate and people of Rome on account of my courage, clemency, justice, and piety. After this time I excelled all in influence.

It was good to be king.

The way of the hero exalted many wonderful qualities: courage and excellence and persistence, overcoming obstacles, self-discipline, and self-mastery. But humility was not an admired quality. It was not considered desirable. What was desirable was greatness.

Historian Robin Lane Fox wrote, "Among pagan authors, humility had almost never been a term of commendation. It belonged with ignoble and abject characters.... The humble belonged with the abject, the mean, the unworthy."

———— •◆• ————

But another way was emerging.

A poor rabbi, who never wrote "The Deeds of the Divine Carpenter," said to his friends, "You know that the rulers in this world lord it over their people, and officials flaunt their authority over those under them."

No Roman would have been offended by this observation of Jesus. The whole point of making it to the top of the pecking order is you get to peck. But what Jesus said next would offend:

> "Not so with you. Instead, whoever wants to become great among you must be your servant, and whoever wants to be first must be your slave—just as the Son of Man did not come to be served, but to serve, and to give his life as a ransom for many."

This is what might be called "the way of the saint."

A saint doesn't try to grab worth through an endless race of achieve-ment, but receives worth by grace.

A saint does not choose as an ultimate value self-fulfillment, but self-giving love.

A saint does not seek glory, but gives glory to a glorious God.

A saint does not impose her will, but surrenders it to a good God.

A saint does not resent serving, but embraces it.

On Jesus' last night, almost the final moments of his life, he was so concerned for his followers to embrace humility that he acted it out in something like a parable. "Jesus knew that the Father had put all things under his power, and that he had come from God and was returning to God; so he got up from the meal, took off his outer clothing, and wrapped a towel around his waist. After that, he poured water into a basin and began to wash his disciples' feet, drying them with the towel that was wrapped around him."

Jesus expressed an alternate view of greatness through his clothes. Removing his outer garment and wrapping a towel around himself is what a slave would do. Jesus wore the uniform of a slave.

> *A saint does not choose as an ultimate value self-fulfillment, but self-giving love.*

His occupation followed a different trajec-tory than the Roman prescription. Jesus worked most of his life with his hands, doing menial labor as a carpenter. No hero in Greek or Roman literature did this. But Jesus did. One of his last acts was to wash feet.

Washing feet was an important part of ancient life. It was an act of hospitality, hygiene, and a religious ritual of cleansing, but it was demeaning. It was done only by slaves. Yet it was considered so demean-ing that while Gentile slaves might have to do it, a Jewish master was not to compel a Jewish slave to wash his feet. There are a few exceptions.

There is an apocryphal story in Israel of a couple named Joseph and Asenath who lived in Egypt in the time of the pharaohs. Asenath is the bride, and she is so in love with her husband that when he comes home, she wants to wash her husband's feet. He is stunned by this.

He says, "No. Get up. A servant will do that."

She says to him, "No. You are my lord from now on. Your feet are my feet. Your hands are my hands. Another woman will never wash your feet."

Isn't that a beautiful story? No? My wife didn't think so either, because we never read about any husband offering to wash his wife's feet.

In another extraordinary story, some disciples love their rabbi so much that they try to wash his feet. But there are no stories of a higher-status person washing the feet of a lower-status person. We never read of a rabbi washing his disciples' feet. Except this rabbi, who by the way said he was the Messiah.

Jesus' legal status was about to become an embarrassment. Within a few hours he would be betrayed by Judas, arrested, convicted, and executed as a criminal. That would be his final status in the Roman Empire.

Jesus washes the feet of Judas. The so-called divine Augustus never washed anyone's feet. A culture built on honor is beginning to implode, but almost no one back then realizes that.

—◆—

Seating was always about expressing status and honor. Jesus was at a table, which is where the guests were, but he got up from the table the way a servant would do. This is a picture of what Jesus taught earlier: "For who is greater, the one who is at the table or the one who serves?" It wasn't a hard question: The great ones sit; the humble ones serve.

We still have echoes of this. At a banquet a special guest has a title: the guest of *honor*. A guest of honor doesn't just sit; he or she sits at a special table, the *head* table. You never go to a banquet where the guest of honor is a busboy.

Who is greater? "Is it not the one who is at the table? But I am among you as one who serves." That is, *I am among you as the busboy.*

Next time you go to a restaurant, look around and ask yourself, *In God's eyes, where are the great ones? Where's Jesus?* We all know about how life works and who's wearing what label and who can afford what on the menu and who has how much in their wallet. Where is greatness in God's eyes?

We are often told in biographies of the great that they do not suffer fools gladly; they have little time for the slow or the dim bulbs. But not Jesus. He had a feeling for people others discounted. Biblical scholar

Dale Bruner said Jesus today would probably like to hang out in Greyhound bus stations. One of the most impressive aspects of Jesus is how he was impressed by unimpressive people.

We are often told that the great do not suffer fools gladly. But not Jesus. He had a feeling for people others discounted.

Jesus subverted the pursuit of impressive titles. "You call me 'Teacher' and 'Lord,' and rightly so, for that is what I am. Now that I, your Lord and Teacher, have washed your feet, you also should wash one another's feet."

Titles are only opportunities to serve.

Jesus died stripped of his robe, convicted by the law, and given the mocking title "king of the Jews." He wore the garb of a slave, took the position of a slave, did the work of a slave, and suffered the death of a slave. A *personis mediocribus*.

What was noted about Jesus is that he chose this. What may be the earliest writing about him said that "he humbled himself." In the Roman Empire, someone might *be* humbled, by losing money or status or title. No one deliberately *humbled himself.*

Until now.

———•◦•———

Sometime after that day, a community was formed. Rome didn't know how to categorize it or what to do with it. In ways that were hard to understand, it subverted some of what was thought most admirable and most necessary to maintain order. "... in Christ, taught the Christians, all were equal and the distinctions of rank and degree were irrelevant. In church meetings, educated people had to sit as equals among other men's slaves and petty artisans."

Slaves would come into a gathering of Jesus' followers and someone else—maybe a freedman, maybe even a citizen, or maybe even an aristocrat—would wrap a towel around his waist, kneel down on the floor, and wash the feet of the slaves.

Plato said, "But do you think that anyone is happy who is in the condition of a slave, and who cannot do what he likes?" Society was arranged vertically. But at the bottom of that society, a great leveling force was beginning to disrupt things: happy, voluntary slaves.

Joseph Hellerman offered a moving explanation to an oddity in the book of Acts. At Philippi, a Roman colony, Paul is arrested and badly beaten. After he is released, he protests that he is a Roman citizen. The officials are apologetic and frightened to hear this; they have violated Roman law by beating a Roman citizen.

But this raises the obvious question: Why didn't Paul tell them he was a Roman citizen *before* they beat him? Who sits on a "Get out of jail free" card?

Paul is forming a little outpost of Jesus' community. When the church would get started, Paul knew there might be a couple of elite people in it, but not many. Mostly it will be the non-elite. But they are supposed to be a family now. Everything inside them—all their customs, training, thinking, language, habits—have taught them that life is about the pecking order, the *cursus honorum*. You keep people down. You try to climb up. Now Paul is going to try to make a family so they become brothers and sisters. How could that be done?

Paul also knew that these nobodies would suffer for their faith. They would have little power. Paul knew he could have used his status as a citizen to avoid suffering; the low-status members of the church would not have that option. He saw in this predicament a painful and glorious opportunity.

So Paul did something irrational. He "humbled himself." He refused to consider citizenship in Rome something to be used to his own advantage. Rather, he made himself like a non-citizen, like a nobody, a *personas mediocribus*.

Celsus, one of the early critics of Christianity, said that all they could draw to themselves were "stupid, ignorant, weak people." Slaves, women, and children. He was concerned that the way of the hero, the excellence and greatness that had taken centuries to emerge, could be lost.

I understand the appeal of elitism. For some of us, humility is not a virtue that comes naturally.

Paul wrote to the church at Rome, "Do not be proud, but be willing to associate with people of low position. Do not be conceited." How am I doing at that one?

— ◆ —

The area of Silicon Valley where I live features a remarkable and wonderful culture: courage, initiative, enterprise, risk-taking, and intelligence. But I'm not sure we do well at producing humble people.

The gravitational pull of the ego is relentless. I sometimes wonder whether those of us in the church are just as preoccupied with honor and status as anyone else, just cover over it with a thin veneer of spiritual language. We develop our own cult of celebrities. We prefer the wealthy or attractive or successful. There is an old story that Thomas Aquinas was being shown the glories of the Vatican by Pope Innocent IV. The pope said, referring to the story of a lame beggar in the book of Acts, "The church no longer has to say, 'Silver and gold have I none.'" And Aquinas replied, "Yes, but no longer is the church able to say, 'In the name of Jesus of Nazareth, Rise up and walk.'"

We often do not live in the way of Jesus.

It is strange how our heroes have changed.

Jim Collins wrote the hugely influential *Built to Last* in celebration of the highest kind of leadership, what he calls level 5 leaders. They combine two qualities. One is the persistence of a tenacious will; this is just the sort of virtue the Romans would have exalted. The other virtue is humility. The second virtue displays itself in leaders who view themselves as servants, who sacrifice their own egos for the benefit of the many. Collins says they are more like Lincoln (who was also called "Father Abraham") than Douglas MacArthur (who was called by one biographer the "American Caesar"). How did our heroes change?

> *It wasn't only a man who died on a cross. In a strange way, a culture was dying too, though no one knew it yet.*

Australia's Macquarie University did a research project exploring how humility went from a despised weakness to an admired social virtue. "[T]he conclusion was clear: the modern Western fondness for humility almost certainly derives from the peculiar impact on Europe of the Judeo-Christian worldview. This is not a 'religious' conclusion; Macquarie is a public university.... It is a purely historical finding."

It wasn't only a man who died on a cross. In a strange way, a culture was dying too, though no one knew it yet. In that culture, honor meant status; shame meant worthlessness. Crucifixion was the ultimate shame.

Jesus was crucified. For his followers, this mean that either he was not as great as they had thought, or the whole notion of greatness itself would have to be redefined. It would have to become *cruciform*—re-shaped by the cross.

Historian John Dickson wrote that while Christians are a long way from cornering the humility market, "it is unlikely that any of us would aspire to this virtue were it not for the historical impact of his crucifixion on art, literature, ethics, law and philosophy. Our culture remains cruciform long after it stopped being Christian."

The way of the hero has been touched by the way of the saint.

——— ·•·———

In 2011 I visited an orphanage in a township outside the city of Durban, South Africa—a township where more than a million human beings live in poverty and violence, crowded together in little huts and shacks on hills. The orphans are the victims of AIDS.

The number of people with AIDS in South Africa is the highest in any country. In some of the townships, the incidence is up to 80 percent. Hundreds of thousands of homes are headed by children because both parents are dead from AIDS. The violence is unbelievable. Our host told us that in these townships, over half of all women have been raped by the time they are twelve years old. This is made worse by a prevalent myth that a man with AIDS can be cured by having sex with a virgin.

The orphanage is run by people who do what they do in the name of Jesus. The people we stayed with are devoting their lives to help these penniless, orphaned AIDS victims. One victim is a little girl named Somie, about ten years old, adorable, multilingual, and sharp as a tack. She does reception work for this facility. As our hosts raved about how well she serves, she put her hands over her face when they were praising her. So shy!

Somie has two little brothers that she brought to this orphanage. She said to them, because she feels so responsible for them, "Now don't be naughty so they don't drive you away. Behave yourselves." We were shown the plastic bag of medicines that Somie has to take every day. But since she has HIV, she will not live long enough to grow up and have her own children or family.

In the room next to these children was a two-year-old boy named Phillip. He is beautiful and precocious. He can recite all of the Lord's Prayer. He loves to show visitors around the compound and introduce them to everybody. He is HIV positive. His mother died, and he was left alone. We saw where rats had come and gnawed off parts of his fingers.

You and I are not morally superior to members of the ancient world. We are no better because we live later. But we live in a world that has changed in this regard. We live in a world where the lowliest of the low are seen differently than they were two thousand years ago.

———•◦•———

He entered the world wearing swaddling clothes and exited it in the towel of a slave.

Think of him whatever we may. Greatness looks different now.

CHAPTER 7

Help Your Friends,
Punish Your Enemies

It is a Sunday morning, and two people walk onto the platform for me to interview at our church. The woman is soulful and lively hearted. In her late fifties, she is plagued by arthritis, so she leans on the arm of a strong young man of quiet dignity. Her name is Mary; his name is Oshea. In 1993 Mary's only son was killed during an argument at a party.

Oshea is the man who killed Mary's son. Mary and Oshea live next door to each other.

Forgiveness is not a natural act.

———•▪•———

In Bath, England, at the hot springs that formed a combination spa/ Roman worship center two thousand years ago, scores of prayers have been excavated that ancients paid to have written down and offered there. They are called "curse tablets" because by far the most common kind of prayers was a curse. People would give the name of someone who hurt them, tell what their crime was, then specify how they wanted the gods to harm them. "'Docimedus has lost two gloves. He asks that the person who has stolen them should lose his mind and his eyes in the temple at the place where the goddess appoints.' No matter how much you love your gloves, this seems a tad harsh."

A more eloquent example of these prayers discovered all over the ancient Mediterranean world comes from a curse tablet in Rome:

I invoke you, holy angels and holy names ... tie up, block, strike, overthrow, harm, destroy, kill, and shatter Eucherios the charioteer and all his horses tomorrow in the arena of Rome. Let the starting-gates not [open] properly. Let him not compete quickly. Let him not pass. Let him not make the turn properly. Let him not receive the honors.... Let him not come from behind and pass but instead let him collapse, let him be bound, let him be broken up, and let him drag behind. Both in the early races and the later ones. Now, now! Quickly, quickly!

The Roman gods were there to help you get what you want. If you got hurt, what you wanted was to get even.

Imagine another category that might be called a "bless my enemy tablet":

Eucherios hurt me badly. Would you deliver me from my prison of hatred and resentment; would you help Eucherios to find genuine repentance; would you forgive his sin and mine; would you heal our relationship?

How many "bless my enemy tablets" do you think they have found at Bath?

None.

People did not pray prayers like that to Zeus or Bacchus. Fierce loyalty to your friends and fierce opposition to your enemies were considered noble. The gods were there to help you get what you want. And if you got hurt, what you wanted was to get even.

———— •┼• ————

Jesus was citing conventional wisdom when he noted, "You have heard that it was said, 'Love your neighbor and hate your enemy.'"

Of course they had heard it said. The Greek writer Xenophon said a man should give help to his friends and give trouble to his enemies. On his death bed Cyrus of Persia gave his final advice: "Take note of my last words: If you do good to your friends, you will also be able to punish your enemies." Some Stoic philosophers observed that anger is beneath human dignity and warned about surrendering to a spirit of vengeance.

But literature professor David Konstan said that forgiveness as we know it did not exist in ancient Greece and Rome. People had various means to appease anger and reestablish relationships, but those means were dictated more by standards of honor, status, and shame than by sin, atonement, and grace. (As a rough analogy, when my dog does something wrong, it will put itself in its cage and act guilty until it sees my anger is assuaged. It's not repenting; it's just doing pain management.) Ancient conventional wisdom said, "Help your friends and punish your enemies." One monograph on the subject is simply titled "Helping Friends and Harming Enemies." But Jesus said: "I tell you, love your enemies and pray for those who persecute you, that you may be children of your Father in heaven. He causes his sun to rise on the evil and the good, and sends rain on the righteous and the unrighteous."

Anger, hurt, bitterness, and resentment are a huge force in life, and no one floats above them.

People sometimes wonder: Is it possible to forgive when the other party is not repentant? You might distinguish between forgiveness as letting go of my right to hurt you back and reconciliation as that which requires the sincere intentions of both parties. I am not commanded to pretend to trust someone who is untrustworthy.

But underneath it all is the command to love. I am called to love the repentant person who hurt me. I am called to love the unrepentant person who hurt me.

Jesus goes on: "If you love [only] those who love you, what reward will you get? Are not even the tax collectors doing that? And if you greet only your own people, what are you doing more than others? Do not even pagans do that?"

He speaks of greeting someone, the homiest and smallest of behaviors. When you greet someone, you are acknowledging their existence and welcoming them into your world. In our day, it often involves the single word, "Hey!" We will be celebrated by future generations for our eloquent civility.

In Jesus' day, the greeting was *Shalom 'alekah*, which means, "Peace be with you." It is not enough to avoid killing someone. Jesus teaches that we are to greet—to pray, wish for, and hope for *shalom* (God's wholeness and peace)—for our enemy. This is so associated with Jesus that no less a thinker than German political theorist Hannah Arendt, the first woman appointed to a full professorship at Princeton University, claimed that forgiveness and love of enemies is a distinctively Christian contribution to the human race: "the discoverer of the role of forgiveness in the realm of human affairs was Jesus of Nazareth."

One day Jesus drops a bomb. It's early in his ministry, things are going well, and he has drawn a crowd so large that he must teach from a boat in a lake so all can hear. That evening he says to his disciples, "Let's go over to the other side."

That's the bomb. The "other side" is something of a technical term. Jesus is not talking just about geography. The other side of the lake was the region of Decapolis, the "ten cities." This was largely enemy territory. Its inhabitants were pagan people.

There was a rabbinic tradition about "the other side" in Jesus' day. It

> *Decapolis was filled with everything Israel was not. The Jews regarded the "other side" as the place where Satan lived.*

said that Decapolis — the "other side" — is where the seven nations of Canaan settled. It was filled with pagan temples (some still being excavated), featuring exaltations of violence or sexual expression or greed that was everything that Israel was not. Moreover, the pig, the most unclean animal in Israel, was regarded as sacred and used in worship on the other side.

The Jews regarded the other side as the place where Satan lived. It was dark, evil, oppressive, and demonic. No one would go to the other side — especially no rabbi.

In the Hebrew Scriptures, God had promised to drive "the Canaanites, Hittites, Hivites, Perizzites, Girgashites, Amorites and Jebusites" out of the Promised Land. These were known as the seven nations of Canaan, and they were still referred to this way even in Jesus' day. Paul related that God overthrew the seven nations in Canaan and gave their land to his people as an inheritance.

Decapolis was also a center of Roman power in Jesus' time. It housed a legion of six thousand Roman soldiers. The symbol of a Roman legion was a boar's head.

— ·◆· —

Jesus casually suggested one day, "Let's go over to the other side."

What was he doing? Didn't he know that the kingdom is for *our* side?

It's almost as if he didn't know that this is the *other* side. It's almost as if he thought it's *his* side. It's almost as if he thought every side belonged to him, or that he belonged to every side. It's almost as if he thought that all the peoples of the earth were now going to be blessed through him —even the seven nations of Canaan.

"Let's go over to the other side," Jesus said. The disciples were not happy about this, but they went.

When they landed, the large crowds the disciples had grown used to on their side were absent. Their reception committee was a single, deranged, tormented, tomb-dwelling, self-mutilating demoniac, so disruptive that he had been thrown out of his own community.

He fell on his knees before Jesus. "What do you want with me?... In God's name don't torture me."

Jesus asked the evil spirit, "What is your name?" And the response was, "Legion, for we are many."

Legion is a loaded word in this story. There was a legion of foreign soldiers, and this was where they lived. That word is a reminder of enemies all around. The spirits asked to be sent into pigs, which then rushed to their destruction.

Any Israelite would think of the story recorded in 1 Maccabees, how Jewish patriots were forced by Rome to eat the flesh of pigs, and when they resisted, they were slaughtered. So the pig is also the symbol of Roman power of the legion. And the tormented man was delivered from the legion.

The people's response was fascinating. We are told that those tending the pigs ran off and reported the man's deliverance widely. The people on the other side came over to see what had happened. They saw the crazed man dressed and in his right mind.

They didn't respond to this miracle like those in Galilee or Jerusalem. They didn't start bringing Jesus their sick children or crippled friends. They begged him to go away.

Why? Because he had power, but he wasn't one of them. He was from the wrong side. And he might use his power to hurt them.

Jesus agreed to go. The man who had been demon-possessed begged to go with him. Jesus, who up to now had been telling everyone, "Follow me," said no. He said, "Go tell your story."

Imagine this man's feeling when that boat rowed away and he wasn't in it. But he did what Jesus asked. He told people in Decapolis how much Jesus had done for him. "And all the people were amazed."

Here's the rest of the story. Jesus returned to Decapolis a short time later. This time great crowds came to see him. "They ran throughout that whole region and carried the sick on mats to wherever they heard he was. And wherever he went—into villages, towns or country side—they placed the sick.... They begged him to let them touch even the edge of his cloak, and all who touched it were healed."

In other words, the seven nations of Canaan were praising the God of Israel. The first time Jesus went over to the other side, nobody was home except for one pathetic wretch. The second time he came, it was one of the most dramatic responses in all of the New Testament. People were more receptive to Jesus here than any other place he had ever gone.

They had heard that this Jesus cared about someone on "their side."

This theme of Jesus' loving "the other side" goes on just beneath the surface. It's part of what might be called the "dueling crowd-feeding stories."

In Mark 6, Jesus fed a crowd on Israel's side of the lake. Twelve baskets of food were left over—think twelve tribes of Israel. God cares for his people.

In Mark 8, Jesus fed a crowd on "the other side," and seven baskets of food were left over. Why the variation?

This is just a guess, but it's almost as if Jesus was saying: "Good news is coming for the twelve tribes. But good news is coming for the seven nations of Canaan, too. Twelve tribes, seven nations—it really doesn't matter to me. I love them all. It's good news for this side and good news for the other side."

— .•. —

Whose side are you on?

Love of enemies is perhaps Jesus' teaching that is most famous and most violated.

We human beings are side-takers. We all tend to divide the human race into *us* versus *them*. This happens for religious reasons but can also happen because of ethnicity, culture, and language. Two of the most powerful words in the human race are *us* and *them*.

If someone is in my *in* group, I will tend to magnify their good qualities and overlook their negative qualities. If somebody is in the *out* group, I look for the bad and overlook the good. I look at each member of "us" as a unique individual. I tend to look at everybody who is one of them as all alike.

In a classic study, researchers divided a group of boys at a camp into Group W and Group X just to look at the power of *us* versus *them*. They would take one kid, give him a little bit of money, and tell him he was going to divide it up between two boys from two different groups: "You will give some of your money to this boy from Group X, and then give some to this boy from Group W."

The plan was to get an initial baseline and then introduce some antagonism between the two groups and see how much antagonism was required before kids started giving more money to the boy in their group. They could not even get a baseline. Researchers were stunned. They said their clearest finding is that boys will discriminate against other boys as soon as they are randomly assigned to a different group.

Jesus seems to have regarded himself as the Man for All Sides, but his followers often collapse back into Us vs. Them.

If you are thinking girls would do any better, it's because you *are* a girl, and you're assuming *your* in-group is superior, and that just confirms the core idea. Us vs. Them is as old as Cain and Abel ("Now Abel kept flocks and Cain worked the soil").

Jesus seems to have regarded himself as the Man for All Sides, but his followers often collapse back into Us vs. Them. The name "Christian" was apparently a derisive nickname given to believers by pagans; the historian Tacitus spoke of "a race of men detested for their evil practices, by vulgar appellation commonly called Christians." Christians returned the favor: the word "pagan" was coined by Christians from the Latin word *pagani*. It could mean "rube" or "civilian"; Christians used it to refer to those who had not enlisted by baptism to become soldiers for Christ.

We who follow Jesus have not just struggled with making non-Christians into *them*; we sometimes famously do it with each other.

A man was walking along San Francisco's Golden Gate Bridge when he saw a woman standing by herself, obviously feeling lonely. He ran up to tell her God loved her. A tear came to her eye. Then he asked her, "Are you a Christian, Jew, Hindu, what?"

"I'm a Christian," she said.

He said, "Me too! Small world. Protestant or Catholic?"

"Protestant."

"Me too! What denomination?"

"Baptist."

"Me too! Northern Baptist or Southern Baptist?"

"Northern Baptist."

He said, "Me too! Northern Conservative Baptist, or Northern Liberal Baptist?"

"Northern Conservative Baptist."

"That's amazing! Me too! Northern Conservative Fundamentalist Baptist, or Northern Conservative Reformed Baptist?"

"Northern Conservative Fundamentalist Baptist."

"Remarkable! Me too! Northern Conservative Fundamentalist Baptist Great Lakes Region, or Northern Conservative Fundamentalist Baptist Eastern Region?"

She said, "Northern Conservative Fundamentalist Baptist Great Lakes Region."

"A miracle," he said. "Northern Conservative Fundamentalist Baptist Great Lakes Region Council of 1879, or Northern Conservative Fundamentalist Baptist Great Lakes Region Council of 1912?"

She said, "Northern Conservative Fundamentalist Baptist Great Lakes Region Council of 1912."

He shouted, "Die, heretic!" and pushed her over the rail.

Miroslav Volf noted that the tendency to exclude the *other*, which religious leaders in Jesus' day often regarded as great *virtue*, was regarded by Jesus as great *sin*. This often surprised the disciples.

One day on his way to Jerusalem, Jesus wanted to stop in a Samaritan village, but it was not welcoming. His disciples asked, "Lord, do you want us to call down fire from heaven to destroy them?" They thought Jesus would be pleased by this offer. *We're going to take a stand. We're going to be on Jesus' side.* Jesus' followers sometimes think this way.

Jesus turned and admonished them. He was protecting the Samaritans and rebuking his followers. What an odd little story! In fact, the New Testament is full of these odd little Samaritan stories. Jesus befriended a five-times-married Samaritan woman, and she became a great evangelist of his. He healed ten lepers, and only the Samaritan returned to thank him. He told a story about an Israelite, a priest, a Levite, and a Samaritan —and the hero is the Samaritan.

Jesus treats people on the other side as if they are people on our side. He doesn't just love us. He seems to love Samaritans.

In fact, while there are very few Samaritans around these days, they are more widely remembered than most extinct ancient peoples, almost always with the adjective "Good" attached. Because of someone who was supposed to be their enemy.

Jesus treats people on the *other* side as if they are people on *our* side. He doesn't just love us. He seems to love Samaritans. And not just them.

There is a saying in *The Godfather* (a movie whose title is, ironically, one more reminder of the life of Jesus): "Keep your friends close, and your enemies closer."

With an entirely different meaning, theses words perhaps come from the heart of the God whom Jesus proclaimed.

The heroic figure in *Conan the Barbarian* was actually paraphrasing Ghengis Khan when he gave his famous answer to the question, "What is best in life?" Namely, "to crush your enemies, see them driven before you, and hear the lamentations of their women."

An alternative idea came from Galilee: What is best in life is to love your enemies and see them reconciled to you.

———•◆•———

When Jesus was approached by soldiers to be arrested and killed, Peter picked up a sword and cut off the ear of a man named Malchus. Jesus told Peter to put his sword away, then he picked up the ear and put it back on Malchus's head. We imagine the dialogue: "I'm sorry about my disciple Peter. I've been working on him for three years, haven't gotten very far. I apologize about the ear thing."

Imagine when Malchus got home for dinner that night, and his wife asked, "How did work go today?" Malchus: "Well, my ear got cut off, but the strangest thing happened. The man who I came to have crucified healed me. Why would he do that?"

This odd little story was regarded as so important that it was included in all four gospels. Dale Bruner put it this way: "Jesus' enemies are not His only problem. Jesus' over-zealous followers have historically been as painful to Him."

For Jesus, the categories break down like this: It's not *us* and *them*. It's *perfect* and *not perfect*. It's *holy* and *sinful*. Which puts all of humanity on the same side: the wrong side. But Jesus was determined to make that *his* side.

This doesn't mean that Jesus agreed with everybody all the time, or was relativistic, or feared conflict. In fact, this very commitment was a large part of what got him killed. But he never succumbed to the in-group bias. He continually communicated an intent to love those who should have been *them*. Those of us in the church often get this wrong. Other religions, other ethnicities, other cultures, other sexual behavior, other politics, other denominations—what have we *not* allowed to turn people into *them*? It must, as Anne Lamott used to say, "make Jesus want to drink gin straight out of the cat dish."

Jesus does not say, "If you follow me, everyone will like you and you will have no enemies. Find a church where everybody will applaud you all day long." We are not given the option of an enemy-free existence.

Dietrich Bonhoeffer, who knew something about enemies, wrote,

Jesus Christ lived in the midst of his enemies. At the end all his disciples deserted him. On the Cross he was utterly alone, surrounded by evildoers and mockers. For this cause he had come, to bring peace to the enemies of God. So the Christian, too, belongs not in the seclusion of a cloistered life but in the thick of foes. There is his commission, his work.

Bonhoeffer went on to quote Luther:

"The kingdom is to be in the midst of your enemies. And he who will not suffer this does not want to be of the Kingdom of Christ; he wants to be among friends, to sit among roses and lilies, not with the bad people but the devout people. O you blasphemers and betrayers of Christ! If Christ had done what you are doing who would ever have been spared."

One of the early Christian heroes was Stephen, who was killed for his faith, but died with words strange in the ancient world, "Lord, do not hold this sin against them."

Followers of Jesus began to resist serving in the Roman military. If they did have to serve, they would refuse to kill. They resisted in part to avoid the emperor-worship that was an aspect of military life. But they also resisted to avoid bloodshed. The church father Origen responded to one critic by saying it would be better for Christians to pray as an "army of piety" for the safety of the emperor and the well-being of the people than to serve in the military. It is thought that the practice of pacifism began there.

Followers of Jesus began to resist serving in the Roman military, in part to avoid emperor-worship, but also to avoid bloodshed.

This concept of pacifism would be picked up by people like the Quakers and the Amish, where the practices of nonviolence and love for enemy would be soul-shaping. In October 2006, the world was moved when five children were shot to death in a schoolhouse in Lancaster County, Pennsylvania, and the Amish community forgave the gunman, donating money to the gunman's widow and children.

One of the atrocities of apartheid was a theological justification for keeping white South Africans in one of the highest living standards in the world while black South Africans suffered in untold ways. One of the heroes of resistance was an Anglican clergyman named Desmond Tutu, who radiated joy in the midst of suffering. At a large rally in a dangerous setting watched by hostile officers, he once beamed to the scowling lawmen: "Since the love of Christ will ultimately prevail, we invite you to join the winning team!"

The reality of this love for enemies was so powerful, for example, that we read about Maurice, a pagan military commander of the Roman army, who was so impressed by followers of Jesus being willing to die that he refused to carry out any further executions, an act that led to his own execution.

———•·•———

The teachings of Jesus inspired a writer named Leo Tolstoy, who wrote a book called *Resurrection* that was banned in Russia but that inspired a British-trained lawyer to start a Tolstoyan community in South Africa. The last full letter Tolstoy ever wrote to a non-relative was to this lawyer to praise the self-sacrificing, enemy-loving approach of Jesus.

That lawyer's name was Mahatma Gandhi. He eventually went back to India and didn't become a Christian, but there is no way to understand the nationalist movement Gandhi fostered apart from the Sermon on the Mount and the suffering love of Jesus.

Here is more irony: How often have attempts to "side" with Jesus caused people to belittle the teachings of other religions to try to make Jesus look more superior? We caricature the teachings of Islam or Buddhism without taking the time to give them a fair hearing in the name of Christianity. In doing so, we place ourselves against the One we claim to support.

Jesus' teachings and Gandhi's strategies in turn inspired Martin Luther King Jr., who gave what was perhaps the best-known American speech of the twentieth century: "I Have a Dream."

It was the language of the prophets from a preacher of the gospel of Jesus that inspired the conscience of a nation.

Taylor Branch wrote that King was speaking from a prepared text. At one point King cited words from the prophet Amos: "We will not be satisfied till justice rolls like the waters. We will not be satisfied till righteousness rolls like a mighty stream." The crowd could not keep quiet. They started to applaud. They started to yell back, "Tell it! Tell it! Amen!" like a church crowd.

Martin Luther King could not go back to his prepared text. This moment is quite noticeable watching the video. He stops looking at his text. Singer Mahalia Jackson, who was sitting behind him at the time, is said to have piped up as she might in a church choir: "Tell them about the dream, Martin." He started singing to a nation as a prophet would do. "I have a dream!"

King went from Amos to Isaiah, saying that "one day all children of God will be judged no longer by the color of their skin but the content of their character. I have a dream today. I have a dream that every valley will be raised up, and every mountain will be brought down. The glory of God will be revealed, and all flesh will see it together. I have a dream!" It was the language of the prophets from a preacher of the gospel of Jesus that inspired the conscience of a nation.

Charles Colson told this story:

In a large open area of a Rwandan prison, Anglican Bishop John Rucyahana spoke to a crowd of killers responsible for the 1994 genocide. "Close your eyes," he instructed them. "Go back in your mind to 1994. What did you see?" he asked. "What did you smell? What did you hear?"

Many in the crowd began to weep. He told the men to see their victims' faces. The sobs grew louder. "Now," said Bishop John, "that which made you cry, that you must confess."

It's amazing enough that Bishop John, himself a Tutsi, would speak to the Hutu perpetrators of the genocide. It's even more amazing when you consider that John's own niece, Madu, was brutally raped and killed during the genocide. But Bishop John had a reason to reach out to these men in compassion—for he, too, had found forgiveness of his sins through Jesus Christ.

He helped start the Umuvumu Tree Project, which has brought together tens of thousands of perpetrators and victims of the genocide, offering offenders the opportunity to confess their crimes and victims the chance to forgive. Many have done so.

———•◦•———

Let's return to the story about Mary and Oshea. How did a mother of an only child end up living next door to the man who took her child's life?

After her son died, Mary tried saying all the right things. She was a daughter of the church, she said at the trial, and thus forgave her son's killer. She meant it sincerely. But as time passed, it became clear that she had not forgiven. Bitterness and resentment ate at her like a cancer.

The church did not help her much. After her son's death, her pastor told her that the reason her son had been killed was that Mary did not pray enough. So she left that church. But she could not leave her pain. People in her church told her to move on, to let go of the past. *Aren't you over that yet?*

One pivotal moment came when Mary stumbled onto a story in which two women meet in heaven. They can tell from their crowns that each was a mother. Each wants to know the other's story.

> "I would have taken my son's place on the cross," said one.
> "Oh, you are the mother of Christ," said the other mother, falling
>   to her knee.
> Kissing a tear away, the first mother said, "Tell me who your son
>   is, that I may grieve with you also."
> "My son is Judas Iscariot."

That was the end of the poem — but only the beginning of a journey. Mary decided that her calling is to help the mothers of murdered children and the mothers of children who have taken life to come together and heal together. But she would have to come to grips with her own heart first.

After twelve years, she decided that in order to be free she would need to meet with the object of her pain, to see if she had really forgiven him. She approached people in the restorative justice program of the Department of Corrections. They warned her, "You will not see the sixteen-year-old boy who shot your son. He has been in prison twelve years. He is a man now. Prison life has molded him for more than a decade." Still, she said, she must try.

They approached Oshea. Not interested. "Why should I meet with this woman? She will just want to hurt and blame me." He was not yet ready to look at any reality beyond the interpretation that allowed him not to blame himself.

Mary waited nine months. She approached the officials again, and they asked Oshea again. Something had been at work in his mind. He said yes.

Mary went with her friend Regina to the meeting. "It's a good thing God sends us two by two," Mary said. "When I got halfway up the ramp, I said, 'God, I cannot do this.' I would have gone home. Regina pushed me the rest of the way up the ramp."

Mary began that first conversation with Oshea with a carefully prepared thought: "I don't know you. You don't know me. Let's just start there."

The idea that she wanted to know him before judging him loosened something in his spirit. He decided he would trust the process. They talked for hours.

By the end of the first interview, Oshea asked Mary if he could hug her.

She said yes.

When his arms went around her, the floodgates burst. She sobbed. Oshea immediately had second thoughts about the hug: *I had been in prison twelve years, around hardened criminals; this was the scariest moment of my life.*

But from that moment, a bond started to form between Mary and Oshea. She would visit; they would talk. She had to be willing to understand his side of what happened. He had to be willing to see what he had robbed her of.

In December 2009, Oshea was released. Mary decided to throw him a "welcome out" party. She asked some nuns who live near her to help. They are locally known as "the sisters in the hood."

Mary's landlord had an idea. "What if you were to invite Oshea to live here, in this apartment building, in the apartment next to you?"

"He'd never do that."

"But what if you asked?"

She did. Now he lives a doorjamb away. He goes to school and works a job.

"Sometimes," Oshea says, "when I'm down, discouraged, when things aren't working, I look at Mary's face. And I say, 'Hey, she gave me another chance. I need to give myself a chance.'"

We sometimes speak of forgiveness as a tool for the victim's release from pain. And it is that. But it is more. Oshea and Mary have given each other gifts that neither would ever have known without the miracle of forgiveness.

It happened because a long time ago someone said, "Love your neighbor" and "Love your enemy."

And an enemy became a neighbor.

CHAPTER 8

There Are Things
That Are Not Caesar's

Leadership, says Harvard's Ron Heifetz, is the art of disappointing people at a rate they can stand.

In the last week of his life, Jesus exceeded the disappointment rate. He explained his refusal to wield the power the crowds wanted: "My kingdom is not of this world." His vision of a sphere above political power would eventually change human kingdoms. Our understanding of limited government is part of his legacy.

But first it got him killed.

———•◦•———

People often think of Palm Sunday as an innocent children's parade. It was not. Years before Jesus' birth, Israel's great temple had been desecrated by foreign powers. Under the Maccabees, Israel won a measure of freedom, which included control of the temple. Palm branches were used for its rededication.

So palms became a symbol of Jewish nationalism. During two major wars against Rome, Israelite rebels illegally minted coins and put palms on them. The palm branch was a political symbol like *elephant* or *donkey* or *Uncle Sam* in America. Waving a palm branch in front of Rome was like waving a red flag in front of a bull.

It was a declaration of war. The "triumphal entry" was, for the crowds, a military statement. John indicates this by the shouts of the crowd. They begin by quoting Psalm 118: "Hosanna! [Lord, save us!] Blessed is he who comes in the name of the Lord!" In Psalm 118, the next line is, "From the house of the LORD we bless you." That is not what the crowds say.

What they say is, "Blessed is the king of Israel!" In other words, "Blessed is the one who is going to overthrow Pilate, Herod, and Caesar." Those are fighting words. But Jesus would not fight. The hosannas would stop abruptly. He disappointed people at a rate they could not stand. The title "King of Israel" hung ominously over Jesus from his birth, as it would over his death. The idea that he was a king would confuse everyone. Especially kings.

— · ◆ · —

We have already seen the tension between Herod the Great and the little baby "born king of the Jews." The tense relationship between Jesus and kings would only get worse when Jesus grew up. Herod died not long after Jesus was born. His estate was a mess; he left seven different wills.

Three of Herod's sons — Archelaus, Herod Antipas, and Herod Philip — went to Rome to try to carve up the pie and get as much territory as they could to govern. (There is a proliferation of Herods in the New Testament, including a granddaughter named Herodias. It's a little like heavyweight boxing champion George Foreman naming his five sons George Jr., George III, George IV, George V, and George VI.)

Archelaus asked Caesar to make him king. Caesar's soldiers had recently executed three thousand Jewish patriots in the temple area during Passover. The Israelites sent a delegation to tell Caesar they did not want Archelaus to rule them; they asked to be put under the authority of Syria.

Caesar made Archelaus ruler anyway. When Archelaus returned home, he had the Jewish delegation brought before him and executed.

We are told that during Jesus' boyhood, "when he [Joseph] heard that Archelaus was reigning in Judea in place of his father Herod, he was afraid to go there.... he went and lived in a town called Nazareth."

Now we begin to see Jesus getting in trouble with that Palm Sunday crowd.

He went on to tell them a parable, because he was near Jerusalem and the people thought that the kingdom of God was going to appear at once. He said: "A man of noble birth went to a distant country to have himself appointed king and then to return....

"But his subjects hated him and sent a delegation after him to say, 'We don't want this man to be our king.'

"He was made king, however, and returned home."

The story does not have a happy ending. The king says,

"Those enemies of mine who did not want me to be king over them—bring them here and kill them in front of me."

After Jesus had said this, he went on ahead, going up to Jerusalem.

———•◦•———

This trip up to Jerusalem was a risk, for Jerusalem at Passover was a dangerous place for people who talked kingdom talk.

When Israelites heard the phrase "kingdom of God," they did not think of a place where human beings would go after they died. They thought about a day when God would crush Rome and restore the temple and give Israel their own king.

The great crisis of Israel in Jesus' day—as it had been for many centuries—was, "Where is God and his kingdom?"

There already was a kingdom, but it was in Rome. Caesar was said to be divine. Rome had a saying that would later be appropriated by the church: "Caesar is lord."

This trip up to Jerusalem was a risk, for Jerusalem at Passover was a dangerous place for people who talked kingdom talk.

Roman coins bore a graven image of Caesar. They had an inscription: *divi filius*—"son of god." A devout Israelite would not even carry a Roman coin, because it was considered a violation of the commandment against graven images. But to Rome, religion was a critical tool of the state to serve the common good.

So Herod took the prerogative of naming as high priest whoever was most cooperative, rather than a member of the traditional priestly family. Herod locked the sacred vestments up in the fortress Antonia, and the high priest had to endure the humiliation of asking permission to wear them into the

Holy of Holies each year then giving them back to Rome. Herod was trying to lock up a kingdom that wouldn't stay locked.

The longing in Jesus' day was the longing for the kingdom of God. *The* question in Jesus' day was, "How will it be brought to earth?"

There were three main responses to that question. Jesus would differ with all three.

———•◦•———

The Zealots decided to *revolt*. The Zealots were an extreme national-ist party dedicated to bringing in the kingdom of God by overthrow-ing Romans using any means, including violence. They were freedom fighters—or terrorists—depending on your politics.

The Essenes decided to *withdraw*. This group is not mentioned in the Bible, although the Dead Sea Scrolls were found in a community probably made up of Essenes. They believed everything had become so corrupt—not just Rome, but also the rest of Israel and the temple system—that the only response was to *withdraw completely* and devote themselves to a life of purity. They slept in caves. They were so austere that they refused to relieve themselves on the Sabbath; they would take a ritual bath before every meal. They were the "sons of light," and all others were the "sons of darkness." They believed their purity would cause God to destroy their enemies and give them the kingdom.

The Sadducees decided to *assimilate*. They were pragmatists. They did not believe in angels or the resurrection. They were interested in the here and now. They looked at the Romans and figured, *If you can't beat them, join them*. They worked with tax collectors and paid allegiance to Caesar. Therefore the positions of importance in Israel went to them. "When in Rome...."

So if you lived in Israel, these were the three main options to the great crisis of the day: revolt, withdraw, assimilate.

———•◦•———

Jesus got into trouble with every one of these groups.

A centurion asked Jesus for help, and Jesus replied that he had "not found anyone in Israel with such great faith."

Imagine the Zealots' reaction to Jesus' praising a Roman soldier. Jesus said, "If anyone forces you to go one mile, go with them two miles." This is a direct reference to the hated law that allowed Roman soldiers to force civilians to carry their packs for one mile. Zealots did not put Jesus' "Go the Extra Mile" saying on greeting cards. Jesus' trouble was just beginning.

The Zealots are wrong. The kingdom of God will not come through violence. But the Zealots were not the only group Jesus offended.

Jesus touched lepers, spoke with prostitutes and Gentiles, and ate with sinners. He ignored purity regulations. *The Essenes are wrong. The kingdom of God will not be realized through withdrawing into a religious subculture.*

> *If Jesus said "yes," people would hate him for giving in to Rome. If he said "no," Rome could always find another cross.*

At the same time, Jesus refused to be co-opted by Rome as the Sadducees were. One day Jesus was asked, "Teacher, ... we know you are a man of integrity and that you teach the way of God in accordance with the truth. You aren't swayed by others, because you pay no attention to who they are. Tell us then, what is your opinion? Is it right to pay the imperial tax to Caesar or not?"

A man named Judas of Galilee led a revolt about just this issue when Jesus was a boy. He and about two thousand followers were crucified by Rome, and the crosses were left up as a subtle warning to pay taxes.

If Jesus answered the question with "yes," people would hate him for giving in to Rome. If he said "no," Rome could always find another cross.

> "You hypocrites, why are you trying to trap me? Show me the coin used for paying the tax." ... he asked them, "Whose image is this? And whose inscription?"
>
> "Caesar's," they replied.

The details matter. Jesus did not carry a coin. He did not agree to Caesar's right to be worshiped. He was not a Sadducee.

"Give back to Caesar what is Caesar's, and to God what is God's."

The second half of this statement was going to change the world. The implication is that there were things that were *not* Caesar's. The right to dictate worship did not belong to Caesar. The claim to ultimate allegiance did not belong to Caesar. The valuation of human worth did not belong to Caesar. The religious conscience of a single, powerless Israelite did not belong to Caesar. The title Lord did not belong to Caesar.

To Rome, the existence of the gods immensely *enhanced* Caesar's authority. To Jesus, the existence of God immensely *limited* Caesar's authority. The kingdom of Rome is not the kingdom of heaven. There is another sphere above Caesar's, to which everyone — including Caesar — will give account. An untried idea is being put forward here — one we might call the separation of church and state. The original opponent of this idea was not the church; it was the state.

"There are things that are not Caesar's." By the time Jesus finished this statement, the uncontested power of human rulers had met its match. And Jesus had signed his own death warrant. To Rome this was treason. But it was actually treason of another kind.

Jesus would not worship Caesar. But he would also not hate him or slander him or even ignore him. God had told Abraham *all peoples of the earth* would be blessed by God's people. Jesus didn't just want to bless Israel. Jesus wanted to bless Rome. Jesus wanted to bless Caesar. Anger and violence are not the way; withdrawal is not the way; assimilation is not the way. There is another way. There are things that are not Caesar's.

Jesus went on to connect people whom politics separated.

Simon, you're a zealot; you despise Romans and collaborators like tax collectors — I'll take you. Matthew, you're a collaborator, a despised tax collector. I'll take you. You room with Simon.

Jesus seemed to be a dangerous man.

Here's our strategy. We have no money, no clout, no status, no buildings, no soldiers — things are going exactly to plan. We will tell them all that they are on the wrong track: the Roman money and power elite; the revolters; the withdrawers; the collaborators.

When they hate us — and a lot of them will — when they call us names and throw us in prison, even kill some of us, we won't fight back, we won't run away, and we won't give in. We will just keep loving them. We will just keep inviting them to join our side. That's my strategy. What do you think?

— ◦ —

The pain and suffering of Israel while waiting for the kingdom had actually led to a major breakthrough in human thought.

In the ancient world, all nations worshiped their own gods. Historian Rodney Stark wrote, "In ancient civilizations the concept of a 'state church' didn't really exist because people did not distinguish between them as two institutions." "State church" would have sounded like "governmental mayor"—what other kind is there? Something would have to happen in the world for state and religion to be regarded as separate spheres.

The general understanding was, the better the nation was doing, the higher the status of that nation's god. If your nation was the greatest nation, it proved your god was the greatest god.

It was the death of Israel's dream for national greatness that led to a prophetic vision of a God above all nations, a God who is for *all* nations. Generations earlier, the prophet Jeremiah had told Israel that they were to pray for the prosperity of Babylon, even though Babylon had defeated and exiled them. In other words, God was up to something in exile. God was disappointing people at a rate they could stand.

> *It was the death of Israel's dream for national greatness that led to a prophetic vision of a God who is for all nations.*

God wanted people to be present in whatever country they happened to occupy in a radically new way. They did not have to control it or withdraw from it or assimilate to it. They could love it.

God cares about Babylon. God cares about Rome.

Most people are concerned about what they can get out of Babylon or Rome. I live in the Bay area, where our professional football team is called the San Francisco 49ers. Prospectors discovered gold in California in 1849 and brought people out by the thousands, but they all came to take gold out. Nobody came to put gold back in. People come to California to take, to get discovered, to get rich, to get tan, to get pleasure.

People go to Hollywood because they want to get famous. People go to Silicon Valley because they want to get rich. People go to Fresno because they get bad directions.

Jesus was calling for people to love Rome—to engage in enterprise and education and the arts and statecraft and neighborhoods so that Rome could flourish—but not worship Rome.

The tension between Rome and the church would bring both great pain and great fruit. Rome did not quite know what to make of this Jesus movement. Something unprecedented in the world was taking root, something for which there were no guidelines.

From Rome's perspective, religion was crucial to maintain the common good. The very word *religion* is related to our word for "ligament" —that which holds a body together. Many religions existed within the Roman Empire. But the rulers allowed people to worship other gods and sacrifice to the emperor. Paying homage to local deities was part of a commitment to the common good. If you move to New York, you root for the Yankees.

The idea that there is one true, real, particular God had huge implications for government. By AD 220 Tertullian was already writing: "However, it is a fundamental human right, a privilege of nature, that every man should worship according to his own convictions: one man's religion neither harms nor helps another man. It is assuredly no part of religion to compel religion—to which free-will and not force should lead us."

Robert Wilkins wrote, "At issue here was not simply the traditional religion as opposed to the new religion that had arisen in Palestine. Here was also a *different understanding of religion....* [To Rome] Christianity was loosening the ties that bound religion to the social and political world." Christians were withholding from Caesar that which Caesar reckoned he had a right to.

This explains why some of the most moral emperors, such as Marcus Aurelius, were some of Christianity's worst persecutors. He was not —like Caligula or Nero—an ancient version of Dr. Evil. He was widely admired for his character. (It's good to be fair, even to ancient Romans.) But from his perspective, Christians were withholding from Rome the ultimate devotion needed to maintain what Virgil called the *imperium sine fine,* "the kingdom that will never end."

There are things that are not Caesar's. And one of them is a kingdom that will never end.

—·•·—

Followers of Jesus had to wrestle in a way that no other adherents to a religion ever had with their relationship to the state. A second-century writer, working out the identity of their movement, expressed it like this:

> Christians are not distinguished from the rest of humanity either in locality or in speech or in customs. But while they dwell in cities of Greeks and barbarians as the lot of each is cast ... the constitution of their citizenship is nevertheless quite amazing and admittedly paradoxical. They dwell in their own countries, but only as sojourners.... *Every foreign country is a fatherland to them, and every fatherland is a foreign country.*

This epistle actually speaks of Christians as a "third race"; the common categories of Greek or barbarian don't quite describe them.

A few centuries later, Augustine, following Jesus, distinguished between what he called the earthly city and the heavenly city. Because a human being's ultimate devotion belongs to the heavenly city, the claims of the earthly city are limited. This means the conscience of each individual becomes a kind of sanctuary. No king is able to claim the authority that belongs to God alone. There are things that are *not* Caesar's.

The tension between Jesus and earthly rulers, and the centuries of persecution created a legacy that helped shape the Western world.

Augustine argued, "What are kingdoms but little robberies? For whatever are robberies themselves, but little kingdoms?" He went on to cite the story of a cheeky pirate captured by Alexander the Great who told him, "Because I seize property in a petty ship I am called a robber; since you seize the whole earth with a great fleet you're called an emperor."

The tension between Jesus and earthly rulers, and the centuries of unease or persecution for the church created a legacy that helped shape the Western world. One of the primary differences between Jesus and Mohammed is that Mohammed was a military leader. Historian Bernard Lewis notes: "In classical Arabic and in other classical languages of Islam, there are no pairs of terms corresponding to 'lay' and 'ecclesi-

astical,' 'spiritual' and 'temporal,' 'secular' and 'religious,' because these
pairs of words express a Christian dichotomy that has no equivalent in
the world of Islam."

At the same time, Christians have often forgotten that the first
thing that "belongs to God" is the obligation to love — including the
obligation to love people who follow the way of other religions. A college
teacher of mine wrote a book on Christian persuasion with a cartoon
cover featuring a medieval crusader sitting on a horse with a lance aimed
at the throat of a prostrate Arab, who in turn is saying, "Tell me more
about this Christianity of yours; I'm terribly interested."

In fact, Jesus' followers have often behaved worse when they have
possessed political power than when they were persecuted *by* it. The first
few centuries of caesars treated Christians with neglect at best, oppression at worst. Then one day an even greater challenge emerged.

Caesar got converted.

In the fourth century, the way of Jesus went from being illegal to
being legal to being mandatory. (It is hard to picture Jesus' response
to this: "*Christianity: the official religion of the Roman Empire.*") From
a human standpoint, this must have looked providential. But human
power always submits to the law of unintended consequences.

For the early church, Nero had been a disaster. He stabbed his
mother to death after a failed attempt to drown her, poisoned an aunt
with a laxative, kicked one pregnant wife to death in the stomach and
executed another on a trumped-up adultery charge. He wedded ("dowry,
veil and all") a boy named Sporius, whom he had castrated to make
more feminine, and lived with him as man and wife. Rumored to have
sung an opera while Rome burned, he found a scapegoat in Christians
whom he had burned as human torches.

And yet the church flourished.

Paul told the church at Rome to pray for the authorities, which
included the emperor, who was Nero, who would have Paul killed.

There is a kingdom that is not of this world. There is a love that
is stronger than hate. A few centuries later, the emperor Constantine
was converted to Christianity through a vision of the cross. Many good
things resulted: persecution ended; more morals laws were passed; and

foundations for art, culture, education, and political legacies of western European civilization were laid.

And yet ...

In some ways, becoming the established religion of Rome was a blow from which the church has still not fully recovered. Gatherings that previously met secretly in catacombs were now housed in magnificent public buildings. A clergy that had been recruited on the basis of devotion was now flooded with wealth and status, and bishops began living lifestyles of the rich and famous. Becoming a Christian became a vocational and financial asset. Now that Christians had power, they outlawed and persecuted not only pagans but fellow Christians they regarded as heretics. "Given their monopoly situation, the privileged Christian clergy were content to recreate a Church very similar to the subsidized temple religions of the ancient civilizations."

—◆—

However, the kingdom of Jesus that was "not of this world" kept showing itself in unexpected ways. Late in the fourth century, a brilliant man named Ambrose became bishop of Milan (Augustine marveled that Ambrose could read without moving his lips! — unheard of in those days). When the emperor — Theodius — massacred seven thousand people in Thessalonica to put down a rebellion, Ambrose was appalled and refused to allow the emperor into his church: "You have not thought about your guilt in that great massacre.... Do you not realize how great your crime was? You must not be dazzled by the splendor of the purple that you wear.... How could you lift in prayer hands which are stained with the blood of such an unjust massacre?"

Before Jesus, the idea of a priest of Rome excommunicating the emperor was like a mouse excommunicating the cat. Now the cat gave in. The emperor confessed his guilt to the bishop, who imposed on him a month of public penance. Whatever Theodosius's motives may have been, an idea got reinforced: "Right and wrong are determined by the commands of God and ... these commands apply equally to all people, even to the emperor in his splendid purpose robes." There are things — like the right to slaughter innocent lives to shore up a regime — that are not Caesar's.

In AD 890 an English king named Alfred the Great laid out the Book of Laws or Dooms (*doom* being the English word for judgment or law). It explicitly drew on the law of Moses and Jesus' Golden Rule, and therefore (unlike law in ancient Rome) was to apply to all alike. Or as Alfred charmingly put it: "Doom very evenly! Do not doom one doom to the rich; another to the poor! Nor doom one doom to your friend; another to your foe!" This would become the basis for the English tradition of common law. Alfred's choice to ground it in the tradition of Moses and Jesus was deliberate: "I have not dared to set down many laws of my own," he wrote modestly.

> *The kingdom of Jesus that was "not of this world" kept showing itself in unexpected ways.*

A few centuries later, a group of barons would force a meeting with King John to sign a document that would become known as the Magna Carta. It was written primarily by Archbishop of Canterbury Stephen Langton. Although it was designed to help very few lives at the time except a handful of wealthy barons, it contained an idea that would bring revolution: "Here is a law which is above the King and which even he must not break.... Now for the first time the King himself is bound by the law."

There are things that do not belong to Caesar. One of them is the ability to hold oneself alone above the law.

———•◦•———

Ideas like individual rights, limited sphere of government, separation of the freedom of worship from the power of the state, and freedom of conscience would all be a part of reflecting on what Jesus meant when he talked about "that which belongs to Caesar." It was this connection that moved John Quincy Adams to say, "The highest glory of the American Revolution was this: it connected in one indissoluble bond the principles of civil government with the principles of Christianity." It is not coincidental that the liberty bell in Philadelphia quotes from the prophetic passage that Jesus would cite at the beginning of his own ministry: the Year of Jubilee instruction to proclaim liberty throughout the land. Quaker William Penn and Baptist Roger Williams pioneered political work to embed freedom of religious conscience in law. The influence of Jesus helped create a state where people could choose not to follow Jesus. In this way, and not only in this way, Jesus is present even in his absence.

Often the influence of Jesus' teaching would surface with new power when Caesar got it wrong. In the face of legally entrenched racism, Martin Luther King Jr. defended the idea of human rights on the basis of what he called "somebodiness"—that every human being regardless of race or background is "somebody" of worth.

"Somebodiness" is another one of those properties that does not belong to Caesar.

A theologian named Oscar Romero was appointed bishop in San Salvadore largely because he was viewed as a bland figure who would not rock any boats. But a few weeks after his appointment, one of his priests was murdered. His ministry became a gift to the poor and a challenge to government death squads. He insisted that the cry for justice is grounded in the ideas Jesus taught: "Whoever tortures a human being, whoever abuses a human being, whoever outrages a human being, abuses God's image, and the church takes as its own, that cross, that martyrdom." In this service, shortly after he said these words, he was shot through the heart and killed by a sniper.

> Today about 70 percent of all followers of Jesus live in the southern hemisphere, South America, Africa, and the East.

Historian Philip Jenkins noted that the most striking church change in our day is that a hundred years ago, 80 percent of all followers of Jesus lived in Europe and the United States. Today about 70 percent of all followers of Jesus live in the southern hemisphere, South America, Africa, and the East. Jenkins writes, "Christianity is flourishing wonderfully among the poor and persecuted while it atrophies among the rich and secure."

———— •·• ————

A man I know was one of the few doctors who specialized in his area in Ethiopia at a time when Christians were often persecuted there. Because of his medical specialty, he was well-known and carefully watched and sometimes privileged. Because of his faith, he was in prison several times. The small church that he was part of was vibrant. They shared everything. When they gathered for worship, with shades drawn, their joy was intense. Their knowledge of the details of each others' lives was far deeper than I have seen in any churches I know of in the United States. They lived in constant danger of arrest. There was no such thing in their world as a nominal Christian; that would be like becoming a nominal chain saw juggler. When I would visit a group of Christians in someone's home, they would say, "Teach us," and pull out paper and pen to write down whatever might be of help. This rarely happens to me in the United States.

I talked with this doctor about the government. I said that he must pray often for the persecution and suffering to stop. He asked me with no apparent irony, "Why should I pray to be relieved of suffering?" I could not think of a good answer.

The man who was ruler then is now forgotten, a figure of shame and derision. His face was often featured on posters alongside Marx and Lenin. I was told they were generally referred to as the three stooges. Those who lived their lives in and out of prison are heroes. What kingdom matters? What kingdom is real?

I recently heard a historian remark that Caesar Augustus was the most successful statesman in human history. If you asked Caesar Augustus what his legacy would be — he probably would have talked about Roman law or the *Pax Romana* or roads and aqueducts or the world's great military machine or most impressive empire.

He would never have guessed that the most celebrated and influential event to occur during his reign would be the birth of a baby he never heard of in a province he never saw. He would never have guessed that Caesar's greatest "legacy" would define the category of that which does not belong to Caesar.

CHAPTER 9

The Good Life
vs. The Good Person

Two great questions are often posed about worthwhile living: Who has the good life? and Who is a good person? The first question gets addressed in ads, the second at funerals.

Two brothers led a miserable life. They were self-centered, money-grubbing, mean-spirited, intolerant scoundrels. Then one of them died. His brother paid a minister a lot of money to do the funeral on the condition that the minister must call his dead brother a saint. Ministers sometimes do a lot of gymnastics at funerals. So the minister did the eulogy: "I have to tell you the truth: this man who died was a liar, a bully, a cheat, and a thief. But compared to his brother, he was a saint."

Dallas Willard said that we see how fundamental this question of who is a good person is in obituaries. Obituaries rarely say things like "'She had a fine figure, and a thick head of hair, and wonderfully white teeth.' 'He drove fast cars and dated fast women.' 'He earned hundreds of thousands of dollars in his spare time at home.'"

But our advertisements are filled with promises to give you the very things you wouldn't want listed in your obituary: great looks, great money, great sex, great food, great widescreen TVs. We don't want to miss out on the good life, but we want to be thought of as good people. "Compared to his brother...."

Much of Jesus' teaching addressed these two questions.

In Jesus' day, the word for the "good life" was "blessed." Jesus' statements about who the good life was available to are called the Beatitudes. They became the most famous statements on the good life ever made, and perhaps the most surprising, because he taught that through God the good life is now truly available to anyone regardless of outer circumstances. "Blessed are those that mourn."

On the other hand, Jesus' statement on what prevents someone from becoming a truly good person revolves around a single word that has been called "perhaps the greatest contribution of Christ to human civilization." Jesus has been the harshest critic of religion's ability to distort human goodness. Let's find out how Jesus defined "a good person" by beginning with Jesus the critic.

———•—•——

The movement that Jesus started produced many hypocrites. Given that there are two billion or so Christians in the world, maybe Christianity produced more hypocrites than any other movement in history.

Religious hypocrisy is one of the great barriers to faith for any thoughtful person. Why become a Christian when the church is filled with so many hypocrites and deeply flawed people?

Mark Twain once listened to a greedy, unscrupulous businessman piously drone on about his plan to travel to the Middle East and read the Ten Commandments from the top of Mount Sinai. "I have a better idea," Twain is supposed to have said, "Why don't you stay home in Boston and keep them?"

A book called *unChristian* described a survey that indicated 85 percent of unchurched young adults believe Christians to be hypocritical. Forty-seven percent of young adults *inside* the church say the same thing.

The presence of hypocrites within a movement does not prove that the movement itself is in error.

Hypocrisy is a kind of universal spiritual heart disease. At a recent annual meeting of the American Heart Association in Atlanta, 300,000 doctors and researchers came together to discuss the importance of low-fat diets in keeping our hearts healthy. But during mealtimes, they consumed fat-filled fast food, such as bacon cheeseburgers and chili fries, at the same artery-clogging high rate as people from any other conventions would. One cardiologist was asked, "Aren't you concerned that your bad eating habits will be a bad example?" He replied, "Not me. I took my name tag off."

Of course the presence of hypocrites within a movement does not prove that the movement itself is in error. Every belief system will attract people who do not live up to it. A friend of mine used to teach in a department of a highly regarded university, which shall remain nameless. All the members of this particular department would have self-identified as Marxists. They were committed to opposing capitalist materialism and conspicuous consumption. But one time they went on a department junket, and they ended up renting a big yacht with an open bar and all kinds of high-end luxury pleasures that they were supposed to be against.

They ended up calling themselves Neiman Marxists. Wonderful phrase.

Our modern ideas about hypocrisy come from a stinging critique of religious hypocrites. Scholar Eva Kittay noted that the word *hypocrite* comes from a Greek word commonly associated with the theater. *Hypocrites* were actors on a stage. Actors would commonly wear a mask to show which character they were playing, so that the same actor might play a king in act 1 and a slave in act 2. By extension, the word came to refer to people who assume a pose or play a role. In classical Greek, the word *hypocrite* did not have the sting that it came to have for us.

In the first century, one of the great theaters of the day was built in a town called Sepphoris, less than an hour's walk from Nazareth. There is a good chance that Joseph and his young apprentice son, Jesus, would have found work helping to construct the building projects in Sepphoris. Jesus from boyhood would be familiar with the stage and the *hypokritai*, these actors.

It was Jesus who critiqued religious hypocrisy in a way that shaped history. When Jesus spoke of religious pretense, he used this term for role-playing. Kittay said that it is the New Testament usage that most shapes our thinking about hypocrisy because of the unique emphasis on the condition of the inner person as opposed to mere outer behavior. "The concept of hypocrisy is doubtless shaped by the moral tone it received with the emergence of Christianity, where attention to what is hidden from view (often from one's own view) is paramount."

There is a *public* me visible to everybody in my world. I spend much time managing the image of the public me. Then there is a *private* me, not visible to the world. In fact, I may not know the depths of the private me, because this has to do with my heart; and the heart, Jesus said, is known fully only to God. This is what matters the most. The condition of the heart is the primary emphasis of Jesus' teaching about human goodness.

The good person is the person whose heart—whose inner being—is bathed and pervaded by divine love. Therefore the good person is not simply one who does good things; it is someone who genuinely *wants* to do good things.

It is concern for the heart, for that which is invisible and knowable to God alone, that made the ugliness of hypocrisy, posing, acting in the public realm, so vivid.

Jesus' teaching about the condition of the heart was so compelling that it entered into the moral vocabulary of the human race. The word *hypocrite* is used seventeen times in the New Testament. Every time it is used, it is used by Jesus. I know of few other words that are so singularly his.

> *God, Jesus said, will not tolerate hypocrisy. This teaching launched a revolution in the ancient world.*

"It is clear from the literary records that it was Jesus alone who brought this term *hypocrisy* and the corresponding character into the moral record of the Western world."

It is ironic that even in the richly merited criticism the church receives for producing hypocrites, we pay tribute to the thinker whose teaching gave us the picture of hypocrisy that shapes our moral understanding two thousand years later.

Contrasts between hypocrisy and genuine goodness are laced through much of Jesus' teaching. But one entire talk, placed by Matthew a few days before Jesus' death, is devoted to this single topic. If you are ever bothered by religious hypocrites, if you've ever wanted to post a scathing blog about how they turn your stomach, you'll have to get in line behind Jesus, because I do not know of any address by any enemy of religion that is more stinging in its rebuke.

Jesus began, "Woe to you...." "Woe" didn't just mean trouble was coming; it meant trouble was coming in the form of divine judgment. God, Jesus said, will not tolerate hypocrisy.

This teaching launched a revolution in the ancient world. The human race has *always* been concerned with what makes someone a good person. Christianity has no corner on the market there, and people imply as much only through ignorance or arrogance.

—•·—

Societies like Sumer, Egypt, and Greece all had moral codes. However, their morality was not rooted in religion. The gods wanted to be acknowledged and appeased, but they did not design the ethical framework for human life. "Greek gods do not give laws." They could not, for they themselves were some of the biggest violaters. The gods had the same set of appetites and flaws as their human counterparts. Historian Mary Lefkowitz wrote, "The life of the gods is a highly idealized form of what human life would be if mortals were deathless, ageless, and strong." The gods of Homer behave alarmingly like supersized versions of Homer Simpson. Robin Lane Fox wrote,

> From Britain to Syria, pagan cults aimed to honour the gods and avert the misfortunes which might result from the gods' own anger at their neglect. Like an electric current, the power of the gods had great potential for helping and harming; unlike electricity, it was unpredictable and mortals could do no more than attempt to channel its force in advance.

Jesus would make available to the world the great teaching of Israel: ethical monotheism. There is one God, and he is the source and judge of all that is good.

This idea of a God who gives moral commands and judges the earth would eventually become so widespread that in our culture—whether we believe or not—this is the being we think of when we hear the word *God*. But it has not always been so. It is an idea, nurtured through Israel, that entered broader world consciousness mostly through the movement of Jesus.

Jesus addressed much of his teaching about the true nature of goodness to scholars known as Pharisees. In our day the word *Pharisee* has become a caricature. We often think ourselves superior to them. In reality they were the most admired spiritual leaders of their day.

In other words, Jesus was talking about a condition that is a hair's breadth away for anybody who takes faith in God seriously. Jesus knew this condition would infiltrate any movement of faith, including his. Thomas Cahill wrote that "any Christian who imagines himself morally superior has only to glance at the subsequent history of Christian persecution of Jews to realize that Christians have been far more successful at rejecting Jesus than any Jew has ever been."

> "Woe to you, teachers of the law and Pharisees, you hypocrites! You shut the kingdom of heaven in people's faces. You yourselves do not enter, nor will you let those enter who are trying to.
>
> "Woe to you, teachers of the law and Pharisees, you hypocrites! You travel over land and sea to win a single convert, and when you have succeeded, you make them twice as much a child of hell as you are....
>
> "Woe to you, blind guides!...
>
> "Woe to you, teachers of the law and Pharisees, you hypocrites! You give a tenth of your spices.... But you have neglected the more important matters of the law — justice, mercy and faithfulness....
>
> "Woe to you , teachers of the law and Pharisees, you hypocrites! You clean the outside of the cup and dish, but inside they are full of greed and self-indulgence....
>
> "Woe to you, teachers of the law and Pharisees, you hypocrites! You are like whitewashed tombs....
>
> "Woe to you, teachers of the law and Pharisees, you hypocrites....
>
> "You snakes! You brood of vipers! How will you escape being condemned to hell?"

I am struck, as someone who regularly preaches to people of faith, by the courage of this man. I cannot imagine the tension. No wonder he made enemies.

I am struck that he used the strongest warnings of judgment and hell, not as warnings aimed at people *outside* his community of faith, but at the people *inside*.

He used images and arguments common in his day to communicate his understanding of human nature and human hearts. Take the unclean cup. Jesus was not talking about general dishwashing principles. Ritual cleanliness was an important part of religion. The Mishnah (teachings about how to keep the law) went to some lengths to teach about this, starting with, "All utensils have an inside and outside." The disciples of Shammai and the disciples of Hillel actually debated the correct order for cleaning the outside and the inside.

Jesus was using a well-known ritual to point to its deeper meaning: *All persons have an an inside and an outside. And it is the inside of persons that most concerns God.*

"It was in fact a great revolution in human history when the Jewish and Christian God revealed Himself as one who sees directly into consciences, and is not misled merely by external acts."

> *The messed-up inside of the cup is simply fallenness; it's the washed-up outside that marks hypocrisy.*

According to Jesus, hypocrisy is not just the failure to live up to what we aspire to. Everybody does that. The core of hypocrisy is deception — mean-spirited and selfish, although sometimes even unconscious, deception.

The messed-up inside of the cup is simply fallenness; it's the washed-up outside that marks hypocrisy. Why would someone whitewash a tomb? To make people think there's life in it, not death. It's not just that religious people neglect justice and mercy and faithfulness. On top of that, they give a tithe of their spices, this tiny area of their financial lives, to convince people of how faithful they are.

I deceive you to get you to think I'm better than I am. I hide my secret dislike for you behind a polite smile. I pretend to help you when I'm hoping you fail. I portray myself as loving when inside I'm full of judgment or selfishness. I may even convince myself I'm devout or loving or kind. I can be hypocritical without knowing it. Just as we have yet to discover the outer limits of the universe, so we have yet to discover the outer limits of the human capacity for self-deception. Case in point: "Eighty-five percent of medical students think it is improper for politicians to accept gifts from lobbyists. Only 46 percent think it's improper for physicians to accept gifts from drug companies."

———◦——

Because of Jesus' emphasis on the heart, goodness does not begin with right behavior. It begins with openness to the truth about the mess in my inner being. "If you hold to my teaching, you are really my disciples. Then you will know the truth, and the truth will set you free."

The truth will set you free. But first it will make you miserable.

Let's try a thought experiment. Imagine picking your car up from a tune-up. The technician says: "This car is in great shape. Clearly you have an automotive genius to take great care of your car." Later that day, your brakes don't work. You find out you were out of brake fluid. You could have died.

You go back to the shop and ask, "Why didn't you tell me?"

"Well, I didn't want you to feel bad. Plus, to be honest, I was afraid you might get upset with me. I want this to be a safe place where you feel loved and accepted." You'd be furious! You'd say, "I didn't come here for a little fantasy-based ego boost! When it comes to my car, I want the truth."

You go in for a checkup. The doctor says to you, "You are a magnificent physical specimen. You have the body of an Olympian. You are to be congratulated." Later that day while climbing the stairs, your heart gives out. You find out later your arteries were so clogged, you were one jelly doughnut away from the grim reaper.

You go back to the doctor and say, "Why didn't you tell me?"

"Well, I knew your body is in worse shape than the Pillsbury doughboy, but if I tell people stuff like that, they get kind of offended. It's kind of bad for business. They don't come back. I want this to be a safe place where you feel loved and accepted." You'd be furious! You'd say to the doctor, "When it comes to my body, I want the truth!"

In the ancient world, truth-telling was the task of philosophers. Temples existed to appease the gods. Jesus was bringing the power of truth-telling to the realm of religion.

I was talking to two people in a local coin-op laundry. It was clear that neither of them had very much money. They were also both very enthusiastic members of different churches in the area. So I told them I was a pastor. That was a status enhancer in the Laundromat. It's usually not a status enhancer, but it was there. They asked me, "Where do you work?" I told them.

The immediate response was, "There are a lot of rich people who go to that church." That was kind of a conversation stopper.

They didn't want me to feel bad, so one of them said, "I hear they do a lot of good things there, though." It was the "though" that got me. I realized how easily I find identity in "ministering to successful people." When I look through the eyes of somebody who lives in poverty, suddenly my perspective becomes really different. The very affluence I am tempted to be secretly proud of becomes embarrassing in the presence of need. I don't look through that perspective very often, because the heart is deceitful above all things.

> *In Jesus' world, wrongdoing is not so much the violation of a moral principle as it is hurt and disappointment to him.*

In Greece, the great truth-tellers who confronted human beings with their ethical shortcomings were orators like Demosthenes or philosophers like Socrates. In Israel, the diagnosis would come through Jesus, and it would change the way wrongdoing was perceived.

In Jesus' world, human wrongdoing is not so much the violation of a moral principle as it is hurt and disappointment to a Friend, who is also our Creator. This gives sin a haunting weight beyond the human capacity to fix it. "Foreign to Plato was the cry of Saint Paul, 'For what I do is not the good I want to do; no the evil I do not want to do — this I keep on doing.'"

This led to another approach to healing: that because of our creatureliness and fallenness and self-deception, we cannot heal ourselves. C. S. Lewis wrote that most of us admit that some "morality" or "decent behavior" has a claim on our life, but we hope to cling to our natural life with whatever is left over, which means we live a life of either pretense or misery.

> In the end, you will either give up trying to be good, or else become one of those people who, as they say, "live for others" but always in a discontented, grumbling way — always wondering why the others do not notice it more and always making a martyr of yourself. And once you have become that you will be a far greater pest to anyone who has to live with you than you would have been if you had remained frankly selfish.

The Christian way is different: harder and easier. Christ says, "Give Me All. I don't want so much of your time and so much of your money and so much of your work: I want You. I have not come to torment your natural self, but to kill it. No half-measures are any good. I don't want to cut off a branch here and a branch there, I want to have the whole tree down.... Hand over the whole natural self, all the desires which you think innocent as well as the ones you think wicked — the whole outfit. I will give you a new self instead. In fact, I will give you Myself: My own will shall become yours."

It turns out that the good life is only available to the good person.

————•◆•————

By the fourth century, as Christianity became the state religion of Rome, people began to find it easier to be nominal Christians than nominal pagans. So some followers of Jesus began to make their way into the desert to find a way of life where self-examination and transparent confession were once again practiced. This became codified in guidelines like the Rule of Benedict, which have been used for centuries.

Other such expressions popped up. In the early twentieth century, a movement called the Oxford Group arose to recapture the power of such practices as honest self-examination and transparent confession. An American businessman by the name of Rowland Hazard who was suffering from alcoholism sought treatment from the Swiss psychiatrist Carl Jung. Jung (whose father was a minister) told Hazard that his case was nearly hopeless (as with other alcoholics) and that his only hope might be a spiritual conversion with a religious group. Hazard eventually found his way to an Oxford group, and there found the power to live a sober life. That brought a chain of connections that eventually led him to William G. Wilson (better known as "Bill W."), who partly under Hazard's influence became co-founder of Alcoholics Anonymous, which expressed the Oxford Group principles in a somewhat secularized form through the Twelve Steps.

This is not to say that recovery programs would not have existed apart from Jesus, but that, as a matter of fact, the Twelve Steps flowed out of the stream that Jesus initiated nineteen hundred years earlier.

Around that same time, a wonderful story was written about how entering into a new pattern of life and relationships can bring about transformation. It was written by Max Beerbohm, who called it "The Happy Hypocrite: A Fairy Tale for Tired Gentlemen."

George Lord had led a wasted life: greed, gambling, superficial relationships, broken promises to women, too much alcohol. He is having a lavish meal with his lover when he sees a young, innocent woman and promptly falls in love. He desperately wants to marry her, but she has vowed only to marry a man with the face of a saint. Not long after, he passes by a mask shop and has the owner create a lifelike wax mask that creates precisely the image he is hoping for. He returns to the woman who has won his heart; he proposes and she accepts.

That moment marks the beginning of a moral conversion. He signs the wedding certificate George Heaven. He donates much of his money to the poor. He repays everyone he has cheated. He is humble before people whom he had never noticed before. He enters into the way of life of a saint.

Sometime later his old lover sees him and comes to unmask him before his wife. A struggle ensues, his mask is tossed to the ground, and his old lover laughs in triumph. He must turn and face his wife.

But when he does, he is shocked by her question: "Why did you have a mask created that looks precisely like your own countenance?" While he had entered into the way of a saint, an unknown unseen power had been at work.

He had grown into his face.

It is ironic to me that perhaps no religion has produced more hypocrites than Christianity. It is also painful to me—there is so much hypocrisy in me. It is both convicting and comforting that no one has ever diagnosed and denounced hypocrisy with more power—no one has ever even offered hypocrites themselves more hope—than Christianity's founder.

CHAPTER 10

Why It's a Small World after All

Holden Caufield, the teenage narrator of *Catcher in the Rye*, wrote about his attraction to Jesus but his ambivalence about his followers:

> I'm kind of an atheist. I like Jesus and all, but I don't care too much for the other stuff in the Bible. Take the Disciples, for instance. They annoy the hell out of me, if you want to know the truth. They were all right after Jesus was dead and all, but while He was alive, they were about as much use to Him as a hole in the head. All they did was keep letting Him down. I like almost anybody in the Bible better than the Disciples.

Holden used to get into arguments about the disciples with a Bible-quoting classmate named Arthur:

> He kept telling me that if I didn't like the Disciples, then I didn't like Jesus and all. He said that because Jesus *picked* the Disciples, you were supposed to like them. I said I knew He picked them, but that He picked them at *random*. . . .
>
> I'd bet a thousand bucks that Jesus never sent old Judas to Hell. . . . I think any one of the Disciples would've sent him to Hell and all —and fast, too—but I'll bet anything Jesus didn't do it.

Jesus picked some people at random, and they were about as much use to him as a hole in the head. The Bible's word for this is *election*. The annoying bride of Christ.

—•—

One day early in his ministry (Mark placed this account a few verses into his first chapter), Jesus saw Simon and Andrew fishing and invited them to be his disciples. "At once" they followed him. A little farther along he saw two more men, James and John. "Without delay" he called them, and they responded as well.

> *It was not unusual for rabbis to have disciples. A man couldn't really be a rabbi without them.*

It was not unusual for rabbis to have disciples. A man couldn't really be a rabbi without them. It's like the old definition of leadership: "He that leadeth when no one followeth only taketh a walk."

What *was* unusual is that Jesus recruited these men. It was customary for disciples to initiate the application process. For the rabbi to make the first move smacked a little of desperation. Harvard does not troll for students at a community college.

Jesus may have done this recruiting to reflect an idea deeply embedded in Jewish life — that calling begins with God. Jesus chose twelve disciples just as God chose the twelve tribes of Israel. This does not mean, as people often think, that God loves Israel *more* than he loves other peoples, or that he wants Israel to have an inside track to heaven. He chooses Israel *for* the world, not *instead* of it, when the Scriptures declare of Israel, "All peoples on earth will be blessed through you." The "randomness" of election is something Israel is reminded of to help them remember not to grow exclusive or arrogant. He chose them "at random."

God could have chosen anybody.

Jesus' band of disciples stayed together for three years. They traveled and learned and prayed together. They saw Jesus weep and grow tired. But when it came to following him, they got it wrong about as often as they get it right. Often you get the sense that Jesus could have ministered a lot easier on his own.

Scott Peck wrote that the Jesus of the Gospels — not the child-patting, sweet-smiling, calm-strolling figure in most people's minds — is perhaps the best-kept secret of Christianity: "I was absolutely thunderstruck by the extraordinary reality of the man I found in the Gospels. I discovered a man who was almost continually frustrated. His frustration leaps out of virtually every page: 'What do I have to say to you? How many times do I have to say it? What do I have to do to get through to you?'"

After Jesus' death, the overwhelming odds were that this little group would disband. After he was executed, their hopes were dashed, and to try to carry on the movement would put their own lives in greater danger. As a fact of history, however, they did carry on. And so much hinges on that one fact that we'll save it for a later chapter.

But it was not because they were a group of extraordinary individuals. Early on two of them were teaching in the temple area. They were called in for examination by the Sanhedrin. Two fishermen being questioned by the intellectual elite would be like two parking lot attendants getting quizzed on quantum mechanics by the faculty at MIT.

But it was actually the MIT faculty that got flummoxed. They observed that these two fisherman were "unschooled, ordinary men," and they "took note that these men had been with Jesus."

This little group of people who followed Jesus formed a kind of alternative community. They rearranged their way of life. They met together daily. They learned from the teachings of Jesus passed down to his disciples. They prayed, they served, they "ate together with glad and sincere hearts." They gave whatever possessions they had to help each other. And as for outsiders, in the memorable translation of Eugene Peterson, "People in general liked what they saw."

The disciples came to understand themselves to have a mission or a calling. (Our notion of someone having a "calling" is not a secular idea; it comes from the story of Jesus and the notion that people are "called" by one greater than themselves.) Their task was to form a community that reflected the presence and power of the God they learned about from Jesus, extend the love of this community to everyone, and invite anybody who was interested to join them.

When persecution came and they were scattered, they took this as a summons to spread the word.

— •❖• —

Rome, and ancient peoples in general, did not know what to make of this movement. There simply had been nothing like this before. Try to empathize with an ancient member of the empire who sought to understand a group for which there was no category.

In the ancient world, there were nations, families, ethnic groups, guilds, tribal religions, philosophical schools. The church was none of these. Paul says this about the church: "Here there is no Gentile or Jew, circumcised or uncircumcised, barbarian, Scythian, slave or free, but Christ is all, and is in all. Therefore, as God's chosen people, holy and dearly loved, clothe yourselves with compassion, kindness, humility, gentleness and patience."

Christianity was not regarded by Rome as a religion, because by definition religions were associated with cities and tribes. If you moved to a new city, you could bring your gods with you, but you would also embrace the gods of the new city. Religion was social and political: "One did not speak of 'believing in gods' but in 'having gods.' The idea of 'conversion'—that is, a conscious and individual decision to embrace a certain creed or way of life—was wholly foreign to the ancients."

The idea of conversion itself would come to the world through Jesus.

> Christians were actually called atheists by Romans because of their neglect of the Roman gods.

To that world, the movement of these followers of Jesus was like Churchill's description of Russia: "a riddle wrapped in a mystery inside an enigma." Christians were actually called atheists by Romans because of their neglect of the gods.

Christians spoke of one another as "brother" and "sister," and this too was strange to the ancient world. Because of this language, Christians were suspected of incest. Because of their taking Communion, they were charged with cannibalism. These charges came to a Roman official known to history as Pliny the Younger. He was so perplexed by this movement that he tortured two deaconesses for information and then had them executed for their "inflexible obstinacy."

The Romans actually tended to understand the church to be a burial association. The poor in the Roman Empire would sometimes form associations and pay a small amount to make sure they would have a funeral feast and a decent burial. Because members of the church made sure that even the poorest among them were buried when they died, they were initially thought to be another such association.

But no burial association ever spread like this one.

Ever been on a ride called "It's a Small World after All"? That song will drive you insane after you've been on the ride long enough. Where did the idea come from of the world gathered together—people of every gender, every nationality, every status—like a family? Where before Jesus was there a movement that actively sought to include every single human being, regardless of nationality, ethnicity, status, income, gender, moral background, or education, to be loved and transformed?

Not only had there never been a community like this before, but there simply had never been the *idea* of a community like this before. It was Jesus' idea. And it was happening.

> While pagan priests and magistrates competed in their "love of honor," Christians termed it "vainglory.".... To the poor, the widows and the orphans, Christians gave alms.... Pagans had never seen any spiritual merit in the status of the poor.... Whereas pagan trade societies and most of their religious groups segregated the sexes among their membership, Christians included men and women alike. In the Greek world, slaves were generally excluded from these pagan groups: Christians even admitted slaves of pagan masters.

> Tertullian said, "It is our care of the helpless, our practice of loving-kindness that brands us in the eyes of many of our opponents. 'Only look,' they say, 'look how they love one another.'"

———◆———

For a long time, the church's biggest problem was its suffering. Then, suddenly, its biggest problem was its success.

By the end of the fourth century, Christianity was the law of the land. When Christianity became accepted in Rome, it experienced phenomenal growth, which ironically changed its character. Persecution ceased, wealth flowed into the churches, patronage created a stampede into the priesthood, and conversions became motivated by a desire to gain a favor or a job or a promotion. Now people who worshiped the old pagan gods began to suffer; the church moved from being the persecuted to the persecutor. As Jaroslav Pelikan said, it became "easier to be a nominal Christian than a nominal pagan."

But there were some within the church who hungered for something deeper than a nominal Christianity. And a new, unexpected movement sprang up.

A young Christian named Anthony heard the story of Jesus telling the rich young ruler to sell all he owned and follow him. So Anthony abandoned everything and moved to the Egyptian desert. Although there had been monks and hermits before, Anthony was the first to "join the geography of the land with the struggle of his soul." He lived a remarkably long life and was finally martyred by Rome when he was over a hundred years old (wasn't it a little late by then?). His influence was staggering; Christians by the hundreds left wealth and comfort behind to seek to follow the way of Jesus. One desert community sprang up in Egypt that was reported to contain twenty thousand women. A saying emerged, "There are as many monks in the desert as there are laymen in the rest of the world," a harbinger of Yogi Berra's restaurant description: "It's so crowded nobody goes there anymore."

Through these monastic communities, people again began to seek the way of Jesus above all. People experimented with placing their time and their work and their prayer and their possessions under the larger goal of unity with God that eventually led to the "rules"—we would speak of them as a "way of life"—of Augustine and Benedict.

The desert people had their own set of problems. They often encouraged a dual-track spirituality that shut out ordinary people from spiritual depth. The desire to be a spiritual "athlete" is never far from self-righteousness. Spiritual disciplines became untethered from wisdom or purpose. Simeon Stylites is said to have lived thirty years bound by a rope to a column thirty feet high. His flesh putrefied around the rope and teemed with worms. When the worms fell out, he would put them back and say, "Eat what God has given you."

But at their best, the desert people became "alternative communities for the common good." These groups that became known as Dominicans and Franciscans and Benedictines and Jesuits were filled with people whose energetic pursuit of a holy life affected the political and educational development of the Western world and created communities that have championed causes for the poor and disenfranchised.

———•◦•———

The sense of mission would send first Patrick to Ireland and eventually thousands around the world, until by the year 1000, Christian communities ranged from Greenland to China. "The tremendous achievement of winning the Teutonic and Slavic people to Christianity and then to civilization was brought about by the continual self-sacrifice and heroic labors of hundreds of monks in all parts of Europe." In these and other ways, a small group of followers who attempted to renounce the world ended up reshaping it.

In the thirteenth century, the son of a noble family, who aspired to be a knight, received instead what he understood to be a calling: "Go and repair my church, which is in ruins." Francis of Assisi left behind money and security, and began to attract followers—three, then twelve, then three thousand within a few years. He combined simplicity with great joy; his *Canticle of Brother Sun* was said to be the first significant work in Italian vernacular. Many hymns praising God for creation ("All Things Bright and Beautiful") are reworkings of his poem. G. K. Chesterton said it was as if Europe had to pass through centuries of being purged of nature worship so that it could return to nature and worship God.

In various ways, a small group of followers who attempted to renounce the world ended up reshaping it.

George Fox was a spiritually frustrated cobbler in seventeenth-century England who wandered from one religion to another until, he said, "I heard a voice which said, 'There is one, even Jesus Christ, that can speak to thy condition,' and when I heard it my heart did leap for joy." George Fox went on to teach that all people had direct access to God through the Inner Light—the Spirit of Jesus. The doctrine of the Inner Light, said historian Dorothy Bass, "in the seventeenth century … was a revolutionary idea that upended the traditional order of society." This would lead to new opportunities for women to lead in the church and to a deep commitment to peace making. Quakers in the colonies would bring the earliest protests against the racist form of slavery present there.

Imagine a world with no church. No Notre Dame. No Saint Paul's.

No storefront church in Watts. No house churches in China. Then all the people: No Peter. No Paul. No Timothy. No Augustine. No Aquinas. No Francis of Assisi. No Mother Teresa. No Martin Luther or Martin Luther King Jr. No Dietrich Bonhoeffer. No Joan of Arc. No John Milton, John Wycliffe, John Wesley, John Calvin, John the Baptist, John the apostle, Pope John XXIII, Johnny Cash.

—·•·—

And yet, as Holden Caulfield wrote, Jesus' followers are often about as much use to him as a hole in the head.

A kind of parable about this comes from one of my favorite scholars/ writers, who wrote *The Message* paraphrase of the Bible. Eugene Peterson grew up in a very devout Pentecostal Christian home, but when he started first grade, he felt the tension of life with non-Christians. A second-grade bully named Garrison Johns picked Eugene out to be his victim. Peterson wrote:

> I had been prepared for the wider world of neighborhood and school by memorizing, "Bless those who persecute you," and "turn the other cheek." I don't know how Garrison Johns knew that about me —some sixth sense bullies have, I suppose. Most afternoons after school, he would catch me and beat me up. He also found out I was a Christian and taunted me with "Jesus-sissy."
>
> I arrived home most days bruised and humiliated. My mother told me this had always been the way of Christians in the world and that I had better get used to it. She also said I was supposed to pray for him. One day I was with seven or eight friends when Garrison caught up with us in the afternoon and started jabbing me. That's when it happened. Something snapped. For a moment, the Bible verses disappeared from my consciousness, and I grabbed Garrison. To my surprise and his, I was stronger than he was. I wrestled him to the ground, sat on his chest, pinned his arms to the ground with my knees, and he was helpless at my mercy. It was too good to be true. I hit him in the face with my fists. It felt good, and I hit him again. Blood spurted from his nose, a lovely crimson in the snow.
>
> I said to Garrison, "Say uncle." He wouldn't say it. I hit him again. More blood. Then my Christian training reasserted itself. I

said, "Say, 'I believe in Jesus Christ as my Lord and Savior.'" He wouldn't say it. I hit him again. More blood. I tried again. "Say, 'I believe in Jesus Christ as my Lord and Savior,'" and he said it.

Garrison Johns was my first Christian convert.

And this is the man who wrote *The Message*.

"They were about as much use to Jesus as a hole in the head."

John Somerville lists some of the most visible sins of the church: the Crusades, the Inquisition, the religious wars of 1550 to 1650, the persecution of witches, slavery, racism, oppression of women, anti-Semitism, and opposition to science.

Christians will point out that all human beings—inside the church or out—are deeply scarred by sin. It even takes a certain humility to be able to recognize sin. A friend of mine from a deeply Reformed tradition likes to say, "No one who recognizes the total depravity of human beings can be all bad."

> *"No one who recognizes the total depravity of human beings can be all bad."*

G. K. Chesterton wrote, "The Church is justified, not because her children do not sin, but because they do." Maybe he's right. But that's a lot of justification. To anyone outside the faith who says the church looks like a mess, I can only say, "You should see it from the inside."

———•·•———

And yet ...

Somehow Jesus keeps shining through.

Jesus started small. Often his followers are at their best doing small things. One man I know got an idea to start a ministry where tech-savvy guru volunteers (also known as teenagers) would take video-chat equipment in vans to assisted-living facilities so elderly residents could see and talk to their grandchildren and family members or friends who might live a continent away. He calls it "Squeals on Wheels."

Sometimes people go around the world. I had dinner with a missionary-anthropologist named Dan Shaw. He knew he wanted to be an anthropologist since he was ten years old. He devoted many years of his life to translating Scriptures for a people group in Papua New Guinea.

He faced a difficulty: they believed in the supernatural and saw spirits and gods in many places, but they had no word for a Big God who was ruler and creator over all.

Dan got to know them and found over the years that in extended families there was a figure called *hi-yo*, a father figure who would arbitrate disputes and make sure everyone was cared for and decide what was fair. Dan began his translation of Genesis: "Back before the time of the ancestors, hi-yo created the heavens and the earth."

People said, "Wow. We had no idea. He is *hi-yo* over everything."

Dan asked, "What if he's *hi-yo* for everyone? Not just for you. Also for your enemies. For the cannibals across the river."

"Oh no. We'd have to make peace with them."

And peace happened.

One day, however it happened, Jesus invited Peter and Andrew and James and John to follow him. What would our world be like if he had not done that?

At the end of their time together, they had not caused much of a stir. If you could have been there on the day after he died, if you could have seen the Roman Empire with its *Pax Romana* and its 250,000 miles of roads and its extension from Asia to Africa to Europe and its history of dominance and its social status that was envied throughout the Mediterranean.... And then if you could have seen a few dozen failed, frightened, demoralized, defeated, confused former followers of an executed carpenter...

If someone had asked you to place a bet on which group would still be around in two thousand years, all the smart money would have been placed on the Roman Empire. Which is as extinct as the dodo bird.

Who was this man?

CHAPTER 11

The Truly Old-Fashioned Marriage

The words *Jesus* and *sex* both tend to evoke strong emotions one way or another.

In our day, people often think the idea of reserving sexual intimacy for a husband and wife in a marriage is old-fashioned. Actually, the reality is precisely the opposite. Sexual activity ranging far outside a marriage covenant is a much older social arrangement. Seeking to reserve sexual intimacy for marriage is, historically, the new kid on the block.

In the ancient world outside of Israel, sex was not regarded as an activity restricted to marriage for moral reasons. It had little to do with religion, although some fertility cults practiced temple prostitution because they believed human fertility made nature itself fertile. Lack of self-control was disdained by some philosophers. But for the most part, the sexual motto of the ancient world was *carpe diem*.

At least if you were a man.

Generally speaking, Roman laws and social norms were designed to protect the sexual adventures of married men. A first-century writer now known as Pseudo-Demosthenes wrote about the truly old-fashioned marriage: "We have mistresses for our enjoyment, concubines to serve our needs, and wives to bear legitimate children."

Larry Yarbrough noted that since most literary evidence comes from propertied, elite males, it's interesting to speculate what Mrs. Pseudo-Demosthenes might have thought of that statement.

To modern ears, "sexual double standard" sounds obviously unfair. To the ancients it did not. A married woman who had sex outside her marriage was guilty of adultery. A married man was not—unless he had sex with the wife of another man. And in that case, the violation was against the other husband; it was a property crime. Moreover, a man was outlawed for condoning his wife's adultery.

In the ancient world, sexuality was celebrated as a means of procreation and as an appetite to be gratified, much like appetites for food and drink. Greek physicians often diagnosed women with "hysteria," which comes from the Greek word for "uterus," a condition they said was caused by a *wandering* uterus. They said hysteria could be cured by intercourse. The Roman physician Rufus prescribed sex to adolescents as a cure for melancholia, epilepsy, and headaches. One imagines he had a thriving practice.

The ancients were as capable as anyone of love, attachment, sexual desire, self-control, and jealousy. Domestic tranquility was admired and advertised often enough that a husband could write on his wife's tombstone that they had been married for thirty years *s.u.q.*, and know everyone would understand that meant *sine ulla querella* ("without any quarrel"). "But, though passersby would have known what he meant, would they have believed him? Should we?"

To the extent that marriage found meaning in a larger context, it was political and economic. In wealthy families of Egypt and much of the Near East, brothers often married sisters in order to keep property within the family. In Rome the household was considered the foundation of the city, and the city was the foundation of the empire. Early Rome required Romans to be married and raise children because they were needed for the spread of the empire. It was a civic duty, like paying taxes.

> *Early Rome required Romans to be married and raise children.... It was a civic duty, like paying taxes.*

Caesar Augustus outlawed marriage between members of different classes because, as we saw from Cicero, "rank must be preserved." Furthermore, slaves were technically not even allowed to marry. Up to half of the population of the Roman Empire may have been slaves, so marriage was something of an elitist institution.

The gods had little to say about marriage. The rules for a public cult in Pergamum demanded a day's interval after sex with one's wife but two days after sex with someone else's wife. Zeus's sexual history (one writer describes him as "the ultimate player") did not suggest that restraint was an Olympian virtue.

The silence of the gods about sex also led to a very different world of sexuality and children. Particularly in Greek culture, sexual relationships between adult men and younger boys, often between ages twelve and sixteen, were taken for granted. The Roman emperor Commodus is said to have had three hundred young boys available for sex. The Christian writer Tatian said that Romans "consider pederasty to be particularly privileged and try to round up herds of boys like herds of grazing mares."

Slave girls were made available for sexual purposes at the decision of the *paterfamilias*. Freeborn girls were often married by their families as early as possible: A study based on inscriptions indicated that 20 percent of pagan girls were married before the age of thirteen (in the Christian community it was about a third of that). Generally the husband was a decade or so older.

———•———

The teaching of Jesus placed marriage and sexuality in a fundamentally different framework than that of the ancient world outside of Israel. It came from the teachings of Judaism and would pass through Jesus to the broader world.

One day when he was around thirty years old, Jesus and his friends showed up at a wedding. Weddings in Israel typically lasted seven days. Families were known to invite large numbers of people, sometimes entire villages. The rabbis said that God's attendance at Adam and Eve's nuptials demonstrated the importance of weddings; they would even suspend their school so disciples could attend one.

Refusal to come to a wedding was considered an insult. It was customary to have so much food at a wedding that there would be leftovers. Someone who invited a neighbor to attend his wedding without showing proper hospitality was listed among thieves. So running out of wine at a wedding was a serious problem.

We are not told what thoughts went through Jesus' mind when he accepted the wedding invitation at Cana. Jesus was unmarried, which

was highly unusual. Rabbis often marveled at how the first commandment in the Torah was not "Love God," or "Don't worship idols" but
rather "Be fruitful and multiply." Rabbis were expected to model this
themselves—and Jesus was a rabbi.

The Bible says nothing about whether Jesus ever thought marriage
might be for him. It's hard to imagine a rabbi who did not. It does not
tell us about any women he was attracted to, although it does say he was
tempted "in every way" like the rest of humanity, so any picture of Jesus
as serenely floating above hormones and desire would be ruled out.

When the wine ran out, Jesus' mother asked him to intervene.

He replied, "Woman, why do you involve me? My hour has not yet
come."

Philip Yancey noted that if Jesus had acted, it would mean his time
had come, and from that moment his life would have changed. A man
reputed to have miraculous powers would draw crowds of injured and
poor and sick. He would also draw attention from authorities. "A clock
would start ticking that would not stop until Calvary."

Jesus acted. The host relaxed, the feast resumed, the crowd rejoiced.
And a clock started ticking.

Only Jesus understood that a chain of events had been set in motion
that would lead to a confrontation with enemies that would not allow
his survival. A normal life was now forever lost to him.

Is it possible that at a wedding Jesus saw how impossible marriage
could ever be for him?

———•———

On another day, Jesus would lay out his interpretation of the Torah's
instruction about marriage.

Jesus said: "Haven't you read that at the beginning the Creator 'made
them male and female,' and said, 'For this reason a man will leave his
father and mother and be united to his wife, and the two will become
one flesh'? So they are no longer two but one flesh. Therefore what God
has joined together, let no one separate."

Marriage, Jesus was saying, is not at its heart just an economic or
social institution. It is a God-directed covenant that reflects the human

capacity for self-transcendence and community. It is a joining of spirit and flesh. It does not serve the state; it precedes the state.

Jesus connects marriage to creation. In Genesis God is making creation good by separating: he separates the light from the darkness, the dry land from the sea, the heavens from the earth. But now, with the man and the woman, he takes what was separate and *joins* them. And so Jesus says what God has joined let *man* not separate.

To marry is to enter into an act of divine creation: "what God has joined together." It is understood to be a spiritual reality. Sexuality—one flesh—is the most intense and physical expression of it.

In Rome weddings were often unstructured, and of course there were many nonmarital sexual arrangements. In the church, the wedding became formalized around its foundation.

Walter Wangerin wrote, "Marriage begins with a promise." A man and a woman stand in a church or a chapel or a backyard before each other, before witnesses, and before almighty God. They make a vow. They say a promise. They give their word. That's what a marriage is built on.

A promise freely offered, fully embraced, joyfully witnessed, painstakingly kept—that's what makes a marriage. Sometimes people will say: "I don't need a piece of paper." It was never about the paper. In Jesus' day they didn't have paper. It's about the promise: "as long as we both shall live."

> *A promise freely offered, fully embraced, joyfully witnessed, painstakingly kept—that's what makes a marriage.*

A man and woman give their word—in a world of change and instability, there is now one inviolable certainty they can rely on—for better or worse, richer or poorer, in sickness and in health. When you are young and sexy and the air is filled with the scent of Chanel N°5, and when you are old and your teeth are gone and the air is filled with the scent of Bengay—you can count on this promise.

This is my solemn vow.

The reason a wedding vow is such a moving, wonderful, frightening sentence is that it is a lifetime promise. It transcends attraction and utility. It has been placed in the context of a covenant. It is a little echo of what God does when he makes a vow of unending love.

The promise, according to Jesus, is not just to avoid adultery or divorce. It is to pursue oneness on every level: physical, intellectual, and spiritual — a oneness that does not diminish the individuality of the other but makes it flourish.

Jesus' words would move Shakespeare to write of this love:

> So they lov'd, that love in twain
> Had the essence but in one;
> Two distincts, division none:
> Number there in love was slain.

Two distinct people, two sets of desires and appetites, joined together in the unity of loving commitment to one another. There is something transcendent about marriage. Love does what math cannot; two become one yet rejoice that they are two. "Number there in love was slain."

Sex had a new meaning and a new context.

In the ancient world, one's primary loyalty was to parents. But the man and the woman are to leave their parents to create a new primary loyalty — a union, and their union with each other is to be expressed through sexual intimacy, one flesh. In other words, sex is kind of a sacrament. It is an outward sign that points to an inward reality, to a spiritual state.

In sexual intimacy, somehow two are knit together or connected at the soul with the other. Sex has a spiritual meaning as well as a biological function. When two people are engaged in sexual intimacy, their bodies are making a promise whether they intend to or not. It's not just sex.

"Adam and his wife were both naked, and they felt no shame." That was a passage that never got taught when I grew up in church. It points to the goodness of the human body and the freedom of redeemed sexuality — two truths that the church would often struggle with over the centuries.

For the God Jesus presents, unlike the gods of Mount Olympus, does have a point of view on human sexuality. "Adam made love to his wife Eve, and she became pregnant and gave birth to Cain. She said, 'With the help of the LORD I have brought forth a man." Notice that Eve does not mention Adam. I have wondered if that dinged his male ego a little. "Hey, I was there too."

The mention of God is deliberate: God is involved. Sexual intimacy for Eve was a rich phenomenon that involved a connection to her husband, a connection to her son, and a connection to God. Sex, in light of Jesus' teaching, always involves God, because God is the creator of humans. Therefore God is inevitably deeply concerned that sex be expressed, enjoyed, savored, and relished in accordance with his design.

One of the ways we learn how a culture thinks about sexuality is the language it uses to describe the sexual act. "Having sex" connotes the notion that it's a commodity one can possess or control. "Doing it" expresses a casual or animal understanding of sex.

Jesus taught that the main word for sex in the Torah is the Hebrew word *yada*. *Yada* is generally translated "to know, to observe, to study closely, to be a student of." When there's *yada*, there's also a relationship. It's not a sterile, abstract, distant knowing. There's also caring. There's a commitment. *Yada* is personal, experiential knowing.

The word *yada* is used in the book of Hosea where God promises to betroth his people to him forever, "and you shall know (*yada*) the LORD."

G. K. Chesterton once wrote that if incompatibility were all that was needed for divorce, no one would stay married. "I have known many happy marriages, but never a compatible one. The whole aim of marriage is to fight through and survive the instant when incompatibility becomes unquestionable. For a man and a woman, as such, are incompatible."

> *When there's* yada, *there's also a relationship, caring, and a commitment.* Yada *is personal, experiential knowing.*

Jesus' teachings on marriage and adultery have become widely known (even if not followed). But imagine the response in an ancient world where the double standard was codified in Roman law when they heard this teaching: "You have heard that it was said, 'You shall not commit adultery.'"

If you were in Israel, you would have "heard that it was said." If you were a man who lived anywhere else, you would not have "heard that it was said." And you might not be all that thrilled about it. But it gets worse: "But I tell you that anyone who looks at a woman lustfully has already committed adultery with her in his heart."

These words are the beginning of the end of the sexual double standard.

Jesus is *not* saying that to look at someone and experience sexual attraction is wrong. This is one of many places where he is addressing the core issue of what it means to be a good person—which is to have a good heart, not merely right behavior. The good person is not someone who simply avoids adultery. The good person is one who has learned not to relate to women as sexualized objects, who would not commit adultery even if he could get away with it.

Notice that Jesus does not place primary responsibility for men's sexual behavior on women. He does not say: "Design a society where women are kept indoors or covered in burlap so they don't seduce men with their beauty."

Each one will guard their own heart.

—⋅◆⋅—

Writer Naomi Wolf, an author with no religious ax to grind, published an essay several years ago musing on the hurts that the soul absorbs through casual sex with multiple partners and the loss of a sense of faithful love that can endure through life. A pastor friend, Andy Stanley, said he once asked a woman who could not believe Jesus was serious about reserving sex for marriage, "Has sex outside marriage made your life better or just more complicated?" This question has a way of touching a tender place in the soul.

In a broader way, something like this went on in the ancient world. For Greco-Roman culture, the idea of reserving sexual intimacy wasn't quaint and old-fashioned; it was new and revolutionary. As a whole, it never did get established terribly well. And to this day, no one I know doesn't struggle with it.

But the framework that Jesus taught—the idea that marriage is a covenant relationship between and man and a woman, that sex has a spiritual component, that fidelity is a quality to be prized in men as well as women, that children are to be protected rather than exploited sexually—would come to shape our world.

Corinth was a harbor town, well-known in the ancient world for the availability of a wide variety of sexual options. There was a temple in

Corinth devoted to the Greek goddess of love, Aphrodite. One writer says there were a thousand temple prostitutes. A Greek writer named Aristophanes actually coined the term *korinthiazo* as a euphemism for having sex. What happened in Corinth stayed in Corinth.

The apostle Paul wrote to the small church in Corinth: "Flee sexual immorality."

His readers understood his meaning. Sexual intimacy is reserved for married people, period. In the words of theologian Beyonce, "Better put a ring on it."

The epistle to Diognetus notes of Christians that they shared their table but not their bed. In other words, as I once heard Tim Keller say, the ancients were stingy with their money but generous with their bodies; the Christians were stingy with their bodies but generous with their money.

Jesus would have an impact on singleness as well. Jesus himself lived a single life. He taught that both women and men can remain unmarried out of dedication to God, which ran counter to most Jewish and non-Jewish traditions. Singleness was normalized.

———•◆•———

Marriage existed for centuries in the West primarily as a spiritual, not just civil, institution. The oldest wedding vows extant in English are from the Book of Common Prayer. It is this spiritual dimension that gives marriage its greatest solemn beauty:

> We are gathered together here in the sight of God to join together this Man and this Woman in holy Matrimony; which is an honourable estate, instituted of God in Paradise, and into which holy estate these two persons present come now to be joined. Therefore if any man can shew any just cause, why they may not lawfully be joined together, let him now speak, or else hereafter forever hold his peace.
>
> (And also, speaking unto the persons that shall be married, he shall say,)
>
> I require and charge you both, as ye will answer at the dreadful day of judgment when the secrets of all hearts shall be disclosed, that if either of you know any impediment, why ye may not lawfully joined together in Matrimony, that ye confess it. For ye be well

assured, that so many as be coupled together otherwise than God's Word doth allow are not joined together by God; neither is their Matrimony lawful.

In our day, churches continue to be preferred wedding sites — often even among irreligious people — because they reflect the notion that there is something deeply spiritual and not simply economic about marriage. When our daughter Laura got engaged, her fiancé, Zach, organized an elaborate process to reflect the depth of the promise they would make. The moment came when the two of them were alone on the top floor of a tall building overlooking San Francisco.

> It is the spiritual dimension that gives marriage its greatest solemn beauty.

Laura saw a table set up with rose petals and champagne and strawberries, and she thought this was supposed to be a special moment for somebody else, not for her. She thought, *We'd better get out of here*. So she turned to Zach to tell him they had to leave. She didn't know this was *her* moment. When she turned around, Zach was down on one knee, and he was holding up a ring.

He said, "Laura Kathleen Ortberg, will you marry me?"

And she said, "Are you serious?"

So he had to say it again, and then she said, "Yes. Yes, I will marry you."

Nancy and I performed the ceremony, and we were struck again by the spiritual solemnity of the institution. Of course, not every word was somber. I realized that, though I have often seen it in movies, I have never actually said, "If any one knows any reason why this marriage should not take place...." My brother-in-law stood up and pretended to be Laura's parole officer and said he had a number of reasons. The groom's family was surprised.

But even that old "If anyone knows" caveat underscored the role of community in marriage. The social and economic and sexual aspects of the promise were woven together as a spiritual reality. The movement Jesus started gave us the ceremony and the words that move people two thousand years later. The idea of marriage as a promise to pursue oneness and fidelity between two souls largely remains.

————•◦•————

The church has also had a history of wrongness and weirdness when it comes to sexuality. In order to avoid lust, some monks would proudly keep a record of how many years it had been since they had seen a woman (it is impossible to imagine Jesus doing this). Origen mistook Jesus' ironic words about physical mutilation as a means to spiritual goodness and castrated himself. Jesus' whole point was that mutilating the body is *not* the way to goodness because it doesn't change the heart.

Oops.

Augustine described his sexual history much like we would talk about an addiction; he called it an "iron chain" that bound him. He found himself divided; he wanted to follow God but was unable or unwilling to change his sexual behavior. He wanted to but did not want to. He wrote that he used to pray, "Lord, make me chaste, but not yet."

Some of Augustine's writings take a dim view of the body in general. Duane Friesen wrote that sexual passion was, for Augustine, one of the most vivid signs of the fall, because in sexual passion that body was not in full control of reason. Augustine theorized that before the fall, human beings were able to procreate with no passion at all:

> Surely, every member of the body was equally submissive to the mind, and surely, a man and his wife could play their active and passive roles in the drama of conception without the lecherous promptings of lust, with perfect serenity of soul.

If the double standard Rome applied to men and women was weakened, it was sometimes replaced by a double standard for people who had power and people who lacked it. Henry VIII had little interest in the Reformation until his wife, Catherine of Aragon (who had initially been married to Henry's dead brother), failed to produce an heir, and he had been attracted by Anne Boleyn. He cited retroactive guilt for marrying his elder brother's widow, based on Leviticus 20:21, and asked the pope for a divorce. The pope was reluctant to anger the Holy Roman emperor Charles V, who happened to be Catherine's nephew.

The Church of England was born out of many noble struggles for reform, but this particular event was not one of them. Because Henry

VIII had money and power, he had access to marital options unavailable to most of the rest of Christendom.

Christians have sometimes spoken about "Christian marriage" as a monolithic institution with a detailed playbook. The reality is that what counted as a good Christian marriage in Roman times differed enormously from medieval years, when many Christians considered marriage an inferior option to celibacy.

Martin Luther argued that vows of celibacy went against common sense and that only men over seventy could honestly make them. The advent of Viagra would probably cause even that number to be adjusted upward. Luther once called marriage a "hospital for lust."

Luther's own marriage to former nun Katherine von Bora (he had her kidnapped from a convent in the back of a fish seller's wagon among barrels of herring) shifted European understanding of marriage yet again. Before the Reformation, men and women stood or sat on opposite sides of the congregation. After it they sat together in families. The family was now seen as the primary spiritual community forming the church, a "radical redefinition of the sacred."

> *What counted as a good Christian marriage in Roman times differed enormously from medieval years.*

Writers about the spiritual life have always understood that sins of the spirit are more dangerous than sins of the flesh. But church discipline rarely gets exercised over sins of the spirit. The church often seems tempted to narrow all morality down to sexuality. The college I attended would occasionally expel a faculty member for "moral turpitude." In every case, "moral" meant sex. A long-term joke among the faculty is that they were not allowed to have sex standing up because it might lead to dancing.

Sexual sin all too often has become the primary litmus test for separating the sheep from the goats. Children — particularly girls — have often been raised to be ashamed of their bodies and afraid of their desires. Leaders have often railed on sexual sins as if they are unforgivable, sometimes while secretly using their exalted status for their own hidden sin.

How different are the teachings of Jesus. Over and over it is the most scandalized sinners — including sexual sinners — who are drawn to him.

When Matthew wrote Jesus' genealogy, he included four women—an unusual practice. Two of them were Gentiles. Three of them were tainted by sexual scandal. And a fifth woman he mentioned—Mary—was the object of gossip, since she was pregnant when she got married.

In the book of Hebrews, the eleventh chapter is called the Hall of Faith, and great heroes in the Bible—Noah, Abraham, Moses, Gideon, and David—are all listed there. Then there is this comment, "By faith the prostitute Rahab, because she welcomed the spies, was not killed."

The writer does not mention anybody else's occupation—not David the king, or Samuel the priest, or Abraham the rancher, or Gideon the judge. Why Rahab's?

Grace.

The same Jesus who was a magnet for sexual sinners who had flunked marriage was the same Jesus who redefined what a marriage could be. "Husbands, love your wives, just as Christ loved the church and gave himself up for her." More marriages have been performed, more wedding vows have been made, more nuptial blessings have been asked in his name than any other.

The person who changed marriage in the Western world more than anyone else was himself never married.

CHAPTER 12

Without Parallel
in the Entire History of Art

Some time ago I heard an interview with the woman who runs the largest speakers' bureau in the world. The interviewer asked her, "What is the number one quality that makes someone an effective speaker?" I thought it might be intelligence or eloquence or charisma, but it was none of those.

She said that the primary single quality that makes someone an effective speaker is this: passion. If someone is passionate about a subject —if they believe it matters deeply, if they are genuinely captivated by it —that passion leaks out. Think about a teacher you know who inspired you. She might not have been the smartest or most polished, but she was gripped by the importance of what she taught, and something about that passion was infectious.

To *not* inspire is every speaker's dread. When I first started preaching, I saw someone sound asleep during the first ten minutes of a talk, and I felt my heart sink. I told Nancy on the way home, "Honey, you've just got to get to bed earlier."

We were made to respond to inspiration. Everybody wears an unseen sign that reads: "Inspire me. Remind me that my life matters; call me to be my best self; appeal to whatever in me is most noble and honorable. Don't let me go down the path of least resistance. Challenge me to make my life about something more than the acquisition of money or success."

On the other hand, to lead an uninspired life—to go through the motions, to forget that your children are worth all the effort needed to be an effective parent, to fail to do good work because it's too hard, to live a day as if it doesn't matter—is one of the great tragedies in the world.

Inspiration comes from beyond ourselves. In Hebrew, Greek, Latin, and English, the word *inspire* is connected to the breath that enters us from the outside and makes us alive. Sociologist Peter Berger wrote, "If anything characterizes modernity, it is the loss of the sense of transcendence—of a reality that exceeds and encompasses our everyday affairs." We long for a political leader or reformer with a soaring moral vision. We listen to motivational speakers hoping to be ignited. We crave beauty and art in particular so that we can be transported to a higher plane. When Mickey Hart of the Grateful Dead was asked why the band was so fascinated with multiphonic chanting of Tibetan lamas, he replied, "Because we are both in the transportation business."

We have all heard gifted orators who can inspire for the moment. Their temporary spell is built on skillful rhetoric and manipulation of emotions. Two Greek orators in the fourth century BC supposedly prompted a cry heard among crowds: "When Isocrates speaks, people say, 'How well he speaks!' When Demosthenes speaks, they say, 'Let's march!'"

> *Great causes require inspiration to reform society.... We wait for someone who will call us to march.*

Great causes require inspiration to reform society. Artists require inspiration to create beauty. Individuals require inspiration to overcome lethargy or apathy and come alive.

We wait for someone who will call us to march.

One day Jesus led Peter, James, and John up to a mountain to pray. Many times, in the Bible and elsewhere, mountains are places where people experience God. Mountains are places of vision. A mountain is literally where the physical heavens and earth come closest together.

We are told that while Jesus was praying, his face changed. He became radiant. We often associate inspiration with light. Even in cartoons the universal symbol for an idea is a lightbulb over a character's head. Brides are spoken of as radiant. Researchers have found that when a person is in love, the flow of blood in capillaries near the skin increases; so love literally does cause a person to "glow." When a speaker is wholly captivated by a vision, we will say that he is "on fire."

The three disciples with Jesus on the mountain saw a vision. It was mystical and glorious, a divinely inspired visitation with a transcendent message. Peter said that it was good for them to be there, that they should build three shrines and stay there. The text says he said this because "he did not know what to say." Apparently he did not consider silence an option.

Jesus said no, they would have to leave; there was work to be done. The purpose of that inspiring vision was not temporary ecstasy; it was power for the work. Jesus' transformation on what became called the Mount of Transfiguration was simply the most vivid expression of the vision that was his consistent message: there *is* a transcendent reality. And it is closer than we think. This kind of inspiration infuses what we do with a significance beyond our ability to see.

———•·•———

Jesus inspired.

Jesus inspired a wealthy cheat named Zacchaeus to give away most of his fortune. He inspired a Samaritan woman to become an evangelist, and she inspired so many townspeople that they had Jesus—a Jewish rabbi—stay in their Samaritan town and teach them for two solid days. He inspired Peter to get out of his boat. He inspired a woman named Joanna, whose husband, Cusa, worked for a man named Herod who killed John the Baptist and kept trying to kill Jesus. Joanna used money they made working for Herod to help finance Jesus' ministry. He inspired four friends of a paralytic to punch a hole through a roof to get their friend to him. He inspired a woman who had been bleeding for twelve years to fight through a crowd just to touch the hem of his robe.

The *message* of Jesus that would inspire the world is that there is a transcendent God, and that the character of this God is love. In the ancient world, the spiritual realm was understood to be real but not morally transcendent. Aristotle said, "It would be eccentric to claim to love Zeus." No one wrote songs that said, "Zeus loves me, this I know, for the *Iliad* tells me so." Adherents of Eastern religions generally did not believe in a personal god at all. Whenever someone says, "I believe in a God of love," we hear the echo of the Nazarene.

Novelist Reynolds Price wrote that Jesus says in the clearest voice we have the sentence humanity craves: "the Maker of all things loves and wants me.... In no other book our culture owns can we see a clearer graph of that need." Jesus' friend John would sum it up in a single breath-taking phrase: "God is love."

The very notion of *God*, like the word *mother*, is a loaded term that carries deep emotion with it. Writer Austin Farrer likened the scenario of an orphan considering the possibility that his mother is still alive to the situation of a person considering the possibility that there is a God. "The heart goes out to God, even to a possible God."

To Jesus, this God was not simply possible; he was real. He was not simply strong; he was good.

This vision of a good God transported people into another reality: a universe founded on love. To Augustine, "'to be human is to love.... We are cast into love. We are born and destined to love. It is our nature to love. We can choose what to love; we cannot choose whether to love....' The Stoic God, cosmic Reason, was something to align oneself with; Augustine's God was someone to love."

The ancient world came to love a triad of worth: the good, the true, and the beautiful. These were the sources of lasting inspiration. Jesus inspired the ancient world because he affirmed the goodness of this impulse and located the good, the true, and the beautiful in one person. His vision is no less profound for being concretely accessible to all. God is a Father who feeds sparrows and raises beautiful flowers and numbers the hairs on your head; he is the woman who searches for a lost coin and the shepherd who tracks a lost sheep; he is the father who runs to his wayward son.

> *The greatest question in human existence has always been does God exist, and what is he like?*

The greatest question in human existence has always been does God exist, and what is he like?

In an old story, a teacher asks a little girl what she is drawing, and the child answers, "I'm drawing a picture of God."

"But no one knows what God looks like," says the teacher.

"After I'm done they will," the girl replies.

The ancients often thought of the many gods existing under one supreme God who ruled over all. However, as the Roman Porphyry wrote, "The first God is incorporeal, immovable, and invisible ... neither is vocal language nor internal speech adapted to the highest God." The one supreme God was distant and unknowable.

The message of Jesus is that this God wants to be known. A follower of Jesus named Julian of Norwich wrote, "For it is God's will that we believe that we see him continually, though it seems to us that the sight be only partial; and through this belief he wishes us always to gain more grace, for God wishes to be seen, and he wishes to be sought, and he wishes to be expected, and he wishes to be trusted."

However, it was not simply Jesus' words that moved people; it was the way his message was fleshed out in his life. Historian Paul Johnson wrote:

> Jesus' love of people, as individuals, was in some way his most striking characteristic. He never tired of talking to them and penetrating their secrets. They were drawn to him and only too willing to divulge them. His life was a series of public meetings punctuated by casual encounters which turned into significant events. Jesus not only encouraged these encounters but treasured them. . . . These episodes, though often brief, form the human core of the New Testament and provide a unique satisfaction to the reader. *There is nothing like them in the entire literature of the ancient world, sacred or secular.*

—— ·•· ——

Jesus brought a vision of the extraordinary significance of the ordinary.

When I hear William Wallace scream "Freedom!" to an advancing army, or hear Olympian runner Eric Liddell talk about feeling God's pleasure in him when he runs fast, or read Henry V's Saint Crispen's Day speech ("We few, we happy few, we band of brothers ..."), or even watch the four-year-old kid on YouTube give the Herb Brooks pep talk to the "Miracle on Ice" hockey team ("This is *your* time ...") — I can be deeply moved. But I will not liberate Scotland, run in the Olympics, hold off the French, or out-skate the Russians.

Martin Luther King Jr. would say many centuries later that the man who has found nothing to die for is not fit to live. In Jesus' vision, ordinary people found something to die for.

In the ancient world, life was regarded as cheap enough that death was a kind of blood sport. It is hard for our age to imagine this, but gladiatorial fights to the death were the football league of the empire. People were disappointed if deprived of executions. A Roman nobleman named Symmachus complained that he had purchased twenty-nine Saxon prisoners for use in gladiatorial contests, but they killed themselves before they could be made to fight and die in the arena.

Why did this stop?

Theodoret of Cyrus tells us that the gladiatorial contests were finally ended by the emperor Honorius in 404. The death blow to the contests came when a monk named Telemachus followed the crowd to the arena and, horrified by the bloodshed, tried to put an end to the killing. The crowd was already in a frenzy (think of how angry crowds can get at soccer matches or football games in our day, and imagine mobs watching actual death matches). They turned on the little monk and killed him.

But the death of a single defenseless monk, the sight of his body lying in his blood, sobered the crowd. We are told that they silently left the arena.

Mars might inspire a man to kill in the arena. Jesus inspired men and women to die there.

It is hard to know how accurate the details of this story may be. But what is clear is that these spectacles were appalling to many who followed Jesus in a way that was not shared by their pagan neighbors. And that many gave their lives both inside the arena and out because they were inspired by the life and teachings of one who had lived centuries before. Mars, the Greek god of war, might inspire a man to kill in the arena. Jesus inspired men and women to die there.

According to historian Michael Grant, "the most potent figure, not only in the history of religion, but in world history as a whole, is Jesus Christ, the maker of one of the few revolutions which have lasted. Millions of men and women for century after century have found his life and teaching overwhelmingly significant and moving."

———•◦•———

Jesus' vision, over time, began to grip the imagination of artists. All expressions of religious vision inevitably use art — music, poetry, drama, and dance—because the arts are able to invite our hearts as well as our minds into a deeper reality. Artists, like saints, depend on a visitation from beyond themselves. Art is the language of inspiration, the signal of transcendence. When we delight in beauty, we take a step toward God. Or, as it is expressed in a more earthy way by the troubled character Celie as she is making her way back to God through delight in beauty in *The Color Purple*, "God love everything you love—and a mess of stuff you don't. But more than anything else, God love admiration.... I think it pisses God off if you walk by the color purple in a field and don't notice it."

Because Israel banned images of God and produced no visual art, you might expect the ascendancy of Jesus to mean the diminishing of art. To the contrary.

Yale professor Jaroslav Pelikan noted: "The victory of Jesus Christ over the gods of Greece and Rome in the fourth century did not, as both friend and foe might have expected, bring about the demise of religious art; on the contrary it was responsible over the next fifteen centuries for a massive and magnificent outpouring of creativity that is probably *without parallel in the entire history of art.*"

Within a few decades of Jesus' life, his followers began composing poetry and hymns to try to express this new vision. Icons began as an act of both art and prayer. They were debated for centuries—*iconoclast* means breaker of icons—but John of Damascus argued that "God himself was the first and original image-maker of the universe." In paintings and sculptures and stained glass, Jesus figured so prominently that he remains the most recognizable figure in the world, even though no one knows what he looks like.

In movies Jesus generally speaks with a British accent and has wonderfully symmetrical features, but the second-century Roman writer Celsus actually described Jesus as "short and ugly." There was an early Christian tradition along the same lines, partly based on a passage in Isaiah 53 that describes God's suffering servant as being without "attractiveness," that would draw people to him. It is poignant to reflect on how an unattractive Jesus might have been particularly sensitive to those with physical challenges around him.

Jesus' story inspired artists to probe the nature of both beauty and ugliness. By the fourth century, Augustine was arguing that Jesus must have been "beautiful as a child, beautiful on earth, beautiful in heaven."

Augustine wrote about the use of art and particularly music to inspire the soul. His *Confessions* often move to poetry: "Too late have I loved Thee, Thou Beauty ever ancient, ever new, too late have I come to love Thee."

Augustine himself showed how the Jesus movement changed literature as well as other arts. His *Confessions* was a kind of introspective autobiography that the world had not seen before. In telling the story of his spiritual journey "Augustine was acknowledging for the first time the importance of the self." The Jesus movement revolutionized language. Without Jesus there would be no Dante, whose *Divine Comedy* was the primary shaper of modern Italian, and no Martin Luther, whose German Bible became the primary shaper of the German language. Without Jesus, there would be no King James Bible, which became along with Shakespeare the most important source for the shaping of the English language, and no John of the Cross, "whom many historians and literary critics regard as the finest poet in the Spanish language."

In fact, Pelikan noted that Latin did not achieve the status of a world-class language until Jerome's translation of the Latin Vulgate. "So also the various Reformation translations of the Bible into the vernacular ... became turning points for their languages in turn—a process that has continued, with additional languages, ever since." In other words, the development history of European languages and literacy rests on Jesus more than any other single figure of history.

> *The development history of European languages and literacy rests on Jesus more than any other single figure of history.*

The gospel accounts of Jesus themselves changed literature. Thomas Cahill wrote:

> What makes the gospels—from a literary point of view—works like no others is that they are about a good human being. As every writer knows, such a creature is all but impossible to capture on the page, and there are exceedingly few figures in all literature who are both good and memorable.

Villains always get the best lines. Who can forget a Nero or a Hanni-
bal Lector (or, for that matter, a Judas Iscariot)? And yet the writers
of the Gospels — who left behind no other indications that they ever
attempted the craft of writing outside this single exercise — succeeded
wildly where almost all others failed. Says Cahill, "To a writer's eyes, this
feat is a miracle just a little short of raising the dead."

— ·•· —

There is only one mention of music in Jesus' life: he and his friends sung
a hymn the night before he died. But Pope Gregory insisted music be
used to "lift the soul to God," and Gregorian chants became the rock-
n-roll of the Middle Ages. Modern music notation was invented in the
Middle Ages by monks who wanted to be able to spread music . "Do-re-
mi-fa-so-la-ti-do" were more or less taken, in case you've ever wondered,
as a mnemonic device from a Latin hymn so notes could be learned, so
worship could be enhanced.

Martin Luther said he would "like to see all the arts, especially music,
used in the service of Him who gave and made them." The Lutheran cho-
rale became "one of the Reformation's principle cultural monuments."

Luther in turn deeply influenced composer Johann Sebastian Bach,
who would begin each work by writing, "JJ" — *Jesu, Jusa*, "*Jesus, help me*"
— on his manuscript. (It is a universal prayer for all writers, but often
they wait until they are desperate. I'm praying it right now.) At the end
of a piece, he would write three letters — S.D.G. (*Soli Deo gloria*) — that
meant "To the glory of God" on all his music.

Nathan Soderblom wrote:

The Passion music, which was created within the church and which
experienced a new depth, a new richness, and a new intensity in the
sixteenth century, constitutes in its way the most important addition that has ever been made to the sources of revelation in the Old
and New Testaments. If you ask about a fifth gospel, I do not hesitate
to name the interpretation of salvation history as it reached its acme
in Johann Sebastian Bach.

George Frideric Handel was born the same year as Bach. At his sister's funeral, the sermon topic was "I Know That My Redeemer Liveth,"

which became one of his most famous arias. A classmate from my college days, Susan Bergman, was herself a gifted writer and artist whose life was claimed far too young by a brain tumor. In my last conversation with Susan and her husband, Jud, not long before her funeral service, her speech was labored and halting; the final full sentence I ever heard her say was, "I know that my Redeemer liveth."

Imagine a world with no "Hallelujah Chorus," no *Messiah*, no Mozart's Requiem. Theologian Karl Barth listened to Mozart while writing his massive *Church Dogmatics*. He said that Mozart was the virtual equivalent of a parable.

Nor has Jesus' influence between restricted to what is sometimes called high culture. It would be ironic if the one who identified with sinner, slave, and peasant was remembered for influencing the art of the elite. He is the only human being to have his own Grammy category —gospel music.

Jesus is remembered in the tunes of the hills of Appalachia. A friend of mine was estranged for many years from her father, famous as a one-armed fiddler (he held the bow between his knees) who played with crowd-shocking brilliance throughout Appalachia, but who had given up on God and so was not just the only one-armed Appalachian fiddler; he was also the only Appalachian fiddler who would *not* play gospel tunes. They were reconciled in the end. On her last night with him, by his hospital bed, he asked for his fiddle and played an old gospel tune: "I'll Fly Away." He put down the fiddle, looked at his daughter, and gave a little smile and a nod. He had made peace with God. And had said so in a way words never could.

———•◆•———

Jesus did not just inspire artists across all media, but also influenced the tone of what they produced. Ancient Greeks loved the beauty of the human form. The beauty of the story of Jesus became a more powerful inspiration: "The lanky Good Shepherd of early Christian art wrestled with the muscular Hercules and won."

In fact, Martin Luther, who did not suffer from a shortage of opinions, criticized medieval painters for painting the Virgin Mary so that "there is found in her nothing [lowly] to be despised, but only great and lofty things." Luther felt they should reveal how God is present with the lowly. Albrecht Durer became influenced by Luther, and his art began to be informed by a new vision of beauty.

There is an unverified story connected with one of Durer's most famous works. Durer was from a large, poor family, the third of eighteen children. A friend of his agreed to work in the mines to support Durer for a period. Early on, Durer showed more skill than his teachers, and after several years, he had had made enough money for his friend to also work as an artist. But when he returned home with the news, his friend's hands had been too damaged by mining work to be able to paint with skill anymore.

Durer had seen those hands clasped in prayer many times and wanted to capture the beauty of praying hands.

It is difficult to look at the picture of these hands without thinking of the mystery and beauty and humility of prayer, or the single human name in which prayer gets offered. It is difficult to imagine a world with no Sistine Chapel, no DaVinci's *Last Supper*, no Rembrandt's *Prodigal Son*, no *Pieta*.

> The influence of Christianity has been called the single greatest factor in the development of architecture over the last two millennia.

The church met in catacombs, and it met and still meets in huts, houses, storefronts, and markets. Among hundreds of thousands of chapels, churches, basilicas, missions, abbeys, and cathedrals worldwide are some of the most striking buildings ever erected. One can look from Saint Paul's which still dominates London's skyline to the Roussanou Monastery in Greece, perched so breathtakingly on a giant slab of rock that it can be accessed only by a narrow bridge. The influence of Christianity has been called the single greatest factor in the development of architecture over the last two millennia. All these buildings have gone up due to a Man of whom it was said that while foxes have holes and birds have nests, he had no place to lay his head.

————◦•◦————

Jesus' vision gives a moral and artistic vocabulary for evil.

Artist Hans Holbein created a painting of Christ after the crucifixion that was so haunting that centuries later Dostoyevsky stared at this painting for days. It was part of the inspiration for one of his books. He wrote, "Looking at that picture, [death] has senselessly seized, cut to pieces, and swallowed up—impassively and unfeelingly—a great and priceless Being, a Being worth the whole of nature and all its laws, worth the entire earth, which was perhaps created solely for the coming of that Being!"

Perhaps Pablo Picasso's most famous painting is *Guernica*, his protest of Spanish general Franco's use of Nazi bombers to destroy the city of Guernica. It is a brutal work: a screaming woman holds a dead child, a man falls as a torture victim, a horse is slaughtered, and all is brutality and darkness. A professor of mine told me that a Fascist soldier saw the painting and asked Picasso: "My God, did you do that?" And Picasso said, "No, you did."

This is not to say that all or even most important artists in the West have been believers, only that their art has been shaped by Jesus' story and framework.

Victor Hugo was deeply disillusioned by the church's neglect of the poor, and most of his life he regarded himself as a skeptic. In *Les Misérables*, the desperate convict Jean Valjean is shown kindness by a priest. Nevertheless, he steals some of the priest's silver. Caught by the police, he is returned to the priest and waits for the words that will condemn him. Instead, the priest says, "Yes, I gave him the silver. But Jean Valjean, you have forgotten to take my best gift," and gives him the silver candlesticks that will allow him to begin a new life. Then, out of the hearing of the police, the priest says, "I have purchased your soul for God."

When Nancy and I saw the musical version of *Les Misérables*, she could not stop the flow of tears (and she is not a crier) at the final line: "To love another person is to see the face of God." "Why didn't God put that in the Bible?" she asked.

Later I pointed out Jacob's words to Esau when they are reunited: "To see your face is like seeing the face of God."

"I'm glad God listened to me," Nancy said.

Jesus' vision inspires people to believe that change may yet happen. Leo Tolstoy, whose book *War and Peace* is maybe the most famous book about war in history, wrote, "Men need only trust in Christ's teaching and obey it, and there will be peace on earth."

Dante wrote that above the doors of hell is a single statement: "Abandon hope, all who enter here." He said that in the final vision of God we see "the Love which moves the sun and other stars," a canto that T. S. Eliot said was the highest point poetry ever had or ever could reach.

Eric Metaxas wrote a wonderful biography of Dietrich Bonhoeffer. Bonhoeffer would lose much from an earthly standpoint. He was engaged when he died; he was in prison for the last two years of his life; he never got to be a father; and while still in his thirties, he would be hung on a gallows and would judge the sacrifice well worth it. The last words he was heard to say by a cell mate when he was leaving to be executed were: "This is the end, but for me the beginning of life."

But he had an inside, like you and me, with all the mixture of humanity. Bonhoeffer wrote a poem just one month before he was executed:

> Who am I? They often tell me
> I would step from my cell's confinement
> calmly, cheerfully, firmly,
> like a squire from his country-house.
>
> Who am I? They also tell me
> I would bear the days of misfortune
> calmly, smilingly, proudly,
> like one accustomed to win.
>
> Am I really then all that which other men tell of?
> Or am I only what I know of myself,
> Restless and longing and sick, like a bird in a cage,
> struggling for breath . . .
> weary and empty at praying, at thinking, at making,
> faint, and ready to say farewell to it all?
>
> Who am I? This or the other? . . .
> They mock me, these lonely questions of mine.
> Whoever I am, Thou knowest, O God, I am Thine.

———◆———

Jesus had no place to lay his head yet became the primary shaper of architecture.

We don't know what Jesus looked like, yet he became the most recognizable figure in the world.

> *We don't know what Jesus looked like, yet he became the most recognizable figure in the world.*

He had "no form nor comeliness … no beauty that we should desire him," yet he became the subject of more paintings and sculptures than anyone else.

He never wrote a book, but he became the most written-about person ever and the greatest inspiration for global linguistic development.

He is associated with only one unknown song but is the subject of more songs and music than any other human being.

He died alone. Yet people die for him still.

CHAPTER 13

Friday

On a Friday, Jesus died on a cross.

When we think of Jesus' reputation in our day as a great teacher and exemplary human being, an obvious question comes to mind: *How did this happen? Why did this Jesus die? How did this man — meek and mild, blesser of little children, friend of sinners — end up being executed as an enemy of the state?* It turns out that Friday is the day of mixed motives, odd alliances, secret meetings, cynical PR ploys, political intrigue, and explosive emotions.

Somehow, Jesus' death is central to his story in an unusual way. If you read the biography of any famous person, even if their death was a prominent story (for example, Abraham Lincoln, Mahatma Gandhi, Martin Luther King Jr.), it will be only a tiny part of that biography. But within a few decades of Jesus' life, four biographies were written about him, and the story of his death takes up a disproportionate amount (about one-third) of each one of these biographies.

Why did Jesus die? Let's travel back to the end of Friday and work our way backwards from the crucifixion through the events that led up to it, to come to see how Jesus would have understood what happened on the way to the cross.

———•+•———

LATE AFTERNOON

It's late Friday afternoon. Outside the gates of Jerusalem there are three crosses. On the outside crosses hang the bodies of two thieves.

The middle cross is empty. Its victim is already dead and has been taken down. Over the middle cross hangs a sign: JESUS OF NAZARETH, THE KING OF THE JEWS. It is written in Hebrew (or Aramaic), Latin, and Greek. This sign is somehow at the crux of Jesus' death.

Many powerful forces and characters are at work, and they end up crushing Jesus. But when we try to understand, it's not clear that the people who think they are in charge on this Friday really are in charge. Everybody on Friday has an agenda. *What do they all want? Whose agenda will prevail? Why does Jesus have to die?*

The most obvious force is Rome. Rome would say that Jesus has to die because he is a threat to Rome, and any threat to Rome has to die. Why is this man a threat? Because he's Jesus Christ. People mistakenly think *Christ* is Jesus' last name, but it is a title. It comes from the Greek word *chrio* ("to anoint"), so it means the Anointed One or the Messiah.

Another force is the crowds in Jerusalem. The people are waiting for a leader who will revolt against and overthrow Rome, a leader who will clean up all the corruption in the temple (because it's under Roman power), who will lead Israel into freedom so it can occupy its place as the dream of the world and the envy of the nations.

——•◆•——

There were many wannabe messiahs in the first century. There were different lines of thought about the Messiah: Some emphasized the prophetic, some thought he would be the new Moses, some thought he would be the new David. But everybody agreed he would be trouble for Rome.

We read about a few of these wannabes in the New Testament. Acts 5:36: "Some time ago Theudas appeared, claiming to be somebody, and about four hundred men rallied to him. He was killed." According to Josephus, Theudas was called Messiah (think "Theudas Christ"). He claimed he could part the Jordan River and make the walls of Jerusalem fall down (a modern-day Joshua; the Aramaic version of the name Joshua is Jesus). He was eventually captured by the Romans, and they decapitated him in Jerusalem in front of the crowds.

> *There were different lines of thought about the Messiah.... But everybody agreed he would be trouble for Rome.*

The book of Acts also mentions Judas the Galilean, who appeared in the days of the census and led a revolt. Judas the Galilean, we're told by the historian Josephus, founded the Zealots. He and two thousand of his followers were crucified. The crosses were all left standing in the Galilean countryside because the Romans wanted to send a message: If anybody else got any bright ideas about trying to get people not to pay taxes, Rome had plenty more crosses.

This happened when Jesus was a boy. Judas the Galilean was from the region of Galilee, and Jesus grew up in the town of Nazareth in Galilee, so Jesus would have seen those crosses on which Rome killed people who followed a man who claimed to be Messiah.

How can you know who the real Messiah is? It's a little like Arthur and the sword in the stone. The true king of England would be the man who could pull the sword out of the stone. No one could know until someone tried. Arthur was the only one who could do it; therefore he was king.

The people thought the Messiah would be the man who could beat Rome, and if you were in his shoes, you couldn't know until you tried. The penalty for failure was crucifixion. If you got crucified, you were not the Messiah. There were at least eighteen Messiah candidates that we know of in Jesus' day. They all met the same fate.

They and their followers would often loot Roman arsenals or palaces in Israel. They thought of themselves as kind of like Robin Hood: *It's our stuff, and Romans don't have any right to it. We ought to have it.* Rome regarded them as thieves. The Greek word for these looters was *lestes*. One is known to history as the thief on the cross. He was not up there for shoplifting. He was crucified so Rome could send a message.

Jesus was crucified. And yet he was not this kind of military-leader-messiah-king the people were looking for. He did the things they expected a messiah to do: he announced a new kingdom, he displayed great power, he claimed great authority. But he deliberately, repeatedly rejected what looked like his destiny. John tells us that after Jesus miraculously fed a crowd, people intended to come and make him king by force. If he could make a few fish and loaves of bread feed five thousand people, think of what he could do with a few swords and chariots. He fled to the hills alone. He refused to lift a finger against Rome. He was not a military threat.

So why did he end up on a cross?

———•—

FRIDAY MORNING

We back up to an earlier scene on Friday when the chief priests bring Jesus before Pontius Pilate. Pilate's role is often misunderstood as an act of hand-washing, passive neutrality, so it will help to look at him for a moment.

Pilate's job is a big headache. Nobody in Pilate's line of work wants to end up in the Middle East. He's an ambitious man, but he has a delicate challenge. He must keep the chief priests cooperative but allow them enough distance that the anti-Roman crowds will still accept their authority. He must keep a lid on the Zealot freedom fighters and the nationalist Pharisees and the isolationist Essenes. They often fight each other but are all agreed on their hatred of Rome. Pilate has to try to put a lid on this mess. He lives in brutal times; probably any ruler who is to survive will look brutal in future times.

In Luke 13 people tell Jesus about a group of pilgrims from Galilee whom Pilate had killed while they were at worship. He had mixed their blood with their sacrifices on the altar. The temple was sacred; it was also the main symbol of national identity. That meant it was ground zero for rebellion. It was a dangerous place, and any ruler had to be a dangerous man.

The victims were from Galilee. Jesus was from Galilee. Pilate was a dangerous man.

Another time Pilate sequestered (Israel would have said "stole") money from the temple to build an aqueduct. When a group of patriots protested, Pilate had them executed. Eventually, sometime after Jesus' death, Pilate had so many people executed that the unrest grew unmanageable and Caesar fired him. That was the last history would hear of him. An ancient writer named Philo said Pilate's rule was marked by bribery, insults, robberies, supreme cruelty, executions without a trial, and a furious, vindictive temper.

So the chief priests bring Jesus to Pilate. They have carefully thought through the charge they will lay before him: "We have found this man [Jesus] subverting our nation. He opposes payment of taxes to Caesar and claims to be Messiah, a king."

This is how the game is played. The chief priests clearly are not concerned with helping Caesar squeeze more cash out of Israel. The American Heart Association doesn't sponsor fund-raisers for tobacco companies. The chief priests don't want to pay taxes to Caesar. They're just trying to put pressure on Pilate to make Pilate do what they want Pilate to do.

> *Pilate resists the chief priests, not out of sympathy for Jesus, but because he never wants to do what they tell him to do.*

This Jesus is a problem for Rome. Caesar won't like him. You'd better do something.

Pilate resists the chief priests, not out of any sympathy for Jesus, but because he always resists the chief priests. He never wants to do what they tell him to do. By definition, if they get stronger he gets weaker.

When Pilate finds out Jesus is from Galilee, he tries to pass the buck to Herod, who actually has jurisdiction over Galilee. But Herod is not taking the bait, so Pilate turns to the crowd. He reminds them of the custom of releasing a prisoner at Passover and offers them a choice between the harmless Jesus or Barabbas. Mark and Luke both tell us that Barabbas had been involved in riots—movements against Rome. John uses the word *lestes*, which tells us Barabbas would be regarded by the crowds as a patriot and freedom fighter.

So we understand why the crowd says, "Give us Barabbas." Barabbas may be a murderer, but Barabbas is willing to kill Romans. Better to free him than the passive Messiah.

Finally, in a famous scene, Pilate washes his hands. It's not that Pilate has a sensitive conscience or he's worried about Jesus. He knows the charge against Jesus is trumped up, but Pilate has bigger problems than the fate of some dime-store Messiah. His challenge is to maintain the upper hand over the chief priests and over the temple. Theoretically, Pilate is in control.

But the chief priests have a trump card. "If you let this man go, you are no friend of Caesar. Anyone who claims to be king [that is, Jesus] opposes Caesar.... We have no king but Caesar."

What does Caesar want? Oddly enough, Caesar wants grain. He has an empire to feed, and the empire is growing increasingly dependent on grain from Egypt and from the Middle East. (Grain was to the Middle East in that day what oil is to the Middle East today.) Caesar needs someone to make the trains run on time, keep the population quiet, and get him the food he needs to run an empire.

Why did Jesus die? In a real sense, he died for corn. For the food needed to prop up Caesar's empire.

For Pilate, the situation is even more delicate. Pilate's patron in Rome is Caesar's chief lieutenant Sejanus. Caesar has recently had Sejanus arrested and executed on suspicion of treason. He has also executed several of Sejanus's associates. There can be no more dangerous charge to Pilate than "You are no friend of Caesar." He is either Caesar's friend or Caesar's corpse.

Pilate cannot risk having Caesar think he is soft on anti-Rome terrorists, so he turns to Jesus and asks, "Are you the king of the Jews?" It is an intensely dramatic moment. Jesus may still go free if he just says no, if he will assure Pilate he is no threat to Caesar.

This was the question that hung over Jesus his entire ministry. Ironically, any day before this one, all Jesus had to do one time was say, "Yes. I'm the Messiah." All of Israel (or a good chunk of it) would have risen up in arms and died for Jesus. As recently as Palm Sunday the chance lay open before him. He would never claim the title.

Now, when there are no crowds around to rally to him, when he's in the hands of Pilate, when there is no chance of an army rising to defend him, when there's no chance of his being misinterpreted as a military figure—now when it's too late for him to be saved, Jesus says, "Yes, yes, that's me. It is as you say. I'm the one they've been waiting for. I am their king."

Jesus knows what is going to happen to him. Pilate pronounces the sentence. But Pilate doesn't want to pronounce it. What motivates Pilate throughout is probably a combination of concerns over career and public safety, of political maneuvering and sheer survival. But even though he technically is legally in charge, he doesn't want the crucifixion to happen.

So who's really making this happen?

——— •◦• ———

FRIDAY, BEFORE SUNRISE

We back up further. Why do the chief priests want Pilate to act?

Jesus had developed a large and volatile following among the people. People were talking about him. The Pharisees and the chief priests had a meeting. One of them said, "Here is this man [this Jesus], performing many signs. If we let him go on like this, everyone will believe in him." And here is the key concern: "and then the Romans will come and take away both our temple and our nation."

This was not an idle fear. In fact, that is exactly what happened in AD 70. There was one revolt and one messiah too many. The Romans laid Jerusalem to waste, destroyed the temple, and devastated the population. In many ways, Israel's suffering from that day has not yet ceased.

The chief priests, like Pilate, knew Jesus was not a military threat. They understood he was a threat of another kind. He was claiming that the kingdom of God everybody had been waiting for was somehow now present on earth. Only it wasn't in the temple. It wasn't in the sacrifices. It was through Jesus, through this one man, through what he said, through how he lived and loved. He was telling everybody that God's presence was now available to the world through him. Not only had no one ever done this before, but no one had ever *thought* something like this before. This could not stand.

So before the hearing with Pilate, there was another one with the Sanhedrin, a kind of supreme court made up of chief priests and Pharisees. This happened we're told before daybreak so it could be secret, because they had a delicate task in front of them. They had to get the crowds to hate Jesus; they had to get Rome and Pilate to crucify Jesus.

The quickest way to get Pilate to crucify Jesus was to tell him that Jesus was a threat to Rome and Caesar. But if they told the crowds this, the crowds would rally to Jesus. So they had to come up with two charges. They ended up charging Jesus with blasphemy so the crowds would turn against him and with treason so Pilate would kill him.

It was a very hard task, and in fact, they couldn't get it done at this trial. Mark recorded: "The chief priests and the whole Sanhedrin were looking for evidence against Jesus so that they could put him to death, but they did not find any. Many testified falsely against him, but their statements did not agree."

Once again, all Jesus had to do was remain silent. Once again, he did not remain silent. He made no attempt to correct the false witnesses. He sat in silence while they mocked him, but when they asked him, "Are you the Messiah?" he responded: "I am." He went on to speak of them seeing the Son of Man coming on the clouds.

> *Jesus pronounced his own death sentence. He gave the Jews what they could not get from all the false witnesses.*

He was not saying, "You're going to see a body float down from the sky." He was using a well-known image from the Old Testament to say, "You now see God present and at work *uniquely* in me."

And so Jesus pronounced his own death sentence. He gave them what they could not get from all the false witnesses. Jesus did their work for them. Why? We have to back up one more time, before the cross, before the meeting with Pilate, before the trial with the chief priests.

———•◦•———

FRIDAY, SOME TIME AFTER MIDNIGHT

Gethsemane. The story of the human race began in a garden with a man called Adam. The story of the one who would be called the second Adam would end in a garden. When Jesus was in the garden, he still had many options. He could fight like the Zealots. He was young. He had charisma. The crowds would follow him to the death. He could do that.

He could withdraw like the Essenes. He could go into the desert and start a safe little community. Many would follow him.

He could collaborate with the chief priests. Imagine what reform Jesus might bring if he had the temple as the platform for his teaching.

He could try to cut a deal with Pilate. Imagine influencing the Roman Empire from the inside. What might that do for the world?

He could call on his God to be delivered. He could ask to be spared. He could ask for legions of angels. Maybe one more miracle would rally everybody to his side.

He did none of those things.

Setting aside questions about his divinity and identity, this is what

Jesus did. This one lone, deserted, vulnerable man decided, *I know what I must do. I will not fight. I will not run. I will not deal. I will not dazzle. I will die.* Then he prayed, "Not my will but yours be done." He came to believe that the real messianic fate, the real messianic calling, was not to conquer but to die out of love for others, and so he did.

Put aside theories and theology. Jesus knew that rebels were killed by Rome. If he did not die, a rebel named Barabbas would. Jesus died on the cross in place of Barabbas.

Jesus knew the crowds even now were waiting for a word from him to march against the Romans. Many Romans soldiers were just boys from nearby Syria working for the Roman government. Jesus did not say that word. Instead, he went to the cross and died. And a whole legion of Roman soldiers would live. Jesus' death saved them.

Jesus knew that if he fled, his disciples would be gathered up and executed. It had happened before and would happen again. His disciples knew how Rome operated, and that was the only reason they fled in terror from the one they loved. Execution was always the fate of accomplices to fugitive messiahs. Jesus died, and his death saved the lives of his followers.

Jesus knew that if he did say the word, that when the crowds followed him—and they would follow him—Rome would come down and destroy Jerusalem. So he died to save Jerusalem. He died for all these people who were disappointed in him, who didn't understand him, who cried out of their frustration and pain that he should be crucified.

It's as if he said, "I will lay down my life for people who do not understand. That can buy a little time. That can buy a little space. A community can be formed, and out of sacrificial love it can change the world."

As a simple historical reality, it was sin—human darkness in every other person involved—that put Jesus on the cross. But he believed that through love the cross could somehow become not just a symbol of sin and death but also a symbol of even more powerful redemptive love. And whatever else one believes or does not believe about Jesus, that is exactly what happened.

He died.

Out of his remarkable brilliance, breathtaking courage, and inexplicable love, Jesus sized up a situation that defeated every human attempt at correction. He identified exactly what would be needed to bring redemption. It would cost him his life.

Two thousand years later, his death is the most important, most remembered death in the history of the world.

Pilate, who wanted above all to be a friend of Caesar, ended up writing in Hebrew, the language of the people of God; in Greek, the language of the cultured world; and in Latin, the language of the Roman Empire, so that the whole world could read:
JESUS OF NAZARETH, THE KING OF THE JEWS.

Jesus outlasted, outmaneuvered, and out-thought every group, every power. But not just that. Mostly he just out-loved everybody. For Jesus in the garden had one agenda that superseded the agendas of all the others: love. "I'll die on Friday."

> *Jesus identified exactly what would be needed to bring redemption. It would cost him his life.*

On Friday, Jesus died for love. He said it was his choice. It wasn't Pilate's. It wasn't Herod's. It wasn't Caesar's. It wasn't the chief priests'. It wasn't the crowds'. He said, "I lay down my life for the sheep.... No one takes it from me, but I lay it down of my own accord. I have authority to lay it down and authority to take it up again."

The cross has become the most widely recognized symbol in the world. It marks more graves, graces more jewelry, and sits atop more churches than any other design. The making of the sign of the cross is known from basilicas to baseball diamonds. Finding a logo has become big business, but no corporation, country, or cause has produced such an enduring or widespread image.

The cross's very ubiquity causes us to forget what a strange symbol it is. It was the most humiliating means of execution available to Rome. Imagine choosing an electric chair or a gallows or a guillotine as an icon for anything.

The cross was changed from the symbol of a human empire's power into a symbol of the suffering love of God. It was changed from an expression of ultimate threat into an expression of ultimate hope. It came, in a sense, to express the exact opposite of its original purpose

—that the power of embraced sacrifice is greater than the power of coercion.

How did this happen?

Jesus chose it. He chose to die on it. After Friday, neither the cross nor the world could stay the same.

CHAPTER 14

Saturday

So far as we know, there has only been one day in the last two thousand years when literally not one person in the world believed Jesus was alive.

On Saturday morning after Jesus' crucifixion, the disciples wake after not having slept for two days. The city that was screaming for blood the day before is quiet. Crowds have disbanded. Jesus is dead.

What do they do on Saturday?

It's strange that the two days on either side of Saturday are so heavily discussed. Some of the brightest minds in the world have devoted themselves primarily to those two days; they have been across the centuries maybe the two most studied days in history. The Bible is full of what happened the day before, the day Jesus was killed. And the next day, Sunday, is the day believers say gave birth to the most death-defying, grave-defeating, fear-destroying, hope-inspiring, transcendent joy in the history of the world. Pentecostals still shout about it. Charismatics still dance because of it. Baptists still say "Amen!" over it. Presbyterians still study it. Episcopalians still toast it with sherry. Some people think of Sunday in mellower terms, as a metaphor for hope. And others think of it as a dangerous enemy of logic, reason, and mortality. Let's just leave Sunday alone for now.

This isn't Sunday. This isn't Friday. This is Saturday. The day after this but the day before that. The day after a prayer gets prayed but there is no answer on the way. The day after a soul gets crushed way down but there's no promise of ever getting up off the mat. It's a strange day, this in-between day. In between despair and joy. In between confusion and clarity. In between bad news and good news. In between darkness and light.

Even in the Bible—outside of one detail about guards being posted to watch the tomb—we're told nothing about Saturday. Saturday is the day with no name, the day when nothing happened.

Now only a handful of followers remain. Friday was a nightmare day; Friday was the kind of day that is pure terror, the kind when you run on adrenaline. On Saturday when Jesus' followers wake up, the terror is past, at least for the moment; the adrenaline is gone. Saturday is the day they realize they have to go on.

Those who believe in Jesus gather, quietly maybe. They remember. It's what people do. Things he said. What he taught. Things he did. People he touched or healed. They remember what it felt like when this Jesus wanted them. They remember their hopes and dreams. They were going to change the world.

Now it's Saturday.

Maybe they talk about what went wrong. *What in God's name happened?* None of them wants to say this, but in their hearts, they're trying to come to grips with this unfathomable thought: *Jesus failed.* Jesus ended up a failure. Noble attempt, but he couldn't get enough followers. He couldn't convince the chief priests. He couldn't win over Rome to make peace. He couldn't get enough ordinary people to understand his message. He couldn't even train his disciples to be courageous at the moment of great crisis.

> *Saturday is the day your dream died. You have to go on, but you don't know how. Worse, you don't know why.*

Everybody knows Saturday.

Saturday is the day your dream died. You wake up and you're still alive. You have to go on, but you don't know how. Worse, you don't know why.

This odd day raises a question: Why is there a Saturday? It doesn't seem to further the story line at all. We might expect that if Jesus was going to be crucified then resurrected, God would just get on with it. It seems strange for God to spread two events over three days.

In its own way, perhaps Saturday should mark the world as much as Friday and Sunday.

Friday, Saturday, and Sunday lie at the heart of the ancient calendar. They attributed great significance to the notion that this event was a three-day story.

The apostle Paul wrote, "For what I received I passed on to you as of first importance: that Christ died for our sins according to the Scriptures, that he was buried, that he was raised on the third day [Paul adds again] according to the Scriptures." The Old Testament Scriptures are filled with what might be called "third-day stories." When Abraham is afraid he's going to have to sacrifice Isaac, he sees the sacrifice that will save his son's life *on the third day.* Joseph's brothers get put in prison, and they're released *on the third day.* Israelite spies are told by Rahab to hide from their enemies, and then they'll be safe *on the third day.* When Esther hears that her people are going to be slaughtered, she goes away to fast and pray. *On the third day,* the king receives her favorably.

It's such a recurring pattern that the prophet Hosea says, "Come, let us return to the LORD. He has torn us to pieces.... After two days he will revive us; on the third day he will restore us, that we may live in his presence." All three-day stories share a structure. On the first day there is trouble, and on the third day there is deliverance. On the second day, there is nothing—just the continuation of trouble.

The problem with third-day stories is, you don't *know* it's a third-day story until the third day. When it's Friday, when it's Saturday, as far as you know, deliverance is never going to come. It may just be a one-day story, and that one day of trouble may last the rest of your life.

I live in San Francisco. In 2010 the Giants played such nerve-wracking, lead-blowing, nail-biting baseball that their unofficial motto for the season was "Giants baseball: it's torture." Giants fans could laugh in the end because they won the World Series. It was a third-day story. Sunday was coming. I'm a Cubs fan. The Cubs haven't won in over a hundred years. When you're a Cubs fan, it's just Friday. Yesterday was Friday. Today is Friday. Tomorrow is going to be Friday. It's always Friday when you love the Cubs. The secret to surviving as a Cubs fan is the same as the secret to parenting an adolescent: *lower your standards.* That's the only way to get through it. Jesus died Friday, and then came Saturday.

---•◦•---

Is life a three-day story, or is it just one day of trouble repeated over and over?

In the ancient world, there were two views about time: a majority opinion and a tiny dissent. The majority opinion was that history moves in endless cycles. What goes around comes around. The universe has always existed without beginning; Aristotle wrote, "Nothing can come out of that which does not exist."

To the ancients, all indications seemed to confirm this: the sun and the moon and the seasons all run on cycles. Generations come and go, civilizations rise and fall, prosperity ebbs and flows. The ancients did not expect progress or for life to get better. We often have surveys that ask people if they think life will be better for the next generation than it was for the past. Ancients did not take surveys. And if they had, they would not have expected a yes. To the contrary, Plato wrote, "The ancients are better than we, for they lived nearer the gods."

But there was a minority report.

Genesis begins, "In the beginning God created the heavens and the earth." People wonder what was happening before that. Augustine, when asked what God was doing before he created the heavens and the earth, is supposed to have replied that he was creating hell for people who ask questions like that. He also said time is one of those realities he understood until someone asked him to explain what it is. But Augustine took the task of explaining the minority report so profoundly that, according to Christopher Dawson, he was "not only the founder of the Christian philosophy of history," but "actually the first man in the world to discover the meaning of time." Think of the minority report this way: out of great love, God created the heavens and the earth and placed human beings in a garden.

Augustine said time is one of those realities he understood until someone asked him to explain what it is.

The story has a beginning. There is a tree in the garden called the Tree of Life, which suggests God's goodness and provision for these human beings. The story has a middle. Through the fall, the garden has somehow become lost to us. The story has gone wrong. The gospel story has an ending. In the last book of the Bible, the book of Revelation, the Tree of Life makes a return appearance. But this time it is not in a garden exactly; somehow the garden has become a city. Eugene Peterson says this is the great surprise of the story:

> Haven't we had enough of cities on earth? Many people want to go to heaven the way they want to go to Florida—they think the weather will be an improvement and the people decent. But the biblical heaven is ... the invasion of the city by the City.

The Tree of Life in Genesis and then the Tree of Life in Revelation are the bookends of the story of human history.

Finally, the arts, education, economics, and all building activities will be so God-powered and God-honoring that all of God's created order will finally flourish. So the Tree of Life in Genesis and then the Tree of Life in Revelation are the bookends of the story of human history. That tree is at the beginning of our story. This tree will be at the climax of our story. We're not part of a random cosmic accident. We have a story. In the meantime, we live, in Rob Bell's memorable phrase, "between the trees." After the Genesis tree, before the Revelation tree, we live between the trees.

Beginning, middle, end. Creation, fall, redemption. Father, Son, Spirit. Yesterday, today, tomorrow. Friday, Saturday, Sunday. We live between the trees.

But God is eternal. "I am the Alpha and the Omega," and this title recurs: "who is, and who was, and who is to come." Alpha is the first letter of the Greek alphabet. "In the beginning"—stretch as far down that direction as you can imagine, and then go infinitely further—God existed. Omega is the last letter. "Before the mountains were born or you brought forth the whole world, from everlasting to everlasting you are God."

He is moving us from one tree to the other tree.

This was not the view of the ancient world. The Greeks believed in an eternal realm. At least some of them believed in an all-powerful god that was ceaseless and unchanging and dwelled beyond time. But he did not have contact with human beings. He was the unseen, unknowable author of a play that ran without him.

That view is largely dead in our world, at least in the West. Even people who do not believe in God believe in something like progress. During the Enlightenment, some thinkers shucked off the notion of God, but they could not bring themselves to abandon a hope for an age to come. They renamed it "progress." They said it would be delivered by education or technology or science. But they were still the secular heirs of the people of Israel who believed history was leading somewhere.

How did that idea get spread from little Israel to the broader world?

"The time has come." Humble Jesus claimed to be the hinge of history.

One day a man named Jesus began his ministry with a single phrase about what time it was: *"The time has come."*

This is both a statement about himself and a claim about time. History is not an endless cycle. The universe itself, like an NFL team during the draft, is "on the clock." There was a before-time, when the world was being prepared. There will be an after-time, when the world will respond. Now, "the time has come." Staggeringly, Jesus said that the marker of this moment is his own arrival. Humble Jesus claimed to be the hinge of history.

The time has come.

———◆———

Augustine said that the turning point, not just of the history of Israel, but of the history of the entire world, had been reached with the arrival of Jesus. He said that it wasn't just Israel's history of priests and sacrifices and tabernacles that was preparing the way. He said that God is the God of all history, and that by "an order of things and times, which is hidden from us, but thoroughly known to God," history had been moving toward this moment from the beginning, and the rest of human history would flow from it.

Augustine argued that the theory that history repeats itself, that "the same temporal event is reenacted by the same periodic revolutions," has been forever disproven because "Christ died for our sins once for all."

Jesus changed how we think about history. The year was given a new starting point. In Israel a baby was brought to the temple and given a name on the eighth day of life. January 1 is eight days past December 25.

January 1 marks the beginning of the New Year, because that's the day when the name of Jesus came into the world. Every January 1 marks this whether we know it or not. It is expressing something that was changing in people's idea of history. When Luke wanted to tell his audience when Jesus was born, he did so by referring to the reign of Caesar Augustus as emperor and Quirinius as governor of Syria.

———•———

Events were dated by the reign of the emperor. Over time, the power of every Caesar, his grip on the human imagination, faded while another vision grew. By the end of the third century, Rome's old eight-day week had been replaced by the seven-day calendar of Israel and the church. Six hundred years after Jesus, a Scythian monk named Dionysius Exiguus (Little Denis) proposed a new system for reckoning history, centered not on the pagan myth of the founding of Rome but on the birth of Jesus. (In a nice parable of how the church often errs, he miscalculated, so it turns out Jesus was most likely born four years "Before Christ.")

The creation of the calendar as we know it was not just a chronological convenience. It carries a claim that life in this universe is not an accident, not a random cycle, but a story with a storyteller. Its critical event is the entrance into this world of a Jewish carpenter named Jesus. Jesus himself lived and died this little life in this little region. No Caesar ever heard a hint of his existence, but Jesus was called Lord of Lords and King of Kings by his disciple John in the first century. In the first century, while the movement was tiny (a few thousand people), such a claim seemed laughable.

The fact remains two thousand years after the birth of this carpenter that every time any human being anywhere on the planet opens a calendar, unfolds a newspaper, or boots up a computer, he or she is reminded that Jesus Christ has in fact become the hinge of human history. Caesar Nero died in the year of our Lord AD 68. Napoleon (the emperor of the world) died in the year of our Lord 1821. Joseph Stalin died in the year of our Lord 1953. Maybe Jesus was not Lord of Lords and King of Kings, but how strange that now every ruler who ever reigned must be dated in reference to the life of Jesus.

History began to be studied and read differently. In the eighth century, a Northumbrian monk and scholar known to history as the Venerable Bede (greatest nickname of all time; my daughter says she's going to buy a Volkswagen and call it the venerable Beetle) wrote *Ecclesiastical History of the English People*; it is said the

> The story of Jesus reaches a more personal level. It's my time. It's my story.

English owe to him more than anyone else their sense of national identity. He writes of pagan King Edwin, whose adviser told a parable comparing life to a sparrow that flitted through a banquet hall for a moment of light and then exited back to the darkness from which it came. He advised the king to convert to Christianity (which he did), so that life would be more than "a brief flit in the banqueting hall." Life, and the time it takes to live it, are like a shadow.

But the story of Jesus reaches a more personal level. It's not just the time frame of the universe I care about. It's my time. It's my story.

———•◆•———

I said before that Saturday is the day when nothing happens. That's not quite right. Silence happens on Saturday. After trouble hits you, after the agony of Friday, you call out to God. "Hear me! Listen to me! Respond to me! Do something! Say something! Rescue!" Nothing. On Saturday, in addition to the pain of Friday, there is the pain of silence and absence of God. When C. S. Lewis wrote his memoirs about coming to faith in Jesus, he called it *Surprised by Joy*. The book is about how his love of joy led him to faith in Jesus, and he actually took as the title a phrase in a poem by William Wordsworth. When Lewis wrote the book, he was a fifty-seven-year-old bachelor. He had met a woman named Joy whom, after the book was published, he ended up marrying. His friends enjoyed teasing him that he really had been surprised by Joy.

After a lifetime of waiting, Lewis knew love only briefly. Joy died soon after they were married of cancer, a lingering, very painful death. So Lewis wrote another book: *A Grief Observed*. A Saturday book.

> When you are happy, so happy you have no sense of needing God, so happy you are tempted to feel His claims upon you as an interruption, if you remember yourself and turn to Him with gratitude and

praise, you will be — or so it feels — welcomed with open arms. But go to Him when your need is desperate, when all other help is vain, and what do you find? A door slammed in your face and a sound of bolting and double bolting on the inside. After that, silence. You may as well turn away. The longer you wait, the more emphatic the silence will become.... What can this mean? Why is He so present a commander in our time of prosperity and so very absent a help in time of trouble?

A husband, a father, wants more than anything in the world to save his marriage. His wife will not listen and will not help. He is not perfect (not by a long shot), but he wants to do a really good thing. He can't find out why his wife won't respond to him, and he can't stand what it's doing to his children. Heaven is silent.

A mom and a dad find out the child they love has a terminal illness. They pray like crazy but hear only silence. She's getting worse.

You lose a job. You lose a friend. You lose your health. You have a dream for your child. And on Friday, it dies. What do you do on Saturday? You can choose *despair*. Paul writes about this: "How can some of you say that there is no resurrection of the dead?" In other words, apparently some people said, "There is never going to be a Sunday. It's Friday. Get used to it. Do disappointment management, because that's as good as it's going to get." Some people — silently, secretly — live here. You can choose *denial* — simplistic explanations, impatience, easy answers, artificial pleasantness. Hydroplane over authentic humanity, forced optimism, clichéd formulas, false triumphalism.

Paul wrote to Timothy that some "say that the resurrection has already taken place, and they destroy the faith of some." In other words, apparently some said, "It's already Sunday. The resurrection has already happened for all of us, so if you're having any problems, if you're still sick, if your prayers aren't being answered, you just don't have enough faith. Get with the program." Or there is this third option: You can *wait*. Work with God even when he feels far away. Rest. Ask. Whine. Complain. Trust.

Oddly, the most common psalm is the psalm of complaint. The Saturday psalm. *God, why aren't you listening?*

Eugene Peterson wrote about visiting a monastery. While on the way to the refectory for lunch, he and the monks he was visiting walked past a graveyard with an open grave. He asked one of the monks which member of the community had died recently, and he was told, "Nobody. That grave is for the next one." Every day, three times a day, as they walk to eat, the members of that community are reminded of what we spend our

"I don't mind the thought of dying. I just don't want to be there when it happens."

waking hours trying to forget. One of them will be the next one. We don't like thinking about this. Entertainer Woody Allen supposedly once said, "I don't mind the thought of dying. I just don't want to be there when it happens." But God has set eternity in the hearts of human beings. We want to know. Yale professor Carlos Eire wrote a book called *A Very Brief History of Eternity*. He observes that human life is either incredibly significant from a cosmic perspective or incredibly insignificant given its brevity next to the history of the cosmos, let alone eternity. If you represent the entire history of our planet as one twenty-four-hour time period that ran from midnight one day to midnight the next, *Homo sapiens* would make their arrival at 11:59 minutes, 59.3 seconds.

That is the span of humanity. Recorded history is far shorter—less than the pop of a flashbulb. Your life is too brief to be measured.

———•·•———

I once took my daughter to see a production of *Hamlet* staged on Alcatraz. The first scene actually began on the ferry on the way over. Then when we arrived, the one hundred or so audience members walked from one setting to another on Alcatraz, starting in the afternoon, ending in darkness.

In the gray twilight, the ghost of Hamlet's murdered father was up in the guard tower at Alcatraz. On the deserted back side of Alcatraz, in the dark, the actors' voices reached us over the sound of the lonely bells from the ocean buoys. The voice of Hamlet's uncle came to us from a secret passage in the prison: "My offense is rank; it smells to heaven."

In one of the cells, Hamlet began the most famous words of the play: "To be or not to be: that is the question. Whether 'tis nobler in the mind to suffer the slings and arrows of outrageous fortune, or to take arms against a sea of troubles and by opposing end them?... To sleep, perchance to dream—aye, there's the rub...." Why am I here? Is the suffering worth it? Would death bring peace?

Just at that moment, a cell phone rang. The Alcatraz acoustics make it unbelievably loud. My first thought is, *This is absolutely brilliant. It's part of the play. Somebody is calling in with an answer to this great question.*

My second thought was, *That's my phone!* because it was my phone.

In the story of humanity—so vast to us but brief to the universe—we are told that in Jesus a startling moment has arrived. The Author is entering the play.

———•—•———

An ancient homily spoke of this strange day: "What happened today on earth? There is a great silence—a great silence and stillness. A great silence because the king sleeps. God has died in the flesh, and hell trembles with fear. He has gone to search for our first parent as for a lost sheep."

The Apostles' Creed says Jesus descended into hell. Somehow no suffering you go through is suffering Jesus will not endure in order to save you.

From a human standpoint, we think of the miraculous day as Sunday, the day the man Jesus is risen from the dead. I wonder if, from Heaven's standpoint, the great miracle isn't on Saturday. When Jesus is born, the skies are filled with the heavenly hosts praising God because that baby is Emmanuel, God with us. Somehow God in a manger, somehow God in a stable, somehow God on earth. Now on Saturday the angels look down and see what? God in a tomb. The miracle of Sunday is that a dead man lives. The miracle of Saturday is that the eternal Son of God lies dead.

So Jesus Christ defeats our great enemy death not by proclaiming his invincibility over it but by submitting himself to it. If you can find this Jesus in a grave, if you can find him in death, if you can find him in hell, where can you *not* find him? Where will he *not* turn up?

CHAPTER 15

Sunday

On Sunday something got released into the world, and it hasn't been eliminated yet. What was it?

One of the unique aspects of Christianity compared to other faith movements is that it actually traces its origin to one particular event in one moment on one day in history. This is not true for Judaism or Buddhism or Islam or atheism. But one day there was no such thing as a church, and then suddenly overnight there was.

According to the gospel of Matthew, one Sunday morning women found the tomb empty, and they were told that Jesus had risen. They were commanded to go back and tell the disciples the news. Then they had an encounter with the risen Christ that featured a remarkably short conversation.

"So the women hurried away from the tomb, afraid yet filled with joy, and ran to tell his disciples. Suddenly Jesus met them. 'Greetings,' he said. They came to him, clasped his feet and worshiped him."

Doesn't Jesus seem just a little understated here? These women were devastated. They loved him. They came to the tomb. The stone was rolled back, and an angel that glowed like lightning sat on it. All of a sudden this rabbi, whom they loved, who had died, whom they saw buried, appeared to them as one risen from the dead. You wonder, *What profound statement, what amazing explanation will the resurrected Jesus give to mark this moment?*

All he said was, "Greetings." The word used was as close as you can come to the very common, informal way somebody in that day would say, "Hey. How you doing? Nice day, isn't it? What's up?" Dale Bruner's wonderful commentary translates it: "And look! Jesus met them and said, 'Hi!'"

In other words, "What did you expect?"

In other words, "Didn't I tell you?"

A pastor named Skip Viau tried to tell this story in a children's sermon one time. He posed the question, "What were Jesus' first words to the disciples after he was raised from the dead?" Before he could give Matthew's answer, a little girl waved her hand, and Skip deferred to her. "I know," she said. "Ta da!" It's as good a translation as any. Jesus went on to reaffirm their assignment. "Go and tell my brothers to go to Galilee."

———•—•———

Sunday changed everything, but not in the way many people think.

From our point of view two thousand years later, many people think of Easter as a comforting story that says, "Spring is coming. Flowers are blooming. Life is eternal. Everything is going to work out." But the response to the resurrection on the first Easter in the Gospels consistently includes fear. In fact, people were more afraid after the resurrection than they were before. And *none* of the gospel accounts have Jesus or the angels saying, "Now you don't have to worry about dying anymore."

> *Sunday changed everything, but not in the way many people think.*

What Jesus does say to his followers is that there is work to be done. In effect, "The cross didn't stick. Their plan to stop my movement didn't work. It's going to go on. Matter of fact, my plan to love even your enemies, to be willing to sacrifice, suffer, and even die for the sake of love has been vindicated by my Father.

"They're really going to be ticked off now. Pilate and the chief priests have already plotted to squelch this news. They are furious. They are desperate. I'm leaving now. So you go, you women, you disciples. Tell them all that the cross failed, Caesar failed, Pilate failed, the chief priests failed. Now they have you to contend with."

On Sunday their lives didn't get safer; their lives got a lot more dangerous. What got released on Sunday was not comfort. Also, what got released on Sunday was not assurance about life after death.

The ancient world, like our own, had a wide variety of opinions about what happens after death. Some believed that life goes out like a candle. An ancient tombstone epitaph popular enough to have both Latin and Greek versions read: "I was not. I was. I am not. I don't care."

Others believed in a place, sometimes referred to as Hades, where departed spirits go at death. They have a shadowy existence there, but they don't come back to this world. The road to Hades was a one-way street.

In Israel a different belief emerged called *resurrection*. This word was around a long time before Jesus. It existed for the Greeks. They didn't believe it was going to happen, but they knew about the idea. Resurrection was different than a vague, shadowy afterlife.

To believe in resurrection meant believing that the universe has been created by a great God and that he means to heal and redeem it. When that happens, he will forgive his people their sin, establish justice, end suffering, heal creation, and bring the righteous dead to life. Resurrection will be dramatic, obvious, undeniable, and done on a mass scale. It will happen to all of God's children at once, and it will end history.

Because of this belief, *nobody* in Israel would ever think to claim that one individual had been resurrected in the middle of history. If somebody had claimed that, the response would have been, "Has disease been eradicated? Has justice broken out? Has suffering ended? Stop talking nonsense."

It would have been like claiming that George Washington had won his independence from Great Britain but the rest of the colonies were still under King George. Resurrection, like war and square dancing and football, was not an individual sport.

———•◆•———

Jesus followers' believed he was the Messiah, that he would overthrow Rome and usher in God's kingdom. But Jesus died. When this happened, even though he had predicted it, none of his followers said, "Everything is going according to plan now." All four of the Gospels give us very unflattering portraits of what happened when he died. His disciples were disheartened, dismayed, disappointed, disillusioned, and dispirited. And then suddenly they weren't.

They saw an empty tomb, which told them their sightings of Jesus were not hallucinations. They saw a live person, which told them the empty tomb was not a result of body snatching. They remembered what Jesus said not long before he died:

> "The hour has come for the Son of Man to be glorified. Very truly I tell you, unless a kernel of wheat falls to the ground and dies, it remains only a single seed. But if it dies, it produces many seeds. Anyone who loves their life will lose it, while anyone who hates their life in this world will keep it for eternal life."

They began to understand.

My old preaching professor Ian Pitt-Watson used to say there have been only two great revolutions in the history of humankind. Just two that have changed human life on this planet irreversibly and forever.

He said the first revolution began when somebody started to farm. Up until this time, human beings had been hunter-gatherers; they lived from day to day. They moved from place to place. There was no such thing as home. Then someone noticed that if they dropped a seed in the ground and walked away, something happened. Normally that's how we get rid of something. But not here. Something in the dirt calls to something in the seed. "Hey seed! Wake up! Send me a little root."

There have been only two great revolutions that changed human life on this planet irreversibly and forever.

Then something above the earth says to the seed, "Send up a little shoot." And the seed does. The seed becomes a plant or a tree, and it produces fruit. It achieves its destiny.

Ta da!

But it could never happen if the seed didn't die first.

One day some human being noticed this. It was so long ago, we no longer know who this genius was. To deliberately throw away something edible looked foolish. But someone did, and then life happened. Human beings would no longer have to live from day to day. There would be villages and towns and crafts and art and architecture and tools and civilization. There would be home.

All human civilization, Ian said, is built on this one observation. It is not a command. It is just the way things are. "Unless a grain of wheat falls into the ground and dies, it remains a solitary grain of wheat. But if it dies, it will be a rich harvest."

There is a second revolution. This time we know the revolutionary's name. We know where he lived. We know how he lived. We know what he taught. We know how he died. This is, Jesus said, the way life works. You have to be willing to sacrifice something if anything is ever going to be the way it is supposed to be. No sacrifice, no harvest. Only it isn't seeds this time; this time it's you.

—— ·•· ——

What got released on Sunday was hope. Not hope that life would turn out well. Not even hope that there will be life after death. Hope that called people to die: die to selfishness and sin and fear and greed, die to the lesser life of a lesser self so that a greater self might be born. And many people did.

This hope changed things. Pliny the Younger said that followers of Jesus began to meet on Sunday instead of on the Sabbath as had always been the case. John called the first day of the week "the Lord's day." The followers of Jesus began to understand themselves to be a kind of resurrection community. God who had created life was beginning to recreate it. God in Jesus was saying, "Let there be life," all over again.

In the ancient world, the way to overcome death was to be so heroic in one's accomplishments that the memory of one's life would not fade. Comments that may sound vain or self-serving in our day were considered admirable in a society where immortality could only be won through honor. Pliny the Younger wrote to his historian friend Tacitus: "I believe that your histories will be immortal; a prophecy which will surely prove correct. That is why (I frankly admit) I am anxious to appear in them."

But there arose rumors in this Jesus community of another book, where the humblest of names could be entered, where the poorest could never be erased. There was only one requirement for entry: one had to die first.

In the ancient world, the great were separated from the humble in death as they had been in life. "Pre-eminent in life, the rich were also marked off by their way of death." Their funerals were public festivals; their tombs dominated civic burial grounds. The "very special dead" received public honors at commemorations paid for by their own donations. The poor would receive no private grave, no public funeral unless they belonged to a burial association.

The church offered a final resting place regardless of whether the deceased had paid contributions. They believed that, through Jesus, death was a kind of sleep through which we awake to true life. So they borrowed a Greek term for dormitories in which people would sleep to name resting places for the dead; every mention of the word *cemetery* is a reminder of the belief in the resurrection of the dead.

The oldest law of Rome mandated that "no body be buried or cremated inside the city" of Rome. The dead were regarded with dread. They actually got a city of their own, the necropolis, or "city of the dead." Terror and fear kept them from the living. That would shift dramatically with the early church. Graveyards were placed on church grounds. Some saints were buried under the floor of the church so that in an almost literal way the living and the dead were gathered for worship.

"This aversion to the proximity of the dead soon gave way among the early Christians.... The change is remarkable, for it reflects a profound difference between the old pagan attitude and the new Christian attitude toward the dead.... The dead ceased to frighten the living, and the two groups coexisted in the same places and behind the same walls." Why did people move so quickly from the old repugnance to the new familiarity? Because of their belief in the resurrection of the body. Because of Sunday.

———◆———

Over time, the issue of life after death sometimes replaced Jesus himself at the center of the faith of his church. Whether people consider themselves "religious" is often taken as synonymous with whether they believe in life after death. Jesus sometimes becomes reduced to the vehicle that will get people to the good afterlife as long as they subscribe to the right religious affiliation. There was a dark side even to the vividness of the church's teachings about the afterlife. They were often used—as they have been ever since—to manipulate people to become or remain Christians out of self-centered fear. Origen said that "literal terrors of hell were false but should be publicized in order to scare simpler believers."

> *Whether people consider themselves "religious" is often taken as synonymous with whether they believe in life after death.*

During a recent Holy Week a cross with the mocking sign ROFL (a texting abbreviation for "rolling on the floor laughing") was placed on Cross Campus at Yale. It stirred considerable conversation about free speech and respect for religion and whether Christians are privileged or persecuted. Some Christians complained that they are the one group allowed to be bashed in public, a complaint that—even if it were true—sounds oddly unlike the response of the early church.

This was not the first time mocking words had been associated with the cross. According to the scriptural account, Pilate had the words "JESUS OF NAZARETH, THE KING OF THE JEWS." printed on the cross. Jewish leaders complained that it should say, "This man claimed to be king of the Jews." But Pilate said, "What I have written, I have written." Churches often place the Latin acronym for what Pilate had written on crosses: Jesus-Nazareth, King-Jews, giving the Latin letters INRI. But it was not a tribute. It was a roast. ROFL.

Garret Fiddler, a guest columnist in the *Yale Daily News*, noted the irony of the cross as a piece of jewelry: "Really, the cross does not belong on the Christian; the Christian belongs on the cross."

At the heart of Jesus' teaching lies this strange command: "Take up your cross, die to yourself, and follow me." The cross is a reminder that there is something in me that needs to die. It is true for individuals and for nations and for the church. The resurrection hope is the hope that lies on the other side of dying. "It is when Christianity has forgotten this that the faith has been at its worst."

Historian Michael Grant wrote that Constantine, perhaps not surprising for a Roman emperor, found the crucifixion an embarrassment. He saw the cross "not so much an emblem of suffering as a magic totem confirming his own victoriousness." Constantine's vision of the cross called him not to die but to conquer. He had his soldiers paint it on their shields so they could kill their enemies. It was painted on other shields in the crusades; it was drawn on seals to claim empires; it was placed on robes to hold inquisitions; it was burned in yards to terrify the "least of these" in whom Christ was present.

Maybe the cross doesn't belong to us.

———•—•———

The hope of resurrection is woven into a thousand stories. One of the stories I love most is called *The Shawshank Redemption*. (The last word in the title is the first clue of where the story is headed.) The hero, Andy Dufresne, initially underwhelms the narrator Red: "I must admit I didn't think much of Andy the first time I laid eyes on him.... Looked like a stiff breeze could blow him over."

Dufresne is unjustly arrested, tried, condemned, and beaten. But as we watch him through Red's eyes, something like wonder begins to grow. In a brutal world he is kind. He is a man of hidden strengths who creates a library and helps his captors with their taxes. He is anxious for nothing: "Strolls like a man in a park without a care or a worry," says Red. He ascends to a high place (the warden's office) and plays Mozart over the intercom, and for a transcendent moment, every prisoner stands motionless in unexpected glory. And Red confesses: "Those voices soared. Higher and farther than anybody in a gray place dares to dream ... for the briefest of moments — every last man at Shawshank feels free."

Andy is persecuted by the warden, a pharisaical hypocrite who hands him a Bible and tells him "Salvation lies within."

In the end, salvation does lie in the Bible. The Bible is where Andy hides the small hammer with which he chips to freedom. (The cut-out space in the warden's Bible where Andy hides the chisel begins on the first page of Exodus, the story of God liberating his people from bondage.)

Andy descends into hell. He crawls to freedom through five hundred yards of prison sewer pipe half filled with sewage and comes out the other side cleansed by the river and the rain and raising his hands bathed in light and freedom. If you can't see the resurrection, you haven't been watching. His empty cell is the beginning of the end for the regime of the warden. ("Judgment cometh, and that right soon" reads the sign in his office.)

Andy, the Christ figure, and Red, the noble pagan, have a running argument about hope. Andy says that music is important in a prison —maybe more important in a prison than anywhere else, because it reminds hearers that there is an unseen reality the powers of the prison cannot touch.

Red asks what he's talking about.

Hope.

Red says hope is a dangerous thing. Hope can drive a man insane. Andy says hope is a good thing, maybe the best thing, and no good thing ever dies.

Let's pause here a moment.

The ancient Greeks lined up with Red. There is one art form, wrote Alain de Botton, that dedicates itself to telling stories of great failure without judgment or mockery. Tragedy was invented by the Greeks. The first traces of drama come from Greek religious ceremonies involving the sacrifice of goats; the word *tragedy* itself comes from the Greek words for "goat" and "song."

> *The purpose of tragedy is the moral elevation of the audience by reflecting on how the fate of the hero could be their fate.*

The purpose of tragedy is the moral elevation of the audience by reflecting on how the fate of the hero could be their fate. Aristotle said that in a good tragedy, the hero has to be neither perfect nor evil but someone we can identify with. The tragedian's task is to confront us with the inconvenient truth that we are capable of any folly. A good tragedy will leave the spectator sympathetic and humble.

The invention of tragedy was an enormous moral gift to the human race. Tragedy teaches that suffering can help us grow. The ancients taught that reason is noble because it enables human beings to endure suffering with patience and courage and therefore grow stronger. Suffering can build character so that the wise person can be ruled by reason in an uncaring and harsh world.

The apostle Paul appeared to concur with this idea when he wrote to the church at Rome: "We also glory in our sufferings, because we know that suffering produces perseverance; perseverance, character." But at the end he added as a climax what would never have occurred to a noble pagan: *"and character [produces] hope."*

No nonchristian ancient writer would have added that. The goal of life was to seek to live by reason and courage in a universe governed by uncaring necessity. Nietzsche said that Zeus gave hope to men to torture them: "In truth, [hope] is the most evil of evils because it prolongs man's torment."

Hope is a dangerous thing. Hope can drive you insane.

Paul added it for one reason. He believed that Jesus, who came to set the prisoners free, had now triumphed over death. Death is the way to life.

In *The Shawshank Redemption*, though, Red finds out paradoxically that when he leaves prison, life without hope cannot sustain him. His options are suicide or return to prison, except for a promise he made to his friend Andy. He does what Andy had asked. And at the foot of a tree, Red finds that his friend has paid, out of treasure Andy acquired through suffering, for Red to join him off the coast of Mexico, free and full of hope. In the final images, we see Andy, Red's friend, dressed in white, rehabbing a fishing boat at the edge of a long coastline next to the blue Pacific. Red's narration closes the movie:

> I am so excited I can barely sit still or hold a thought in my head....
> I hope I can make it across the border.
> I hope to see my friend and shake his hand.
> I hope the Pacific is as blue as it has been in my dreams.
> I hope....

— ⋅•⋅ —

I think of the change Jesus brought to the world around hope when I think about two tombstones. One of them marks the resting place of Mel Blanc, the famous voice of countless characters in *Looney Tunes* cartoons. In accordance with his instructions, his family inscribed as his final epitaph the words that he had said to end a thousand cartoons: *"That's all, folks."*

The other tombstone is described by Philip Yancey. It marks the grave of a friend's grandmother who lies buried under ancient oak trees in the cemetery of an Episcopal church in rural Louisiana. In accordance with the grandmother's instructions, only one word is inscribed on the tombstone: *Waiting.*

A Staggering Idea

"Once upon a time, the world had meaning."

This wonderful line is the beginning of a book called *Medieval Views of the Cosmos.* The authors point out how maps reflected the worldview of mapmakers in the Middle Ages.

Of course, maps are never totally neutral. Many of us grew up with maps that showed Europe and North America on the top half of the planet, mostly because the people who drew the maps came from Europe and North America. Another map circulating the Web these days shows the United States from the view of Californians: Florida is full of old people; New York is full of loud and obnoxious people; the Midwest is full of religious nutballs trying to convert everyone else.

In the Middle Ages, maps were not intended to be used for travel —people would employ live guides for that. Instead, maps were attempts to reflect on the meaning of the world, rather than just its terrain. That's why mapmakers would often include historical or biblical scenes.

A common feature of medieval maps was the city of Jerusalem at the center of the earth. There was an important reason for this. As N. T. Wright points out, that common feature reflected the ancient belief of Israel that Jerusalem—particularly the temple—was the heart of everything, the holiest place on earth.

Wright notes that some religions have sacred buildings that are a kind of escape from earth. The temple was very different. It was a sign that the God who created the world wants it back.

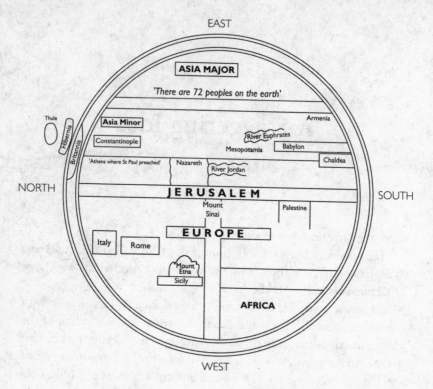

Those mapmakers didn't just want people to know where things were; they wanted them to reflect on how things should be. The map was a reminder that this is our Father's world. He has plans to reoccupy it. He intends to evict sin and rule the earth in justice and love, and to occupy Madison Avenue and Hollywood and the Rift Valley and the United Nations building. He established a play to "occupy Wall Street" way before any human activist every dreamed of it.

The temple was the focal point of everything, because it was a sign that God had established a toehold on the planet. "*The LORD is in his holy temple; let all the earth be silent before him.*"

Heaven and earth are not two separate spheres; they actually overlap and interlock. "The Temple is where heaven and earth meet." For Israel that looked like this:

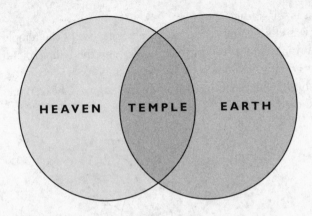

Events like sacrifice and dedicating and naming infants and worship took place in the temple because the temple is the place heaven invades earth, and when heaven invades earth, things happen:

Sins get forgiven.

Nobodies become somebodies.

Outcasts enter a relationship with God.

Human lives are given divine purpose.

Israel believed that God decided that in this one little place, people could get a glimpse of what it would be like for heaven to invade earth — so that they could keep hope alive. Moreover, they were waiting for the day when God's Occupy Earth plan began to expand beyond the temple.

———•·•———

Then Jesus came. He was presented as an infant to God in the temple. He returned to it in the only boyhood story we have about him, saying, "I had to be in my Father's house."

Jesus' association with the temple was very important. It got him killed.

Jesus began to say and do extraordinary things.

> "I tell you that something greater than the temple is here." (Matthew 12:6)

> "Destroy this temple, and I will raise it again in three days." (John 2:19, speaking of his body)

This is staggering.

He was talking and acting as if the whole idea of the temple was to point to him. He was talking as if everything the temple pictured was actually coming true now that he was around. He was claiming that in him—his life, his teachings, his body, his actions—heaven had finally invaded earth.

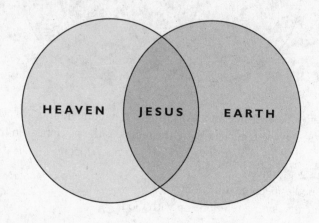

What happens when heaven invades earth?

Sins get forgiven.

Outcasts get taken in.

Nobodies become somebodies—the poor in spirit become blessed; Simon becomes Peter the Rock.

Human beings receive divine purpose: "Go into all the world and preach the gospel."

The cross seemed to put all such talk at an end. But then came the story of the resurrection, in which the ultimate invasion of earth by heaven was said to have happened.

——— ·◆· ———

To the great question behind this book "Who is this man?" came at last —with difficulty, with reluctance, with great joy—an answer. He must be, people said, something more than just a man. Humanity and divinity somehow intersect in this one man. He became like us so that we might become like him.

All of the wonders that we have been exploring through this book turned out to find their fullest expression in him: all roads meet; all threads are woven together in the tapestry of this life.

Heaven is now overlapping earth. Anybody who wants to get in on it can. People invite this man into their lives, and heaven starts invading earth through them. Paul said, "You yourselves are God's temple." In other words, Jesus woke something up, started something new, so that now heaven can invade earth through ordinary human beings.

God wants his will to be done on earth as it is in heaven. God wants a new map of the world. It doesn't require money, degrees, status, looks, talent, connections, or clout. In fact, those probably get in the way as often as they help. Anyone can be part of this.

When someone volunteers somewhere to help a left-out child learn to read, or seriously blesses a person in spiritual turmoil, or confesses holding a grudge against another and instead seeks to forgive, or gets an idea to be generous with their money and actually does so, or takes the time to actually look someone in the eye and love them, or crosses ethnic barriers in love, or shows compassion to an infant, or defends the rights of a vulnerable woman, or treats an overlooked nobody with dignity, or holds on to hope in the face of death … Then, once again, the temple is at the center of life. An ordinary human being becomes the nexus where heaven is invading earth.

———•◦•———

Jesus' life is not an abstract subject to be debated by experts. It is an invitation.

Early in Jesus' ministry, a man named Nathanael was skeptical about claims made on Jesus' behalf: "Nazareth! Can anything good come from there?" he asked.

Jesus was not offended by this. Philip, who was already following Jesus, extended an invitation to Nathanael that still goes out today: "Come and see."

Said another way, put what Jesus said to the test. Run an experiment. We all learn how to live from somebody: our parents, our peers, favorite writers, our appetites, our boss, or a vague combination of these. Try learning how to live from Jesus. Come and see. Whatever your ideas about religion might be, you can try being a student of Jesus. And that's a very good place to start.

Jesus told Nathanael, "You will see heaven open, and the angels of God ascending and descending on the Son of Man." He was referring to the Old Testament story of Jacob's ladder. The place where heaven and earth overlap. Try Jesus. Come and see.

Do you know what Jesus said about anything? Try living accordingly. Take a stab at removing contempt from your life, and see how life runs. See how well you are able to do it. Try living as if there is a heavenly Father who cares for and listens to you. Try living "without worry" one day at a time.

You have to go through tomorrow anyway. Try it with Jesus. Come and see.

The offer still stands.

Sources

CHAPTER 1: The Man Who Won't Go Away

12: G. K. Chesterton, *The Everlasting Man* (New York: Dodd Mead, 1930), 211.

13: Yemelian Yaroslavky: Quoted in Brian Moynahan, *The Faith* (New York: Doubleday, 2002), viii.

13: *"In the fifteenth year"*: Luke 3:1.

13: *"Maybe as few as one"*: See N.T. Wright, *Simply Jesus: A New View of Who He Was, What He Did, and Why He Matters* (New York: HarperOne, 2011), 7.

14: Milton Rokeach, *Three Christs of Ypsilanti* (1964; New York: NYRB Classics, 2011).

14: Jaroslav Pelikan, *Jesus through the Centuries: His Place in the History of Culture* (New Haven, CT: Yale University Press, 1985), 1.

14: Chesterton, *The Everlasting Man*, 9.

15: O. M. Bakke, *When Children Became People: The Birth of Childhood in Early Christianity* (Minneapolis: Augsburg Fortress, 2005).

15: *"Not from this world"*: Translation by N. T. Wright, who beneficially points out that the common rendering "not of this world" confuses the intended meaning because of implies that Jesus' kingdom has nothing to do with this-worldly matters.

16: *"We hold these truths"*: U.S. Declaration of Independence.

16: *"Whatever you did"*: Matthew 25:40.

17: N. T. Wright, *Simply Jesus: A New View of Who He Was, What He Did, and Why He Matters* (New York: HarperOne, 2011).

17: *"People who listened to him"*: Ibid., 9, emphasis mine.

17: *Groups claiming to be "for"* Jesus: Personal communication from Sharon Miller of Docent Research Group. http://www.docentgroup.com/.

17: Eugene Debs: Quoted in Richard Fox, *Jesus in America* (San Francisco: HarperSanFrancisco, 2004), 291.

18: Malcolm Muggeridge: Quoted in Thomas Cahill, *Desire of the Everlasting Hills: The World Before and After Jesus* (New York: Random House, 1999), 304–5.

18: Mary Karr, *The Liars' Club: A Memoir* (New York: Penguin, 2005): quoted in Roy F. Baumeister and John Tierney, *Willpower: Rediscovering the Greatest Human Strength* (New York: Penguin, 2011), 167.

19: Pelikan, *Jesus through the Centuries*, 17.

19: Andrew Walls, "The Expansion of Christianity," *Christian Century* (August 2000), 792: quoted in Timothy Keller, *The King's Cross: The Story of the World in the Life of Jesus* (New York: Dutton, 2011), 123.

19: Ralph Waldo Emerson, speech at Harvard Divinity College, July 15, 1838 (Boston: James Munroe, 1838), 10. (Available online.)

19: H. G. Wells, *The Greatest Men in History*, quoted in Mark Link, S.J., *He Is the Still Point of the Turning World* (Chicago: Argus, 1971), 111.

CHAPTER 2: The Collapse of Dignity

21: *"No one in Herod's period"*: Peter Richardson, *Herod: King of the Jews, Friend of the Romans* (Columbia: University of South Carolina Press, 1996), 12.

23: *"When King Herod heard this"*: Matthew 2:3.

23: *"Was furious, and he gave orders"*: Matthew 2:16–18.

23: *"O Little Town of Bethlehem"*: Words by Phillips Brooks, music by Lewis H. Redner.

23: *"Rachel weeping for her children"*: Matthew 2:18.

24: *"Go and search carefully"*: Matthew 2:8, 9, 11, 13, 19.

24: Plato and Pliny the Elder: Cited in O. M. Bakke, *When Children Became People: The Birth of Childhood in Early Christianity* (Minneapolis: Augsburg Fortress, 2005), 16–18.

24: *"After Herod died"*: Matthew 2:19.

26: Aristotle, *Politics*, bk. 1, chap. 5.

26: Nicholas Wolterstorff, *Justice: Rights and Wrongs* (Princeton, NJ: Princeton University Press, 2008).

27: Martin Luther King Jr.: Source unknown.

27: *"Because every girl"*: George MacDonald, *The Princess and the Goblin*. See, for example, http://derickmathew.blogspot.com.

28: Plutarch: Quoted in Bakke, *When Children Became People*, 30.

28: *"Kopros"*: W. V. Harris, "Child Exposure in the Roman Empire," in *Journal of Roman Studies* 84 (1994): 1–22.

28: *"A gruesome discovery"*: Bakke, *When Children Became People*, 32.

28: *"Who ... is the greatest"*: Matthew 18:1–4.

29: *"An example of conversion"*: See Frederick Dale Bruner, *Matthew: A Commentary*, vol. 2, The Churchbook (Grand Rapids: Eerdmans, 2004), 209.

29: *"And whoever welcomes"*: Matthew 18:5.

29: *"Let the little children"*: Matthew 19:14.

29: Shepherd of Hermas: Quoted in Bakke, *When Children Became People*, 66.

30: G. K. Chesterton, *The Everlasting Man* (New York: Dodd Mead, 1930), 243–44.

32: David Bentley Hart, *Atheist Delusions: The Christian Revolution and Its Fashionable Enemies* (New Haven, CT: Yale University Press, 2009), 175.

CHAPTER 3: A Revolution in Humanity

33: *"Filled with compassion"*: Mark 1:41 from 1984 ed. of NIV (2011 ed.: "Jesus was indignant").

33: *"His heart went out to her"*: Luke 7:13.

33: Elaine Aron, *Highly Sensitive People* (New York: Broadway, 1997).

33: *Jesus in the temple:* Matthew 21:12–13; Mark 11:15–17; Luke 19:45–46; John 2:13–17.

33: *"You snakes!":* Matthew 23:33.

34: *"Most awkward dinner parties":* See Luke 14:1–13.

34: *"If one of you has a child":* Luke 14:5–6.

35: *"If any of you has a sheep":* Matthew 12:11–12.

35: *"Look at the birds":* Matthew 6:26.

35: *"Are not sparrows":* Matthew 10:29–30.

35: *"Gray hair is a crown":* From 1984 ed. of NIV.

36: *"When you give a luncheon":* Luke 14:12–14.

37: *"Blessed is anyone who will eat":* Luke 14:15.

38: *"The poor, the crippled":* Luke 14:21.

38: *"Roads and country lanes":* Luke 14:23.

38: Nicholas Wolterstorff, *Justice: Rights and Wrongs* (Princeton, NJ: Princeton University Press, 2008), 126–27.

38: Rodney Stark, citing ancient quotations in his book *The Rise of Christianity: How the Obscure, Marginal, Jesus Movement Became the Dominant Religious Force* (New York: HarperOne, 1996), chap. 4.

38: Thucydides, *History of the Peloponnesian War*, 2.47–54.

39: Dionysius: Quoted in Stark, *The Rise of Christianity*, chap. 4.

39: *"I was hungry":* Matthew 25:35–36, 40.

39: Julian the Apostate, *Against the Galileans.*

39: Basil: Source unknown.

40: Gregory of Nyssa, from his sermon "On the Love of the Poor": quoted in Nonna Harrison, *God's Many Splendored Image* (Grand Rapids: Baker, 2010), 101–2.

40: Jean Henri Dunant: See, for example, http://www.britannica.com/EBchecked/topic/173580/Henri-Dunant or http://biography.yourdictionary.com/jean-henri-dunant.

40: Theodor Fliedner: See, for example, http://encycl.opentopia.com/term/Theodor_Fliedner or http://www.answers.com/topic/theodor-fliedner.

40: Father Damien: See, for example, http://www.newadvent.org/cathen/04615a.htm or http://www.answers.com/topic/father-damien.

40: Tertullian: Quoted in Stark, *The Rise of Christianity*, 87.

41: *"Non habens personam":* Quoted in David Bentley Hart, *Atheist Delusions: The Christian Revolution and Its Fashionable Enemies* (New Haven, CT: Yale University Press, 2009), 168.

41: *"Beatings and kickings":* See O. M. Bakke, *When Children Became People: The Birth of Childhood in Early Christianity* (Minneapolis: Augsburg Fortress, 2005), 138.

41: *"There is neither Jew nor Gentile":* Galatians 3:28.

41: Thomas Cahill, *Desire of the Everlasting Hills: The World Before and After Jesus* (New York: Random House, 1999), 141.

42: Gregory of Nyssa: Quoted in Harrison, *God's Many Splendored Image*, 97.

42: "How can you": Ibid., 99.

42: Mark Noll, The Civil War As a Theological Crisis (Chapel Hill: University of North Carolina Press, 2006), 97.

42: "I was in prison": Matthew 25:36.

43: Elizabeth Fry: See A. Kenneth Curtis et al., The 100 Most Important Events in Christian History (Grand Rapids: Revell, 1998), 152.

44: Mark Nelson: Personal communication. Nelson is Monroe Professor of Communication at Westmont College.

44: "The poor you will always": Matthew 26:11; Mark 14:7; John 12:8.

44: Kevin Bales: Cited in Harrison, God's Many Splendored Image, 103.

44: Nonna Harrison: Ibid., 104–5.

CHAPTER 4: What Does a Woman Want?

47: "Ancient Greco-Roman world": See Rodney Stark, The Rise of Christianity: How the Obscure, Marginal, Jesus Movement Became the Dominant Religious Force (New York: HarperOne, 1996), 97.

47: "I ask and beg of you": Quoted in ibid., 97–98.

47: Posidippus: Quoted in Mark Golden, "Demography and the Exposure of Girls in Athens," in Phoenix 35, no. 4 (Winter 1981): 316.

47: Amartya Sen, "More Than 100 Million Women Are Missing," in New York Review of Books 37, no. 19 (December 1990).

47: Mara Hvstendahl, Unnatural Selection: Choosing Boys over Girls and the Consequences in a World Full of Men (New York: Public Affairs, 2011).

48: "Tired as he was": John 4:6.

48: "Just then his disciples returned": John 4:27.

48: Lynn Cohick: From a talk given at a Christians for Biblical Equality Conference at Wheaton College, September 25, 2010.

50: "After this, Jesus traveled about": Luke 8:1–3.

51: Socrates: Quoted in Yoel Kahn, The Three Blessings: Boundaries, Censorship, and Identity in Jewish Liturgy (New York: Oxford University Press, 2010).

51: Dietrich Bonhoeffer: Quoted in Leon Morris, The Gospel according to Matthew, Pillar New Testament Commentary Series (Grand Rapids: Eerdmans, 1992), 727n104.

52: "In Christ Jesus you are all": Galatians 3:26–28, emphasis mine.

52: "You are no longer a slave": Galatians 4:4, from 1984 ed. of NIV.

52: "As Jesus was saying these things": Luke 11:27.

52: "Blessed rather are those": Luke 11:28, emphasis mine.

53: "She had a sister called Mary": Luke 10:39.

53: "Martha, Martha": Luke 10:41–42.

54: "I am a Jew": Acts 22:3.

54: John Chrysostom: Quoted in Frederick Dale Bruner, Matthew: A Commentary, vol. 2, The Churchbook (Grand Rapids: Eerdmans, 2004), 767.

55: Celsus: Quoted in Robert Wilkins, *The Christians as the Romans Saw Them* (New Haven, CT: Yale University Press, 2003), 111.

55: *"In Israel, receiving testimony"*: Cited in Tal Ilan, *Jewish Women in Greco-Roman Palestine* (Peabody, MA: Hendrickson, 1995), 163ff. See this book for much other helpful discussion of the status of women in Judaism during the Greco-Roman era.

55: *"When they came back from the tomb"*: Luke 24:9, 11.

55: Pliny the Younger, bk. 10, letter 96.

56: Tim Miller Dyck, "Women Building the Church," in *Canadian Mennonite* 11, no. 9 (April 30, 2007).

57: O. M. Bakke, *When Children Became People: The Birth of Childhood in Early Christianity* (Minneapolis: Augsburg Fortress, 2005).

57: Sigmund Freud: Quoted in Ernest Jones, *Sigmund Freud: Life and Work*, Vol. 2 (New York: Basic Books, 1955), 421.

58: Dorothy Sayers, *Are Women Human? Penetrating, Sensible, and Witty Essays on the Role of Women in Society* (Grand Rapids: Eerdmans, 2005), 68.

CHAPTER 5: An Undistinguished Visiting Scholar

60: *"When Jesus had finished"*: Matthew 7:28–29.

60: *"It is more blessed"*: Acts 20:35.

61: G. K. Chesterton, *The Everlasting Man* (New York: Dodd Mead, 1930), 249.

61: *"Christ, in whom are hidden"*: Colossians 2:2–3.

62: Harvey Cox, *When Jesus Came to Harvard: Making Moral Choices Today* (Boston: Mariner, 2006), 121.

62: Dallas Willard: Chapter 3 of Willard's *The Divine Conspiracy* (San Francisco: HarperOne, 1998) is helpful for this discussion.

63: *"We cannot supply you"*: President Benno Schmidt of Yale University, in a Freshman Address, 1990: quoted in William H. Willimon, *Peculiar Speech: Preaching to the Baptized* (Grand Rapids: Eerdmans, 1992), 42.

63: *"Hear, O Israel"*: Deuteronomy 6:4–5.

63: *"All authority in heaven"*: Matthew 28:18–20.

63: *"Day after day, in the temple courts"*: Acts 5:42.

64: *"Love the Lord your God"*: Matthew 22:37.

64: *"The word mind"*: Here Jesus is following the Septuagint version of the Old Testament.

64: Tertullian: Quoted in Rodney Stark, *The Rise of Christianity: How the Obscure, Marginal, Jesus Movement Became the Dominant Religious Force* (New York: HarperOne, 1996), 87.

64: Saint Jerome: See Thomas Cahill, *How the Irish Saved Civilization* (New York: Doubleday Anchor, 1996), 159.

65: *"Balaam's donkey"*: See Numbers 22:21–35, especially verses 28 and 30.

65: Jaroslav Pelikan, *Jesus through the Centuries: His Place in the History of Culture* (New Haven, CT: Yale University Press, 1985), 120.

65: George Marsden, *The Soul of the American University* (New York: Oxford University Press, 1994), 34.

66: *"I shall really go after the shameful"*: Martin Luther, *The Christian in Society III*, vol. 46 in *Luther's Works*, American ed. (Philadelphia: Fortress, 1957), 211.

66: *"It being one chief project"*: See www.constitution.org/primarysources/deluder/html.

66: Marsden, *The Soul of the American University*, 33.

67: Robert Raikes: See A. Kenneth Curtis et al., *The 100 Most Important Events in Christian History* (Grand Rapids: Revell, 1998), 138–39.

68: Frank Laubach: See, e.g., www.spiritus-temporis.com/frank-laubach/.

68: Diogenes Allen, *Christian Belief in a Postmodern World* (Louisville: Westminster John Knox, 1989), 11.

68: Johannes Kepler: Source unknown.

69: Alfred North Whitehead, *Science and the Modern World* (New York: Macmillan, 1925; repr., New York: Mentor, 1948), 13.

69: Dinesh D'Souza, *What's So Great about Christianity?* (Washington, DC: Regnery, 2007), 83–84.

69: Lynn White: Quoted in Vishal Mangalwadi, *The Book That Made Your World* (Nashville: Thomas Nelson, 2011), 95.

69: Mangalwadi: Ibid., 98.

70: Konrad Burdach: Quotation from Pelikan, *Jesus through the Centuries*, 146.

70: Washington Irving: See Evelyn Edson and Emilie Savage-Smith, *Medieval Views of the Cosmos* (Oxford: Bodleian Library, University of Oxford, 2004), 7–8.

71: Mark A. Noll, *The Scandal of the Evangelical Mind* (Grand Rapids: Eerdmans, 1994), 3.

71: *"Upstart astrologer"*: Martin Luther, *Lectures on Genesis Chapters 21–25*, vol. 22 in *Luther's Works*, American ed. (Philadelphia: Fortress, 1957).

71: Robert Wilkins, *The Christians as the Romans Saw Them* (New Haven, CT: Yale University Press, 2003), 195.

CHAPTER 6: Jesus Was Not a Great Man

74: Francis Ambrosio, "The Heroic Age—The Greek Worldview," pt. 3 in *Philosophy, Religion, and the Meaning of Life*, The Great Courses (Chantilly, VA: The Teaching Company, 2009), lecture on DVD.

74: Cicero: Quoted in Joseph Hellerman, *Reconstructing Honor in Roman Philippi* (Cambridge: Cambridge University Press, 2005), 3.

74: Alasdair MacIntyre, *A Short History of Ethics* (Notre Dame, IN: University of Notre Dame Press, 1998), 78–79.

75: *"The existence of inferiors"*: Quoted in Hellerman, *Reconstructing Honor in Roman Philippi*, 10.

76: *"Remarkably incommodious garment"*: See Hellerman, *Reconstructing Honor in Roman Philippi*.

76: *"Wearing a gold ring"*: James 2:2.

77: *"Vulgar are the means"*: Hellerman, *Reconstructing Honor in Roman Philippi*, 20.

77: *"A slave of Christ Jesus"*: In Romans 1:1, the Greek word *doulos* is more accurately translated "slave" than "servant."

77: *"We preach Christ crucified"*: 1 Corinthians 1:23.

77: *"Anyone hung on a tree"*: Deuteronomy 21:23 NRSV.

77: *"We serve a crucified slave"*: See, e.g., Romans 6:18, 22; Ephesians 6:6.

78: *"A wealthy person might"*: Marcel Mauss, *The Gift* (New York: W. W. Norton, 1990), 41ff.

78: Plutarch, *Cato Maior*, 18.4.

78: Caesar Augustus: Quoted in John Dickson, *Humilitas: A Lost Key to Life, Love, and Leadership* (Grand Rapids: Zondervan, 2011), 92–93.

79: Robin Lane Fox, *Pagans and Christians* (New York: HarperCollins, 1988), 324.

79: *"You know that the rulers"*: Matthew 20:25 NLT.

79: *"Not so with you. Instead"*: Matthew 20:26–28.

80: *"Jesus knew that the Father"*: John 13:3–5.

81: *"For who is greater"*: Luke 22:27.

81: *"Is it not the one who"*: Luke 22:27.

82: Dale Bruner: Personal communication.

82: *"You call me 'Teacher' and 'Lord' "*: John 13:13–14.

82: *"He humbled himself"*: Philippians 2:8.

82: *"In Christ, taught the Christians"*: Lane Fox, *Pagans and Christians*, 336.

82: Plato: Source unknown.

83: Hellerman, *Reconstructing Honor in Roman Philippi*.

83: Celsus: See Robert Wilkins, *The Christians as the Romans Saw Them* (New Haven, CT: Yale University Press, 2003), 93.

83: *"Do not be proud"*: Romans 12:16.

84: Jim Collins, *Built to Last: Successful Habits of Visionary Companies* (New York: Harper Business Essentials, 2002).

84: Douglas MacArthur: See William Manchester, *American Caesar: Douglas MacArthur 1880–1964* (Boston: Little Brown, 1978).

84: *"The conclusion was clear"*: Dickson, *Humilitas*, 99.

85: *"It is unlikely that any of us"*: Ibid., 112.

85: *"The number of people with AIDS"*: For statistics, see, e.g., Avert, an international charity organization, at http://www.avert.org/aidssouthafrica.htm.

CHAPTER 7: Help Your Friends, Punish Your Enemies

87: *"Docimedus has lost two gloves"*: Quoted in David Konstan, *Before Forgiveness: The Origins of a Moral Idea* (Cambridge: Cambridge University Press, 2010), 13.

87: *"I invoke you, holy angels"*: Quoted in John G. Gager, *Curse Tablets and Binding Spells from the Ancient World* (New York: Oxford University Press, 1992), 55.

88: *"You have heard that it was said"*: Matthew 5:43.

88: Xenophon, *The Life of Cyrus the Great*, 8.7.28.

88: Konstan, *Before Forgiveness*, 10ff.

89: "Helping Friends and Harming Enemies": Monograph by Mary Blumenthal, cited in Reiser, "Love of Enemies in the Context of Antiquity," 412.

89: *"I tell you, love your enemies"*: Matthew 5:44–45.

89: *"If you love [only] those"*: Matthew 5:46–47.

89: Hannah Arendt, *The Human Condition* (Chicago: University of Chicago Press, 1958), Part 33.

90: *"The 'other side' "*: Ray Vander Laan, *Discovery Guide: Death and Resurrection of the Messiah*, Faith Lessons vol. 3 (Grand Rapids: Zondervan, 2009), 44.

90: *"The Canaanites, Hittites, Hivites"*: Joshua 3:10.

90: *"Paul related"*: Acts 13:19.

91: *"What do you want with me?"*: Mark 5:7.

92: *"And all the people were amazed"*: Mark 5:20.

92: *"They ran throughout that whole region"*: Mark 6:55–66.

93: *"You will give some of your money"*: Muzafer Sherif and Carolyn Wood Sherif, *Social Psychology*, rev. ed. (New York: Harper & Row, 1969). See section on intergroup conflict.

93: *"Now Abel kept flocks"*: Genesis 4:2.

93: Cornelius Tacitus, *The Annals: The Reigns of Tiberius, Claudius, and Nero*, 15:44, in Oxford World's Classics, trans. by J. C. Yardley (New York: Oxford University Press, 2008).

94: *"Die heretic!"*: This joke was written by comedian Emo Phillips and was voted the funniest religious joke of all time by the website Ship of Fools.

94: Miroslav Volf, *Exclusion and Embrace: A Theological Exploration of Identity, Otherness, and Reconciliation* (Nashville: Abingdon, 1996), cf. chap. 1.

95: *Conan the Barbarian*: Movie directed by John Milius for Edward Pressman Productions, 1982.

96: Frederick Dale Bruner, *Matthew: A Commentary*, vol. 2, The Churchbook (Grand Rapids: Eerdmans, 2004). See his comments on Matthew 26:51ff.

96: Anne Lamott. See, e.g., www.goodreads.com/quotes/7113.Anne-Lamott.

96: Dietrich Bonhoeffer, *Life Together* (San Francisco: Harper & Row, 1954), 17–18.

97: *"Lord, do not hold"*: Acts 7:60.

97: *"Army of piety"*: Quoted in Robert Wilkins, *The Christians as the Romans Saw Them* (New Haven, CT: Yale University Press, 2003), 117.

97: *Shooting in Amish schoolhouse*: See, e.g., www.800padutch.com/amishshooting.shtml.

97: Desmond Tutu: Speech at Fuller Seminary, date unknown.

97: Maurice: See Alvin J. Schmidt, *How Christianity Changed the World* (Grand Rapids: Zondervan, 2004), 32.

98: Taylor Branch, *Parting the Waters: America in the King Years 1954–63* (New York: Simon & Schuster, 1989), 862.

99: Charles Colson, "Love Your Enemies: Forgiveness in Rwanda," at crosswalk.com (February 2, 2009). See www.crosswalk.com/news/love-your-enemies-forgiveness-in-rwanda–11598997.html.

99: *Mary and Oshea:* The story is also told on the Internet, e.g., at http://thecatholic spirit.com/featured/from-death-to-life/.

101: *"Love your neighbor . . . enemy":* See Matthew 5:43–44.

CHAPTER 8: There Are Things That Are Not Caesar's

102: Heifetz: Quoted in Anthony B. Robinson and Robert W. Wall, *Called to Be Church: The Book of Acts for a New Day* (Grand Rapids: Eerdmans, 2006), 42.

102: *"My kingdom is not of this world":* John 18:36.

102: *"Hosanna! [Lord, save us!]":* See Psalm 118:25–26; John 12:13.

103: *"Born king of the Jews":* Matthew 2:2.

103: *Seven different wills:* Peter Richardson, *Herod: King of the Jews and Friend of the Romans* (Columbia, SC: University of South Carolina Press, 1996), 20–21.

103: Foreman: See George Foreman's website, http://biggeorge.com/main/familyman .php.

103: *"When he [Joseph] heard":* Matthew 2:22–23.

103: *"He went on to tell them a parable":* Luke 19:11–15.

104: *"Those enemies of mine":* Luke 19:27–28.

105: *"Not found anyone in Israel":* Matthew 8:10.

106: *"If anyone forces you":* Matthew 5:41.

106: *"Teacher, . . . we know you are":* Matthew 22:16–17.

106: *"You hypocrites, why are you":* Matthew 22:19–20.

106: *"Give back to Caesar":* Matthew 22:21.

108: Rodney Stark, *Discovering God: The Origins of the Great Religions and the Evolution of Belief* (New York: HarperOne, 2007), 101.

108: *"The prosperity of Babylon":* See Jeremiah 29:7.

109: Tertullian, "Apologetic: To Scapula," chapter 2 in *Ante-Nicene Fathers*, vol. 3, trans. Sydney Thelwell (Wikisource).

109: Robert Wilkins, *The Christians as the Romans Saw Them* (New Haven, CT: Yale University Press, 2003), 124.

109: Virgil: Quoted in Jaroslav Pelikan, *Jesus through the Centuries: His Place in the History of Culture* (New Haven, CT: Yale University Press, 1985), 50.

110: *"Christians are not distinguished":* From Epistle of Mathetes to Diognetus 5.5, quoted in *Early Christian Writings*, trans. by J. B. Lightfoot, 1891, italics mine. See www.earlychristianwritings.com.

110: Augustine: *City of God*, quoted in Rodney Stark, *Victory of Reason: How Christianity Led to Freedom, Capitalism, and Western Success* (New York: Random House, 2005), 81.

110: Bernard Lewis: Quoted in Dinesh D'Souza, *What's So Great about Christianity?* (Washington, DC: Regnery, 2007), 48.

111: *"A college teacher of mine":* Emory A. Griffen, *The Mind Changers* (Wheaton: Tyndale, 1987).

111: *He wedded ("dowry, veil and all"):* Brian Moynahan, *The Faith* (New York: Doubleday, 2002), 38–39.

112: "Given their monopoly situation": Stark, Discovering God, 329.

112: "You have not thought about your guilt": Jonathan Hill, What Has Christianity Ever Done for Us? (Downers Grove, IL: IVP, 2005), 157.

112: "Right and wrong are determined": Ibid., 158.

113: Alfred the Great: Quoted in Sir Winston Churchill, The Birth of Britain (New York: Dodd, Mead, 1956), 88ff.

113: "Here is a law": Churchill, The Birth of Britain, 188.

113: John Quincy Adams: Quoted in D. James Kennedy, What If Jesus Had Never Been Born (Nashville: Thomas Nelson, 1994), 82.

114: "Whoever tortures a human being": Marie Dennis, Oscar Romero: Reflections on His Life and Writings (Maryknoll, NY: Orbis, 2000), 114ff.

115: Philip Jenkins, The Next Christendom: The Coming of Global Christianity. 3rd ed. Vol. 3, Future of Christianity Trilogy (New York: Oxford University Press, 2011), 275.

CHAPTER 9: The Good Life vs. The Good Person

116: Dallas Willard, Knowing Christ Today (New York: HarperOne, 2009), 47–48.

117: "Blessed are those that mourn": Matthew 5:4.

117: "Perhaps the greatest contribution of Christ": Willard, Knowing Christ Today, 53.

117: Mark Twain: Quoted in Bruce Cavanaugh, The Sower's Seeds: One Hundred and Twenty Inspiring Stories for Preaching, Teaching and Public Speaking (Mahwah, NJ: Paulist Press, 2004), 55.

117: "A book called unChristian": David Kinnaman and Gabe Lyons, unChristian: What a New Generation Really Thinks about Christianity . . . and Why It Matters (Grand Rapids: Baker, 2007), 41.

117: "At a recent annual meeting": Craig Brian Larson and Phyllis Ten Elshof, 1001 Illustrations That Connect: Compelling Stories, Stats, and News Items for Preaching, Teaching, and Writing, #272, contributed by Stephen Nordbye (Grand Rapids: Zondervan, 2008).

118: Eva Kittay, "Hypocrisy," in Encyclopedia of Ethics, ed. by Lawrence C. Becker (New York: Garland, 1992), 1:582–87.

118: "The concept of hypocrisy": Ibid., 583.

119: "It is clear from the literary records": Dallas Willard, The Divine Conspiracy (New York: HarperOne, 1998), 191.

119: "Woe to you . . .": See Matthew 23:13ff.

120: "Greek gods do not give laws": Stark, Discovering God, 92.

120: "The life of the gods": Mary Lefkowitz, Greek Gods, Human Lives (New Haven, CT: Yale University Press, 2003), 83.

120: Robin Lane Fox, Pagans and Christians (New York: HarperCollins, 1988), 38.

121: Thomas Cahill, Desire of the Everlasting Hills: The World Before and After Jesus (New York: Random House, 1999), 318.

121: "Woe to you, teachers of the law": Matthew 23:13–33.

122: "All utensils have an inside and outside": Mishnah tractate Kelim 25:1, quoted in

Dictionary of New Testament Background, ed. Craig Evans and Stanley Porter (Downers Grove, IL: InterVarsity, 2000), 896.

122: *"It was in fact a great revolution"*: Michael Novak, *No One Sees God* (New York: Doubleday, 2008), 46.

122: *"Eighty-five percent of medical students"*: Ashley Wazana, "Physicians and the Pharmaceutical Industry: Is a Gift Ever Just a Gift?" *Journal of the American Medical Association* 283, no. 3 (January 19, 2000), 373.

123: *"If you hold to my teaching"*: John 8:31–32.

124: *"Foreign to Plato was the cry of Saint Paul"*: Novak, *No One Sees God*, 156.

124: C. S. Lewis, *Mere Christianity* (New York: Macmillan, 1943), 167.

125: *"The Twelve Steps"*: Ernest Kurtz, *AA: The Story* (rev. ed. of *Not God: A History of Alcoholics Anonymous*) (New York: Random House, 1991).

125: *"The Happy Hypocrite"*: See www.gutenberg.org/ebooks/36497.

CHAPTER 10: Why It's a Small World after All

127: *Holden Caufield*: J. D. Salinger, *Catcher in the Rye* (New York: Little Brown, 1945), 130–31.

128: *"At once"* and *"Without delay"*: Mark 1:18, 20.

128: *"All peoples on earth"*: Genesis 12:3; 28:14.

128: M. Scott Peck, *Further along the Road Less Traveled* (New York: Simon & Schuster, 1993), 160.

129: *"Unschooled, ordinary men"*: Acts 4:13.

129: *"Ate together with glad and sincere hearts"*: Acts 2:46.

129: *"People in general liked what they saw"*: Acts 2:47 MSG.

130: *"Here there is no Gentile or Jew"*: Colossians 3:11–12.

130: *"One did not speak of 'believing in gods' "*: Robert Wilkins, *The Christians as the Romans Saw Them* (New Haven, CT: Yale University Press, 2003), 64.

130: *"A riddle wrapped"*: Winston Churchill, radio broadcast, 1 October 1939.

130: Pliny the Younger: Quoted in Robert Wilkins, *The Christians as the Romans Saw Them* (New Haven, CT: Yale University Press, 2003), 23.

131: *"While pagan priests"*: Robin Lane Fox, *Pagans and Christians* (New York: HarperCollins, 1988), 323ff.

131: *"It is our care of the helpless"*: Tertullian, "Apology," in *The Ante-Nicene Fathers*, ed. Alexander Roberts et al. (Grand Rapids: Eerdmans, 1989), vol. 2.

131: *"Easier to be a nominal Christian"*: Jaroslav Pelikan, *Jesus through the Centuries: His Place in the History of Culture* (New Haven, CT: Yale University Press, 1985), 113.

132: *"Anthony was the first to 'join the geography' "*: Dorothy Bass, *A People's History of Christianity* (New York: HarperOne, 2009), 46.

132: *"There are as many monks in the desert"*: Ibid., 47.

132: Simeon Stylites: See Will Durant, *The Age of Faith*, The Story of Civilization, vol. 4 (New York: Simon & Schuster, 1950), 58ff.

132: *"Alternative communities"*: Elizabeth Rapley, *The Lord as Their Portion: The*

Story of the Religious Orders and How They Shaped Our World (Grand Rapids: Eerdmans, 2011).

133: *"The sense of mission"*: Richard A. Fletcher, *The Barbarian Conversion* (New York: Henry Holt, 1997), 2.

133: *"The tremendous achievement"*: Lowrie John Daly, *Benedictine Monasticism: Its Formation and Development through the 12th Century* (New York: Sheed & Ward, 1965), 135–36.

133: G. K. Chesterton, *Saint Francis of Assisi* (Garden City, NY: Doubleday, 1931), 51.

133: George Fox: Quoted in Bass, *A People's History of Christianity*, 224.

133: Bass: Ibid., 224.

134: Eugene Peterson, *The Pastor: A Memoir* (New York: HarperOne, 2010), 47–48.

135: John Somerville, *The Decline of the Secular University* (New York: Oxford University Press, 2006), 135–36.

135: *"No one who recognizes the total depravity"*: Dr. Neal Plantinga at Calvin Theological Seminary.

135: G. K. Chesterton, *The Everlasting Man* (New York: Dodd Mead, 1930), 4.

CHAPTER 11: The Truly Old-Fashioned Marriage

137: Pseudo-Demosthenes: Quoted in Nancy Sorkin Rabinowitz and Lisa Auanger, eds., *Among Women: From the Homosocial to the Homoerotic in the Ancient World* (Austin: University of Texas Press, 2002), 293.

137: Larry Yarbrough, "Paul, Marriage and Divorce," in *Paul and the Greco-Roman World*, ed. Paul Sampley (Harrisburg, PA: Trinity Press International, 2003), 404. If there was any boastfulness in the statement, it would be financial and not sexual; only men of a certain level of wealth would be able to afford that lifestyle. Historian Robin Lane Fox wrote that before marriage a young man could turn to slaves or prostitutes as a sexual outlet; parents might worry about it, not as an inappropriate practice (married men engaged in it too), but because it was expensive. Robin Lane Fox, *Pagans and Christians* (New York: HarperCollins, 1988), 344.

138: *"It was a property crime"*: A number of epitaphs praise a "one-man woman," a woman who had remained sexually faithful to her husband throughout marriage. There are no epitaphs to a "one-woman man."

138: *"A man was outlawed"*: This may not have been strictly observed, for a Roman statesman named Rufinus wrote, "Does anyone throw his woman out naked when he happens to find a lover with her, as if he had not enjoyed adultery himself?" See Lane Fox, *Pagans and Christians*, 346.

138: *"But, though passersby would have known"*: Yarbrough, "Paul, Marriage and Divorce," 405.

138: *"Early Rome required Romans to be married"*: "Family and Household" in *Dictionary of New Testament Background*, ed. Craig Evans and Stanley Porter (Downers Grove, IL: InterVarsity Press, 2000), 680. "The purpose of a Roman marriage was to produce legitimate children." Yarbrough, "Paul, Marriage and Divorce," 406.

138: *"Caesar Augustus outlawed marriage"*: Lane Fox, *Pagans and Christians*, 345.

139: *"The Roman emperor Commodus"*: Alvin J. Schmidt, *How Christianity Changed the World* (Grand Rapids: Zondervan, 2004), 86.

139: Tatian: Quoted in Vivian Green, *A New History of Christianity* (New York: Continuum, 1996), 10.

139: *"Freeborn girls were often married"*: See Lane Fox, *Pagans and Christians*, 348.

140: *"Woman, why do you involve me?"*: John 2:4.

140: *"A clock would start ticking"*: Philip Yancey, *The Jesus I Never Knew* (Grand Rapids: Zondervan, 2002), 168.

140: *"Haven't you read. . . ?"*: Matthew 19:4–6.

141: Walter Wangerin, *As for Me and My House: Crafting Your Marriage* (Nashville: Thomas Nelson, 2001), 8.

142: William Shakespeare, "The Phoenix and the Turtle," in *The Complete Works of Shakespeare*, ed. Hardin Craig (Glenview, IL: Scott, Foresman, 1973), 463.

142: *"Adam and his wife were both naked"*: Genesis 2:25.

142: *"Adam made love to his wife"*: Genesis 4:1.

143: *"And you shall know (yada) the LORD"*: Hosea 2:20 NRSV.

143: G. K. Chesterton, *What's Wrong with the World?* (London: Dodd, Mead, 1912), 68.

143: *"You have heard that it was said"*: Matthew 5:27.

143: *"But I tell you"*: Matthew 5:28.

144: Naomi Wolf: See "The Porn Myth," http://nymag.com/nymetro/news/trends/n_9437/.

145: *"Flee from sexual immorality"*: 1 Corinthians 6:18.

145: *Book of Common Prayer*: The quote is from the 1662 version of the Book of Common Prayer; the spelling is more readable than the original.

147: Augustine: Quoted in Duane Friesen, *Artists, Citizens, Philosophers: Seeking the Peace of the City* (Scottsdale, PA: Herald, 2000), 199.

148: *"Radical redefinition of the sacred"*: Dorothy Bass, *A People's History of Christianity* (New York: HarperOne, 2009), 191.

149: *"By faith the prostitute Rahab"*: Hebrews 11:31.

149: *"Husbands, love your wives"*: Ephesians 5:25.

CHAPTER 12: Without Parallel in the Entire History of Art

151: Peter Berger: Quoted in Huston Smith, *The Soul of Christianity* (New York: HarperOne, 2005), xxi.

151: Mickey Hart: Quoted in ibid.

151: Isocrates and Demosthenes: The historicity of this quote is doubtful and often refers to others instead of Isocrates. But it makes a wonderful point. See, for example, Henri J. Blits at http://presentinghenri.blogspot.com/.

152: *"He did not know what to say"*: Mark 9:6.

152: Aristotle: Quoted in Philip Yancey, *The Jesus I Never Knew* (Grand Rapids: Zondervan, 2002), 267.

152: Reynolds Price: Quoted in ibid., 269.

153: Austin Farrer: Quoted in Diogenes Allen, *Christian Belief in a Postmodern World* (Louisville: Westminster John Knox, 1989), 11.

153: Augustine: Quoted in Nicholas Wolterstorff, *Justice: Rights and Wrongs* (Princeton, NJ: Princeton University Press, 2008), 191.

153: Porphyry: Quoted in Robert Wilkins, *The Christians as the Romans Saw Them* (New Haven, CT: Yale University Press, 2003), 149.

154: Julian of Norwich: Quoted in Dallas Willard, *The Divine Conspiracy* (San Francisco: HarperOne, 1998), 77.

154: Paul Johnson, *Jesus: A Biography from a Believer* (New York: Penguin, 2010), 127–28, italics mine.

154: Martin Luther King Jr.: Speech at the Great March in Detroit, June 23, 1963. See http://mlk-kpp01.stanford.edu.

155: Telemachus: David Bentley Hart, *Atheist Delusions: The Christian Revolution and Its Fashionable Enemies* (New Haven, CT: Yale University Press, 2009), 123.

155: Michael Grant, *Jesus: An Historian's Overview of the Gospels* (New York: Scribner, 1977), 1.

156: *Celie:* Alice Walker, *The Color Purple*, quoted in Duane Friesen, *Artists, Citizens, Philosophers: Seeking the Peace of the City* (Scottsdale, PA: Herald, 2000), 172.

156: *Pelikan:* Jaroslav Pelikan, *Jesus through the Centuries: His Place in the History of Culture* (New Haven, CT: Yale University Press, 1985), 83, emphasis mine.

156: *John of Damascus:* Ibid., 89.

157: *Augustine:* Quoted in Edward Lucie-Smith, *The Face of Jesus* (New York: Abrams, 2011), 14.

157: *Augustine: Confessions*, quoted in Pelikan, *Jesus through the Centuries*, 94.

157: *Augustine:* Quoted in Jonathan Hill, *What Has Christianity Ever Done for Us?* (Downers Grove, IL: IVP, 2005), 106.

157: *"Whom many historians":* Pelikan, *Jesus through the Centuries*, 164.

157: *"So also the various Reformation translations":* Pelikan, *Jesus through the Centuries*, 161.

157: *"What makes the gospels":* Thomas Cahill, *Desire of the Everlasting Hills: The World Before and After Jesus* (New York: Random House, 1999), 284.

158: *"To a writer's eyes":* Ibid.

158: *Martin Luther:* Quoted in Pelikan, *Jesus through the Centuries*, 163.

158: *"One of the Reformation's":* Ibid.

158: *Nathan Soderblom:* Quoted in ibid.

159: *Karl Barth:* See Friesen, *Artists, Citizens, Philosophers*, 172.

159: *"The Lanky Good Shepherd":* Thomas Matthews, quoted in James Davison Hunter, *To Change the World: The Irony, Tragedy, and Possibility of Christianity in the Late Modern World* (New York: Oxford University Press, 2010), 56.

159: *"There is found in her nothing":* Martin Luther, "Magnificat" in vol. 21 of *Luther's Works*, ed. by Jaroslav Pelikan (St. Louis: Concordia, 1956), 84.

160: *"The influence of Christianity"*: See Hill, *What Has Christianity Ever Done for Us?* 79ff.

160: *"Foxes have holes"*: See Matthew 8:20; Luke 9:58.

161: *"Looking at that picture"*: Fyodor Dostoyevsky, *The Idiot* (New York: Macmillan, 1913), 410.

161: *"A professor of mine"*: Ian Pitt-Watson, personal communication.

161: *"To see your face"*: Genesis 33:10.

162: *"Men need only trust"*: Quoted in Janko Lavin, *Tolstoy: An Approach* (London: Methuen, 1944), 101.

162: *Eliot*: T. S. Eliot, *Selected Essays: 1917–1932* (New York: Harcourt, Brace, 1932), 212.

162: *"This is the end"*: Dietrich Bonhoeffer, quoted in Eric Metaxas, *Bonhoeffer: Pastor, Martyr, Prophet, Spy* (Nashville: Thomas Nelson, 2010), 581–82.

162: *"Who am I? They often tell me"*: See, for example, http://www.christianforums .com/t7560086/.

163: *"No form nor comeliness"*: Isaiah 53:2 KJV.

CHAPTER 13: Friday

166: *Judas the Galilean*: Acts 5:37.

168: *"We have found this man"*: Luke 23:2.

168: *"If you let this man go"*: John 19:12, 15.

169: *"Are you the king of the Jews?"*: Matthew 27:11.

170: *"Here is this man"*: John 11:47–49.

170: *"The chief priests"*: Mark 14:55–56.

173: *"Jesus of Nazareth, the King of the Jews"*: John 19:19.

173: *"I lay down my life for the sheep"*: John 10:15, 18.

CHAPTER 14: Saturday

177: *"For what I received"*: 1 Corinthians 15:3–4.

177: *"Come, let us return"*: Hosea 6:1–2.

178: *Aristotle*: Aristotle, quoted in Robert Wilkins, *The Christians as the Romans Saw Them* (New Haven, CT: Yale University Press, 2003), 90.

178: *Plato*: Plato, quoted in ibid., 122.

178: Christopher Dawson: Quoted in Jaroslav Pelikan, *Jesus through the Centuries: His Place in the History of Culture* (New Haven, CT: Yale University Press, 1985), 30.

179: Eugene Peterson, *Reversed Thunder: The Revelation of John and the Praying Imagination* (San Francisco: HarperSanFrancisco, 1988), 174.

179: *"Between the trees"*: From the sermon "Between the Trees" by Rob Bell. Sermon available through Willow Creek Association, 2003, Week 35.See also www .willowcreek.com/wca.

179: *"I am the Alpha and the Omega"*: Revelation 1:8.

179: *"Before the mountains were born"*: Psalm 90:2.

180: *"The time has come"*: Mark 1:15.

180: Augustine: Pelikan, *Jesus through the Centuries*, 28.

180: Augustine: Ibid.

181: *"When Jesus was born"*: See Luke 2:1–2.

182: Venerable Bede: Randy Petersen, A. Kenneth Curtis, and J. Stephan Lang, *100 Most Important Events in Christian History* (Grand Rapids: Revell, 1998), 62.

182: William Wordsworth, "Surprised by Joy—Impatient as the Wind": See, for example, www.bartleby.com/145/ww427.html.

182: C. S. Lewis, *A Grief Observed* (New York: Bantam, 1961), 4–5.

183: *"How can some of you say"*: 1 Corinthians 15:12.

183: *"Say that the resurrection has already"*: 2 Timothy 2:18.

184: Eugene Peterson.

184: Carlos Eire, *A Very Brief History of Eternity* (Princeton, NJ: Princeton University Press, 2010), 10–12.

184: *"My offense is rank"*: Hamlet, act 3, scene 3.

184: *"To be or not to be"*: Hamlet, act 3, scene 1.

185: *"What happened today on earth?"*: Cited in Alasdair McGrath, *The Christian Theology Reader* (Oxford: Blackwell, 2007), 350.

CHAPTER 15: Sunday

186: *"So the women hurried"*: Matthew 28:8–9.

187: Frederick Dale Bruner, *Matthew: A Commentary*, vol. 2, The Churchbook (Grand Rapids: Eerdmans, 2004), 797.

187: Skip Viau: See ibid., 796.

187: *"Go and tell my brothers"*: Matthew 28:10.

189: *"The hour has come:"* John 12:23–25.

190: *"Unless a grain of wheat"*: John 12:24, my paraphrase.

190: *"The Lord's Day"*: Revelation 1:10.

190: Pliny the Younger: Bk. 10 , Letter 97: quoted in Robert Wilkins, *The Christians as the Romans Saw Them* (New Haven, CT: Yale University Press, 2003), 6.

191: *"Pre-eminent in life"*: Robin Lane Fox, *Pagans and Christians* (New York: HarperCollins, 1988), 61.

191: *"No body be buried or cremated"*: Philippe Aries, *The Hour of Our Death: The Classic History of Western Attitudes toward Death over the Last One Thousand Years* (New York: Barnes and Noble, 2000), 30.

191: *"This aversion to the proximity"*: Ibid., 30–31.

192: Origen: See Lane Fox, *Pagans and Christians*, 327.

192: *"Jesus of Nazareth"*: John 19:19.

192: *"This man claimed to be king"*: John 19:21–22.

192: Garrett Fiddler: *Yale Daily News*, April 21, 2011.

192: *"Take up your cross"*: See Matthew 16:24.

192: *"It is when Christianity has forgotten"*: Fiddler, *Yale Daily News*.

192: Michael Grant: Quoted in Philip Yancey, *The Jesus I Never Knew* (Grand Rapids: Zondervan, 2002), 202.

194: *de Botton:* Alain de Botton, *Status Anxiety* (New York: Pantheon, 2004), 149.

194: *Aristotle said:* Ibid., 150.

195: *"We also glory in our sufferings":* Romans 5:3–4.

195: *"and character [produces] hope":* See David Frederickson, "Paul, Hardships and Suffering," in *Paul in the Greco-Roman World: A Handbook,* ed. J. Paul Sampley (Harrisburg, PA: Trinity Press International, 2003).

195: Friedrich Nietzsche, *Human, All Too Human* (Lincoln: University of Nebraska Press, 1984), 58.

EPILOGUE: A Staggering Idea

197: *"Once upon a time":* Evelyn Edson and Emilie Savage-Smith, *Medieval Views of the Cosmos* (Oxford: Bodleian Library, University of Oxford, 2004).

197: *Wright:* See N. T. Wright, *Simply Jesus: A New Vision of Who He Was, What He Did, and Why He Matters* (New York: HarperOne, 2011), 131ff.

198: *"The LORD is in his holy temple":* Habbakuk 2:20.

198: *"The Temple is where heaven":* Wright, *Simply Jesus,* 132.

199: *"I had to be in my Father's house":* Luke 2:49.

200: *"Go into all the world":* Mark 16:15.

200: *"You yourselves are God's temple":* 1 Corinthians 3:16.

201: *"Nazareth!":* John 1:46.

201: *"You will see heaven open":* John 1:51.